A Book Of

HUMAN RESOURCE MANAGEMENT

For
MPM Semester - I
As Per Pune University's New Syllabus
Effective from June 2013

Sunil Lalla
B.A., M.B.A., M.M.M., D.P.L. (Diploma in Taxation Laws)

Neha Shukla
M.B.A.
ISB&M College of Commerce, Pune

N2964

HUMAN RESOURCE MANAGEMENT – MPM : (Sem. - I) **ISBN 978-93-83525-26-3**

First Edition	:	September 2013
©	:	Authors

The text of this publication, or any part thereof, should not be reproduced or transmitted in any form or stored in any computer storage system or device for distribution including photocopy, recording, taping or information retrieval system or reproduced on any disc, tape, perforated media or other information storage device etc., without the written permission of Authors with whom the rights are reserved. Breach of this condition is liable for legal action.

Every effort has been made to avoid errors or omissions in this publication. In spite of this, errors may have crept in. Any mistake, error or discrepancy so noted and shall be brought to our notice shall be taken care of in the next edition. It is notified that neither the publisher nor the authors or seller shall be responsible for any damage or loss of action to any one, of any kind, in any manner, therefrom.

Published By :
NIRALI PRAKASHAN
Abhyudaya Pragati, 1312, Shivaji Nagar,
Off J.M. Road, PUNE – 411005
Tel - (020) 25512336/37/39, Fax - (020) 25511379
Email : niralipune@pragationline.com

Printed By :
Repro Knowledgecast Limited,
Thane

DISTRIBUTION CENTRES
PUNE

Nirali Prakashan
119, Budhwar Peth, Jogeshwari Mandir Lane
Pune 411002, Maharashtra
Tel : (020) 2445 2044, 66022708, Fax : (020) 2445 1538
Email : bookorder@pragationline.com

Nirali Prakashan
S. No. 28/27, Dhyari,
Near Pari Company, Pune 411041
Tel : (020) 24690204 Fax : (020) 24690316
Email : dhyari@pragationline.com
bookorder@pragationline.com

MUMBAI
Nirali Prakashan
385, S.V.P. Road, Rasdhara Co-op. Hsg. Society Ltd.,
Girgaum, Mumbai 400004, Maharashtra
Tel : (022) 2385 6339 / 2386 9976, Fax : (022) 2386 9976
Email : niralimumbai@pragationline.com

DISTRIBUTION BRANCHES

NAGPUR
Pratibha Book Distributors
Above Maratha Mandir, Shop No. 3, First Floor,
Rani Jhanshi Square, Sitabuldi, Nagpur 440012,
Maharashtra, Tel : (0712) 254 7129

BENGALURU
Pragati Book House
House No. 1, Sanjeevappa Lane, Avenue Road Cross,
Opp. Rice Church, Bengaluru – 560002.
Tel : (080) 64513344, 64513355,
Mob : 9880582331, 9845021552
Email:bharatsavla@yahoo.com

JALGAON
Nirali Prakashan
34, V. V. Golani Market, Navi Peth, Jalgaon 425001,
Maharashtra, Tel : (0257) 222 0395
Mob : 94234 91860

KOLHAPUR
Nirali Prakashan
New Mahadvar Road,
Kedar Plaza, 1st Floor Opp. IDBI Bank
Kolhapur 416 012, Maharashtra. Mob : 9855046155

CHENNAI
Pragati Books
9/1, Montieth Road, Behind Taas Mahal, Egmore,
Chennai 600008 Tamil Nadu, Tel : (044) 6518 3535,
Mob : 94440 01782 / 98450 21552 / 98805 82331, Email : bharatsavla@yahoo.com

RETAIL OUTLETS
PUNE

Pragati Book Centre
157, Budhwar Peth, Opp. Ratan Talkies,
Pune 411002, Maharashtra
Tel : (020) 2445 8887 / 6602 2707, Fax : (020) 2445 8887
Pragati Book Centre
Amber Chamber, 28/A, Budhwar Peth,
Appa Balwant Chowk, Pune : 411002, Maharashtra,
Tel : (020) 20240335 / 66281669
Email : pbcpune@pragationline.com

Pragati Book Centre
676/B, Budhwar Peth, Opp. Jogeshwari Mandir,
Pune 411002, Maharashtra
Tel : (020) 6601 7784 / 6602 0855
PBC Book Sellers & Stationers
152, Budhwar Peth, Pune 411002, Maharashtra
Tel : (020) 2445 2254 / 6609 2463

MUMBAI
Pragati Book Corner
Indira Niwas, 111 - A, Bhavani Shankar Road, Dadar (W), Mumbai 400028, Maharashtra
Tel : (022) 2422 3526 / 6662 5254, Email : pbcmumbai@pragationline.com

Acknowledgements

Human Resource Management is one of our most favourite subjects. We are truly grateful to Nirali Prakashan for giving us an opportunity to write a book on this. We sincerely thank Shri Dineshbhai Furia and Shri Jignesh Furia, the publishers, for making this happen. We consider this as a privilege.

We thank Mrs. Nirja Sharma and Mr. Prasad Chintakindi for the care with which they have studied the script and their attention to each and every detail.

We would also like to thank Mr. Akbar Shaikh, Miss Chaitali Takle and Mr. Ravindra Walodare who have painstakingly attended to all the details to make this book appear good.

We are also grateful to all the staff members of Nirali Prakashan, who were involved in the publication of this book.

Authors

Preface ...

Dear Students,

HR is fundamentally an expression of an organisations belief in the employee element of that organisation's success. HR pure and simple is the implementation of a strategy to drive innovation and productivity through mobilising the workforce towards excellence. The ability of HR to add value lies in its ability to leverage the tools that it has at its disposal.

Human Resources (HR) management covers a broad range of fundamental business concepts, including recruiting, compensation and advancement, as well as legal considerations. Human resources management is a specialised career path that can provide a variety of job opportunities. Studying HR management can give students a more solid understanding of the employment process and the issues HR managers face.

We thus welcome you to the all new Human Resource Management book.

This book is designed to be student friendly with several new features keeping up with current trends, relevant research and changes made in the University Syllabus 2013.

The hallmark features comprise a clear writing style, cutting edge content and compelling pedagogy.

The key changes in the new edition are:

1. **Case Studies:** Each chapter contains a relevant case study, which helps to clarify concepts and to answer application-based questions from the examination point of view.
2. **Objective/Multiple Choice Questions (MCQs):** The objective questions and MCQ's will help in reinforcing learning and will help in solving the new online MCQ's examination.
3. **Key Points Highlighted:** All through the chapters key points are highlighted and boxed for easy revision at a glance.
4. **Activities:** Activities at the end of each chapter will help you to connect theory with the real world.
5. **Questions for Discussion:** These questions have been added to test the ability of student's understanding of the concepts and theories discussed in the chapters.

Your suggestions for improvements in the text will be highly appreciated.

Wish you the Very Best

Authors

Syllabus ...

Number of Sessions

1. **Understanding the Concept of Human Resource Management** **(7 + 2)**

   (a) **Human Resource Management:** Definition, Nature, Scope and Importance, Evolution of HRM, Objectives and Functions. HRM and its Environment.

   (b) **PM and HRM:** Difference between PM and HRM, Role of HR Professional/Manager, Qualities of Successful HR.

   (c) **Organisation of HR Department:** Structure of HR Dept., Line and Staff aspects of HRM, Relationship and Linkages with other Functional Deptts.., Personnel Policies and Principles.

   (d) **Model of HRM:** Fombrun model, Harvard model, Guest model, Warwick model.

   (e) **HR's Strategic Role:** SHRM, HR's role as a strategic partner, HR's role in executing strategy, HR's role in formulating strategy, HRIS, Human Capital Management, HR and Employee Performance and Commitment, Managing global HR.

2. **Procurement of Human Resources** **(8 + 2)**

   (a) **Job Analysis:** Nature and need of Job Analysis, Steps in Job Analysis, Methods of collecting information for Job Analysis, Quantitative Job Analysis techniques, Define Job Descriptions, Writing JD's, Define Job Specification, Writing JS's.

   (b) **HRP:** Meaning and significance of matching right abilities to the right job, Importance of HRP, Its Objectives and Process, Factors affecting HRP, HR estimation- HR demand forecast.

   (c) **Recruitment:** Definition and Meaning, Need, Planning of Recruitment, Process and sources of Recruitment, Recruiting yield pyramid, Study of live recruitment process, Succession planning.

   (d) **Selection:** Define selection, Process of selection, Types of tests and selection, Work sampling technique, Test of cognitive ability, Achievement tests, Situational testing.

   (e) **Interview:** Types Interview techniques, Designing and conducting an effective interview, Matching the candidature to the job, Activity on Mock interview.

   (f) **Induction and Placement:** Define Induction, Techniques, requisites and evaluation of induction programmer, Define placement, problems in placements.

3. **Training, Developing, Appraising Employees and Managing Performance** **(8 + 2)**

   (a) **Training:** Define Orientation, Definition and importance of training, Objective and needs, Training process, Gaps in training, Training programme and its evaluation, Analysis of training needs, Methods of training, training for special purposes.

   (b) **Development:** Define Development, Need and importance of development, What is management development, EDP's/MDP's.

- (c) **Performance Management System:** Define PMS, Explain self appraisals, Performance appraisals, Objectives and methods of performance appraisals, Performance counseling, Performance coaching, Performance Mentoring, Performance interviews, Edward Deming's view on PA, Legal issues associated with PA.
- (d) **Job Evaluation:** Define Job evaluation, Scope and process of JE, Methods of JE.
- (e) **Managing Careers:** Career Management process Career planning, Career path, Career development roles, Managing promotions and transfers, Types of promotion and transfer.

4. **Compensation and Productivity Management** (5 + 2)
   - (a) **Wage and Salary Administration:** Define reward, Compensation, Wage, Salary, Establishing pay rates, Compensation trends, Factors affecting employee remuneration, Wage and salary structure, Minimum fair and living wage, Wage policy in India, Preparation of salary structure.
   - (b) **Benefits and Services:** Nature and need of B and S, Types of employee B and S, Fringe benefits, Administration of B and S, Insurance - retirement-flexible benefits programmers.
   - (c) **Incentive schemes:** Nature of incentive schemes, Scope and type of incentive schemes, Wage incentive schemes and plans in India, Team or group variable plans, Incentive schemes for operation employees, Managers and executives, Salespeople.
   - (d) **Productivity Management:** Performance productivity management - through TQM, Kaizen, Quality circles.

5. **Industrial Relations, Separations and Safety Management** (7 + 2)
   - (a) **Industrial Relations:** Define IR, Concepts and objectives of IR, Parties to IR, Approaches to IR, TU and its role in IR.
   - (b) **Dispute Settlements:** Machineries of dispute settlement Grievance procedure, Collective bargaining, Negotiation, Conciliation, Arbitration, Adjudication, Labour courts.
   - (c) **Separations:** Define separations, VRS/CRS, Resignation, Superannuation, Gratuity, Discharge, Dismissal, Suspension, Layoff, Retrenchment.
   - (d) **Safety and Security:** Define employee safety, Types of safety, Safety and Health Programmes, Statutory Provisions of Safety in India.

Contents ...

1. **Understanding the Concept of Human Resource Management**   1.1 - 1.46

2. **Procurement of Human Resources**   2.1 - 2.34

3. **Training, Developing & Appraising Employees and Managing Performance**   3.1 - 3.40

4. **Compensation and Productivity Management**   4.1 - 4.40

5. **Industrial Relations, Separations and Safety Management**   5.1 - 5.74

Chapter 1...

Understanding the Concept of Human Resource Management

Contents ...

1.1 Definitions of Human Resource Management
1.2 Nature, Scope and Importance of HRM
    1.2.1 Nature of Human Resource Management HRM
    1.2.2 Scope of Human Resource Management HRM
    1.2.3 Importance of Human Resource Management
1.3 Evolution and History of Human Resource Management
1.4 Human Resource Management - Functions and Objectives
1.5 HRM and its Environment
1.6 Difference between PM and HRM
    1.6.1 Definition
    1.6.2 Difference between Personnel Management and HRM
1.7 Role of HR Professional/Manager
1.8 Qualities of Successful HR
1.9 Structure of HR Department
1.10 Line and Staff Aspects of HRM
1.11 HR Relationship and Linkages with other Departments
1.12 Personnel Policies and Principles
    1.12.1 Definition
    1.12.2 Function
    1.12.3 Principles of Personnel Policies
1.13 The HRM Models
1.14 SHRM
1.15 HR's Role in Formulating Strategies
1.16 HR's Role as a Strategic Partner
1.17 HR's Role in Executing Strategies
1.18 HRIS
1.19 Human Capital Management
1.20 HR and Employee Performance and Commitment
1.21 Managing HR
- Points to Remember
- Questions for Discussion
- Objective Questions
- Case Study
- Activity
- References and Web Links

Objectives ...

Human Resource Management: Definition, nature, scope and importance, evolution of HRM, objectives and functions, HRM and its environment.

- To define Human Resource Management
- To explain the nature, scope and importance of HRM
- To describe evolution of HRM
- To enumerate objectives and functions of HRM
- To identify HRM and its environment

PM and HRM: Difference between PM and HRM, role of HR professional/manager, qualities of successful HR.

- To define Personnel Management (PM)
- To differentiate between PM and HRM
- To explain the role of HR professional/manager
- To enumerate qualities of successful HR

Organisation of HR department: Structure of HR department, line and staff aspects of HRM, relationship and linkages with other departments, personnel policies and principles.

- To illustrate the Structure of HR department
- To explain line and staff aspects of HRM
- To describe the relationship and linkages with other departments
- To enumerate personnel policies and principles

Models of HRM: Fombrun model, Harvard model, Guest model, Warwick model.

- To illustrate different Models of HRM
- To explain the Fombrun model
- To describe the Harvard model, Guest model, and Warwick model

HR's Strategic Role: SHRM, HR's role as a Strategic Partner, HR's role in executing strategies, HR's role in formulating strategies, HRIS, Human Capital Management, HR and employee performance and commitment, managing HR.

- To explain HR's Strategic Role
- To define SHRM
- To identify HR's role as a Strategic Partner
- To describe HR's role in executing strategies
- To learn HR's role in formulating strategies
- To illustrate HRIS
- To define Human Capital Management
- To describe HR and employee performance and commitment
- To describe managing HR

Introduction

The HR function was initially dominated by transactional work such as payroll and benefits administration. However, the range of responsibilities of the human resource management function has increased substantially in recent years. The effective human resource specialist needs to be not only a skilled practioner, but also a counsellor, negotiator and advisor. Due to globalisation, company consolidation, technological advancement, and further research, HR now focuses on strategic initiatives like mergers and acquisitions, talent management, succession planning, industrial and labour, diversity and inclusion.

It is now expected to add value to the strategic utilisation of employees and the employee programmes that impact the business in measurable ways. The new role of HR involves strategic direction and HR metrics and measurements to demonstrate value.

In start-up companies, HR's duties may be performed by trained professionals. In larger companies, an entire functional group is typically dedicated to the discipline, with staff specializing in various HR tasks and functional leadership engaging in strategic decision making across the business.

HRM is concerned with carrying out the **Same Functional Activities** traditionally performed by the personnel, such as HR planning, job analysis, recruitment and selection, employee relations, performance management, employee appraisals, compensation management, training and development etc. But, the **HRM approach** performs these functions in a **qualitatively distinct way**, when compared with Personnel Management.

During the 1980s, personnel departments were responsible for handing out applications, providing employees with insurance enrolment forms and processing payroll. The role of the personnel department was mainly administrative.

Over the next two decades, the role of personnel administration became more involved with overall business goals. Companies began to recruit human resources leaders who were capable of managing the department from a more strategic position.

Personnel administration, therefore, evolved into a business now referred to as human resources management. Human resources managers are responsible for developing strategic solutions to employment-related matters that affect the organisation's ability to meet its productivity and performance goals.

HR is a product of the human relations movement during the early 20th century, when researchers began documenting 'ways of creating business values through the strategic management of the workforce'.

1.1 Definitions of Human Resource Management

The first definition of HRM is that *"it is the process of managing people in organisations in a structured and thorough manner."* This covers the fields of staffing (hiring people), retention of people, pay and perks setting and management, performance management, change management and taking care of exits from the company to round off the activities.

This is the traditional definition of HRM which leads some experts to define it as a modern version of the Personnel Management function that was used earlier.

Management specialists have defined human resource management as below:

HRM is:

"The Process of analysing and managing an organisation's human resources needs to ensure satisfaction of its strategic objectives"

- Management – Hell Riegel/Slocum

"The policies and practices involved in carrying out the 'people' or human resources aspects of a management position, including recruiting, screening, training and appraising."

- Human Resource Management – Gray Dessler

The other definitions of HRM encompass the management of people in organisations from a macro perspective i.e. *managing people in the form of a collective relationship between management and employees.* This approach focuses on the objectives and outcomes of the HRM function. What this means is that the HR function in contemporary organisations is concerned with the notions of people enabling, people development and a focus on making the "employment relationship" fulfilling for both the management and employees.

These definitions emphasise the difference between Personnel Management and human resource management. To put it in one sentence, personnel management is essentially "workforce" centered whereas human resource management is "resource" centered.

Whatever definition we use the answer to the question **"What is HRM?"** focuses on people in an organisation. Some MNC's (Multinationals) call the HR managers also as People Managers, People Enablers and the practice as people management.

In the 21st century organisations, the HR manager or the people manager is no longer seen as someone who takes care of the activities described in the traditional way. In fact, most organisations have different departments dealing with Staffing, Payroll, and Retention etc. Instead, the HR manager is responsible for managing employee expectations vis-à-vis the management objectives and reconciling both to ensure employee fulfillment and realisation of management objectives.

1.2 Nature, Scope and Importance of HRM

Human Resource Management (HRM) is the function within an organisation that focuses on recruitment, management, and providing direction for the people who work in the organisation.

HRM deals with issues related to people such as compensation, hiring, performance management, organisation development, safety, wellness, benefits, employee motivation, communication, administration, and training.

HRM is also a strategic and comprehensive approach to managing people and the workplace culture and environment.

Effective HRM enables employees to contribute effectively and productively to the overall company direction and the accomplishment of the organisation's goals and objectives.

> *Effective HRM enables employees to contribute effectively and productively to the overall company direction and the accomplishment of the organisation's goals and objective.*

1.2.1 Nature of Human Resource Management HRM

The nature or features of Human Resource Management (HRM) are as follows:

1. **HRM is a Process of four functions:**

    (a) **Acquisition of human resources:** This function includes Human Resource Planning, Recruitment, Selection, Placement and Induction of staff.

    (b) **Development of human resources:** This function includes Training and Development, and Career development. The knowledge, skills, attitudes and social behaviours of the staff are developed.

    (c) **Motivation of human resources:** This function includes giving recognition and rewards to the staff. It also includes Performance Appraisal and handling the problems of the staff.

    (d) **Maintenance of human resources:** This function includes providing the best working conditions for employees. It also looks after the health and safety of the staff.

2. **Continuous Process:** HRM is not a one-time process. It is a continuous process. It has to continuously change and adjust according to the changes in the environment, changes in the expectations of the staff, etc.

    HRM has to give continuous training and development to the staff due to changes in technology.

3. **Focus on Objectives:** HRM gives a lot of importance to achievement of objectives.
   The four main objectives HRM has to achieve are:
   (a) Individual objectives of the staff.
   (b) Group or Departmental objectives.
   (c) Organisational objectives.
   (d) Societal objectives.
4. **Universal Application:** HRM has universal application. That is, it can be used for business as well as for other organisations such as schools, colleges, hospital, religious organisations, etc.
5. **Integrated use of Subsystems:** HRM involves the integrated use of sub-systems such as Training and Development, Career Development, Organisational Development, Performance Appraisal, Potential Appraisal, etc. All these subsystems increase the efficiency of the staff and bring success to the organisation.
6. **Multidisciplinary:** HRM is multidisciplinary. That is, it uses many different subjects such as Psychology, Communication, Philosophy, Sociology, Management, Education, etc.
7. **Develops Team Spirit:** HRM tries to develop the team spirit of the full organisation. Team spirit helps the staff to work together for achieving the objectives of the organisation. Now-a-days more importance is given to team work and not to individuals.
8. **Develops Staff Potentialities:** HRM develops the potentialities of the staff by giving them training and development. This will make the staff more efficient, and it will give them more job satisfaction.
9. **Key Elements for Solving Problems:** Today, we have rapid technological, managerial, economic and social changes. These changes bring many problems. HRM continuously tries to solve these problems.
10. **Long Term Benefits:** HRM brings many long term benefits to the individuals (staff), the organisation and the society. It gives many financial and non-financial benefits to the staff. It improves the image and profits of the organisation. It also provides a regular supply of quality goods and services at reasonable prices to the society.

1.2.2 Scope of Human Resource Management HRM

The Scope of Human Resource Management HRM is discussed below:
1. **Human Resource Planning (HRP):** HRP estimates the manpower demand and manpower supply of the organisation. It compares the manpower demand and manpower supply. If there is manpower surplus then it gives voluntary retirement, lay-off, etc. to some employees. If there is manpower shortage then it hires employees from outside, gives promotion to employees, etc.

2. **Acquisition Function:** Acquisition function includes Human Resource Planning, Recruitment, Selection, Placement and Induction of employees. HRM uses the scientific selection procedure for selecting the right man for the right post. The "right man" is given proper placement and induction.
3. **Placement Function:** HRM also performs the placement function. Placement is done after selection of employees. It means to put the right man in the right place of work. Proper placement gives job satisfaction to the employees, and it increases their efficiency.
4. **Performance Appraisal:** HRM also conducts a performance appraisal. Performance appraisal is a systematic evaluation of the employees' performance at work. It informs the employees about their strengths and weakness. It also advises them about how to increase their strengths and remove their weaknesses.
5. **Career Development:** HRM also helps the employees in planning and developing their careers. It informs them about future promotions and how to get these promotions. It helps them to grow and develop in the organisation.
6. **Training and Development:** HRM also provides training and development to the employees. Training means to increase the knowledge and skills of the employee for doing a particular job. Training given to managers is called development. So, training is given to employees while development is given to managers.
7. **Quality of Work Life (QWL):** HRM also includes Quality of Work Life. **QWL** is a technique for improving productivity and quality of work. It involves labour management co-operation, collective bargaining and participative management.
8. QWL provides good working conditions, job security, good pay and other facilities such as flexible working hours, freedom to suggest changes or improvements, etc. QWL creates a sense of belonging. This benefits the organisation as well as the individual employees.
9. **Employees' Welfare:** HRM provides employee's welfare. Welfare measures include paid holidays, medical insurance, canteen facilities, recreation facilities, rest room, transport facilities, etc. Proper and timely welfare facilities motivate the employees to work hard in the organisation.
10. **Compensation Function:** Employees must be rewarded and recognised for their performance. HRM makes proper compensation packages for the employees. These packages motivate the employees and increase their morale. Rewards are given to individuals, and teams. The rewards may be in the form of higher pay, bonus, other monetary incentives, and non-monetary incentives such as a certificate of appreciation, etc.
11. **Labour Relations:** HRM also includes industrial relations. It includes union management relations, joint consultations, negotiating, collective bargaining, grievance handling, disciplinary actions, settlement of industrial disputes, etc.

12. **Maintenance Function:** HRM also performs the maintenance function. That is, protecting and promoting the health and safety of the employees. HRM introduces health and safety measures. It also provides other benefits such as medical aid, provident fund, pension, gratuity, maternity benefits, accident compensation, etc., to the employees.

1.2.3 Importance of Human Resource Management

An organisation cannot build a good team of working professionals without good Human Resources.

The key functions of the Human Resources Management (HRM) team, include recruiting people, training them, performance appraisals, motivating employees, workplace safety as well as workplace communication, and much more.

The beneficial effects of these functions are discussed here:

1. **Recruitment and Training:** This is one of the major responsibilities of the human resource team. The HR managers first plan strategies for hiring the right kind of people. They design the criteria which is best suited for a specific job description. Their other task related to recruitment includes formulating the obligations of an employee and the scope of tasks assigned to him or her. Based on these two factors, the contract of an employee with the company is prepared.

They also provide training to the employees according to the requirements of the organisation. Thus, the staff members get the opportunity to sharpen their existing skills or develop specialised skills which in turn, will help them to take up some new roles.

2. **Performance Appraisals:** HRM encourages the people working in an organisation, to work according to their potential and gives them suggestions that can help them to bring about improvement in it. The team communicates with the staff individually from time to time and provides all the necessary information regarding their performances and also defines their respective roles. This is beneficial as it enables them to form an outline of their anticipated goals in clearer terms and thereby, helps them execute the goals with best possible efforts.

Performance appraisals, when taken on a regular basis, motivate the employees.

3. **Maintaining Work Atmosphere:** This is a vital aspect of HRM because the performance of an individual in an organisation is largely driven by the work atmosphere or work culture that prevails at the workplace.

A good working condition is one of the benefits that the employees can expect from an efficient human resource team. A safe, clean and healthy environment can bring out the best in an employee. A friendly atmosphere gives the staff members, job satisfaction as well.

4. **Managing Disputes:** In an organisation, there are several issues on which disputes may arise between the employees and the employers. You can say conflicts are almost inevitable. In such a scenario, it is the human resource department which acts as a consultant and mediator to sort out those issues in an effective manner.

They first hear the grievances of the employees. Then they come up with suitable solutions to sort them out. In other words, they take timely action and prevent things from going out of hand.

5. Developing Public Relations: The responsibility of establishing good public relations lies with the HRM to a great extent. They organise business meetings, seminars and various official gatherings on behalf of the company in order to build up relationships with other business sectors.

Sometimes, the HR department plays an active role in preparing the business and marketing plans for the organisation too. Any organisation, without a proper setup for HRM is bound to suffer from serious problems while managing its regular activities. For this reason, today, companies must put a lot of effort and energy into setting up a strong and effective HRM.

1.3 Evolution and History of Human Resource Management

Organisations have many operational functions. HRD is one of them.

In the early 70's there was no division called as Human Resource Department or Division. The only division along these lines was "Personnel", which dealt with the labour related in the organisation.

Personnel Management was introduced by the end of the 19th century. At that time, the focus was on the welfare of labours in the organisations. According to the tasks they have done, the officers at Personnel Department were called as "Welfare Officers". Did you know that the employee welfare tasks were done by women at that time? Interesting, isn't it?!

During the period of 1914-1939, many organisations showed a quick growth and quick changes in needs and wants of the operations. Therefore the tasks done by women shifted to the men's, because of the complexity of tasks. These officers were called as "Labour managers" at that time.

After Second World War, during the period 1945 - 1979, this has changed to "Personnel Management", and the focus was basically on employee administration and legislation.

During the late 70's the economics of the world changed gradually and labour emerged as an important resource. During the decade of the 80's the concept of "Human Resource Management" started and it has gradually shown growth in 90's.

Finally the tasks and operations of personnel management were shifted to the Human Resource Management and it is now functioning in a broad way.

Birth and Evolution of the Discipline

By the time enough theoretical evidence existed to make a business case for strategic workforce management, changes in the business landscape (à la Andrew Carnegie, John Rockefeller) and in public policy (a là Sidney and Beatrice Webb, Franklin D. Roosevelt and the New Deal) had transformed the employer-employee relationship, and the discipline was formalized as "industrial and labour relations".

In 1913, one of the oldest known professional HR associations—the Chartered Institute of Personnel and Development—was founded in England as the Welfare Workers' Association, then changed its name a decade later to the Institute of Industrial Welfare Workers, and again the next decade to Institute of Labour Management before settling upon its current name.

Likewise in the United States, the world's first institution of higher education dedicated to workplace studies—the School of Industrial and Labour Relations—was formed at Cornell University in 1945.

During the latter half of the 20th century, union membership declined significantly, while workforce management continued to expand its influence within organisations. "Industrial and labour relations" began being used to refer specifically to issues concerning collective representation, and many companies began referring to the profession as "personnel administration".

In 1948, what would later become the largest professional HR association—the Society for Human Resource Management (SHRM)—was founded as the American Society for Personnel Administration (ASPA).

Nearing the 21st century advances in transportation and communications greatly facilitated workforce mobility and collaboration. Corporations began viewing employees as assets rather than as cogs in a machine. "Human resources management", consequently, became the dominant term for the function—the ASPA even changing its name to SHRM in 1998.

"Human capital management" is sometimes used synonymously with HR, although human capital typically refers to a more narrow view of human resources; i.e., the knowledge the individuals embody and can contribute to an organisation. Likewise, other terms sometimes used to describe the field include "organisational management", "manpower management", "talent management", "personnel management", and simply "people management".

1.4 Human Resource Management - Functions and Objectives

HRM not only takes care of the present organisational objectives but it also examines and determines the future organisational needs for developing strategies as per the future requirements.

Moreover, after identifying the fact that employee turnover is directly proportional to the employee dissatisfaction, taking care of the needs of the employees also became one of the major considerations of HRM.

> *HRM is looked up as a prominent department and shares its existence with the top management functions and figures of the organisation*

Today, HRM is looked up as a prominent department and shares its existence with the top management functions and figures of the organisation.

Today, HR is an exclusive department in almost all organisations and has a number of important functions to perform.

Functions of HRM are as follows:

1. **Employee Career Goals:** To understand that the employees are also individual and have their own set of needs and goals. The HR has to identify those needs and work upon them to make the employees feel motivated, by providing them time to time training, related to their field of interest. It is to be kept into consideration that if the employee does not find any career advancement in the role he has been assigned in the organisation, his inclination towards performing well, will be really low due to lack of motivation.

2. **Organisational Goals:** To understand and define the overall objectives and goals of the organisation, its mission as well as vision. It also calls for aligning the skills of the workforce with the company's mission/vision statement and encouraging them to work towards achieving those organisational objectives. It not only includes the present organisational requirements but also forecasting the future needs and strategies for fulfilling them.

3. **Training and Development:** To ensure proper availability of latest tools and methods for training the employees according to their respective competencies. Identifying the imperfect areas which require training and working towards filling the gap with the best available training tools. HR should realise that training is not an unnecessary expenditure which can be discarded; instead they should understand that if the employees are properly trained and developed, it can prove to be the best investment made by the company which will definitely furnish quality returns in future.

    HR's job does not just end with the training. They should also scrutinize the post training transformation in the performance of the employees and should provide adequate feedback if further improvement is required.

4. **Recruitment:** Selecting the best workforce from the labour market by using the recruitment options like internal job portals, job websites, advertisements, employment agencies etc. Personal interviews, GD's, aptitude test should be unbiased and very seriously performed, for getting the best of the best. The

candidates should be informed well in advance about the profile of the job, required skills, attitude and the workload a candidate can experience so that they may come with a defined mindset and give their best to the job offered to them. Before moving ahead with recruiting, the HR manager should ensure the adequacy of the funds to be invested on the recruitment procedure.
5. **Staffing:** Staffing involves assigning the right job to the right employee. The HR should understand that the employee will not be able to give his 100% if his talent is not utilised in the right direction. They are also required in making them understand the overall objective, mission and vision statements and also providing them proper resources which will help him / her attain those objectives.
6. Ensuring employee health and safety by abiding to the employee safety and health regulations.
7. Managing grievances.
8. Ensuring provisions for adequate and promised compensation with fixed and variable benefits to keep them motivated.
9. Making strategies for reducing the employee turnover rate.
10. To ensure a positive work environment in the organisation.
11. To continuously stimulate a sense of belonging, responsibility and accountability in employees.
12. Ensuring effective communication between employees and minimising conflicts.
13. To ensure latest appraisal methods, fair and unbiased salary hikes for keeping the employees motivated.
14. To keep a record of the employee profiles and database so that it can be readily available at the time of recruitment and staffing and also ensuring its confidentiality.
15. To keep a bird's eye view on the employee's performance and regularly providing feedbacks on the same.

> ***HRM aligns the employee's skills with the present and future needs of the organisation and utilises it towards the achievement of the desired goal***

It analyses the workforce profile, skills, abilities, qualifications, potential capabilities etc. and assign them various responsibilities as per the requirement of the job and the workers profile. Moreover it also facilitates acquiring, training and retaining the talent.

There are also some objectives for which HRM performs its aforesaid functions in an organisation.

Some of the HRM objectives are as follows:
1. To achieve the organisational goals and objectives.
2. To ensure employee satisfaction at every level.
3. To instil team spirit in employees.
4. To explore employees capabilities for performing a given job.

5. To ensure maintaining the quality of work life.
6. To respect the employees as individuals and also respect their individual career goals.
7. To equip the employees with proper resources.
8. To keep the employees motivated.
9. To encourage the feeling of organisational loyalty in employees.
10. To ensure a positive environment of mutual trust and understanding in the organisation.

1.5 HRM and its Environment

A number of environmental factors affect HRM. Environment provides the macro context and the organisation is the micro unit i.e. the external influences of economic conditions, labour markets, laws and regulations and labour unions. Each of these external factors separately or in combination can influence the HRM function of any organisation.

Changes in the external environment have a profound impact on the personnel

These changes include technological obsolescence, culture and social changes, and policies of the government.

The external environment consists of factors that affect an organisation's human resources from outside it. Let us examine these factors in detail:

- **Technological Innovation:** Rapid technological changes and innovations are taking place all over the world. As a result of these, technical personnel are increasingly required. Hence, procurement of technically skilled employees is necessary to match the changing job requirements.
- **Economic Factors:** Economic conditions influence financial "health" of the organisation. Under favourable economic condition, expansion of existing programmemes and creation of new programme are very likely. With less favourable conditions, cancellation of some programme may be necessary.
- **Employees' Organisations:** Employees' organisations have matched the growth of industrialisation. Labour unions seek to bargain with management over the terms and conditions of employment for their members.
- **Labour Markets:** In labour markets, organisations seek employees (demand and labour), and individuals offer their services to organisations (supply and labour). Labour supply and demand affects all activities, particularly compensation and external staffing.
- **Changing Demand of Employers:** Organisations also undergoes changes and consequently their demands on employees also change. The technological revolution and stiff business competition demands that the existing employees adapt to every changing work situation and learn new skills, knowledge etc., to cope up with the new changes.

- **Legal Factors:** It has to manage its employees according to the legislation of government at the centre and the states. The Important Legislations enacted in India affecting HRM are: Factories Act, Trade Unions Act, Workmen's Compensation Act, The Payment of Wages Act, The Minimum Wages Act, Payment of Gratuity Act, and The Maternity Benefit Act. The government is the custodian of industrial and economic activities.
- **Human Resource in the country:** The structure, values and the level of education of human resource in the country influence the HRM function of any organisation. The influence of manpower in the country can be studied through:
  o Change in the structure of employment with the entry of workforce with different backgrounds.
  o Changes that have taken place in the structure of the workforce over the years and led to the emergence of new values in organisations.
  o Increased level of formal education which has led to changes in the employee attitude.
  o Well-educated employees always challenge and question the management's decisions and want a voice in the company's affairs in their interest.

Thus, many environmental factors affect the performance of specific tasks of HRM.

Changes in the internal and external environmental factors cause difficulties in the job both of line and personnel managers. Considering the complexities and challenges in the HRM now and in the near future managements have to develop sophisticated techniques and competent people to manage personnel effectively.

1.6 Difference between PM and HRM

Personnel Management (PM) is a traditional form of management, where the manager was the person who organised, delegated and divided the work. The management applied the principles for getting things done universally regardless of the type of organisation and situations involved. PM has a limited scope. The norms, laws and strategies of functioning were designed by the management, the head of the company. The task of the personnel managers includes the activity of hiring new employees, to maintain personnel records, and to supervise the labour as an important tool.

Personnel Management involved monitoring employees in the interest of the organisation with negotiation, division of labour, indirect and downward communication and functioning under clear rules, norms and customs of the organisation.

But later, research shows that there may be few instances where certain principles were used in all circumstances. After analysing the various situational variables carefully, the behavioural situations are much more complicated. This was how HRM, Human Resource Management came into existence. Intellectuals identified that man at work is the asset of any organisation and is dynamic in thought process as well as functioning, thus his individual identity should be retained.

> *Historically, it is believed, that PM preceded HRM.*

This was an end to the PM approach that had a universal outlook in dealing with employees.

1.6.1 Definition

Edwin Flippo: "***Personnel Management*** *is concerned with procurement, development, compensation, integration and maintenance of personnel of organisation for the purpose of contributing towards the accomplishments of the organisational objectives.*"

Paul Pigore & Charles Myres: "***Personnel Management** is the line responsibility & staff functions, assisting managers in providing advice, counsel, service and various types of controls to secure uniform administrations of personnel policies designed to achieve organisation's objective.*"

Thus, Personnel Management "is basically an administrative record-keeping function, at the operational level. Personnel Management attempts to maintain fair terms and conditions of employment, while at the same time, efficiently managing personnel activities for individual departments etc. It is assumed that the outcomes from providing justice and achieving efficiency in the management of personnel activities will result ultimately in achieving organisational success.

Human Resource Development - Human resource management is concerned with the development and implementation of people strategies, which are integrated with corporate strategies, and ensures that the culture, values and structure of the organisation, and the quality, motivation and commitment of its members contribute fully to the achievement of its goals.

1.6.2 Difference between Personnel Management and HRM

Personnel management is **workforce centered**, directed mainly at the organisation's employees; such as finding and training them, arranging for them to be paid, explaining management's expectations, justifying management's actions etc. While on the other hand, HRM is **resource-centered**, directed mainly at management, in terms of devolving the responsibility of HRM to line management, management development etc.

Though a management function, personnel management has never totally identified with management interests, as it becomes ineffective when not able to understand the needs and views of the workforce.

Personnel Management is basically an **operational** function, concerned primarily with carrying out the day-to-day people management activities. While on the other hand, HRM is **strategic** in nature, that is, being concerned with directly assisting an organisation to gain *sustained competitive advantage.*

> *Human resource management involves all management decisions and practices that directly affect or influence the people, or human resources, who work for the organisation.*

In other words, Human resource management is concerned with 'people centric issues' in management.

The Human Resources Management (HRM) function includes a variety of activities. The key among them is deciding the staffing needs. Activities also include managing your approach to employee benefits and compensation, employee records and personnel policies. Usually small businesses (for-profit or non-profit) have to carry out these activities themselves because they can't afford part- or full-time help. However, they should always ensure that employees have -- and are aware of -- personnel policies which conform to current regulations. These policies are often in the form of employee manuals.

Although both human resource management (HRM) and personnel management focus on people management, if we examine critically, there are many differences between them. **Some are listed below:**

(1) Nature of relations: The nature of relations can be seen through two different perspective views which are Pluralist and Unitarist. There is a clear distinct difference between both because in personnel management, the focus is more on individualistic where individual interest is more than group interest.

The relationship between management and employees are merely on contractual basis where one hires and the others perform. HRM focuses more on Unitarist, where the word "uni" refers to one and together.

Here, HRM through a shared vision between management and staff create a corporate vision and mission which are linked to business goals and the fulfillment of mutual interest where the organisation's needs are satisfied by employees and employees' needs are well-taken care by the organisation. Motorola and Seagate are good examples of organisations that have belief in this Unitarist approach which also focuses in team management and sees employees as partners in an organisation.

2. Relation of power and management: The distribution of power in personnel management is centralised where the top management has full authority in decision-making and even the personnel managers are not allowed to give ideas or take part in any decision which involves "employees".

HRM, on the other hand, sees the decentralisation of power where the power between top management is shared with middle and lower management groups.

This is known as "empowerment" because employees play an important role together with line and HR managers to make collective and mutual decisions, which can benefit both the management and employees.

In fact, HRM focuses more on TQM (Total Quality Management) approach as part of a team management with the involvement and participation of management and employees with shared power and authority.

The nature of management is focused more on bottom-up approach with employees giving feedback to the top management and then the top management gives support to employees to achieve mutually agreed goals and objectives.

3. Leadership and management role: Personnel management emphasises much on leadership style which is very transactional. This style of leadership merely sees the leader as a task-oriented person. The leader focuses more on procedures that must be followed, punishment from non-performance and non-compliance of rules and regulations and put figures and task accomplishments ahead of human factors such as personal bonding, interpersonal relationship, trust, understanding, tolerance and care.

HRM creates leaders who are transformational. This leadership style encourages business objectives to be shared by both employees and management. Here, leaders only focus more on people-oriented and importance on rules, procedures and regulations are eliminated and replaced with:

- Shared vision;
- Corporate culture and missions;
- Trust and flexibility; and
- HRM needs that integrates business needs.

4. Contract of employment: In personnel management, employee's contract of employment is clearly written and employees must observe strictly to the agreed employment contract. The contract is so rigid that there is no room for changes and modifications. There is no compromise in written contracts that stipulates rules, regulations, job and obligations.

HRM, on the other hand, does not focus on one-time life-long contract where working hours and other terms and conditions of employment are seen as less rigid. Here, it goes beyond the normal contract that takes place between organisations and employees. The new "flexible approach" encourages employees to choose various ways to keep contributing their skills and knowledge to the organisation.

HRM, with its new approach, has created flexi-working hours, work from home policies and not forgetting the creation on "open contract" system that is currently practiced by some multinational companies such as Motorola, Siemens and GEC.

HRM today gives employees the opportunity and freedom to select any type of working system that can suit them and at the same time benefit the organisation as well. Drucker (1996) calls this approach a "win-win" approach.

5. Pay policies and job design: Pay policies in personnel management is merely based on skills and knowledge required for the perspective jobs only. The value is based on the ability to perform the task and duties as per the employment contract requirement only. It does not encourage value-added incentives to be paid out. This is also because the job design is very functional, where the functions are more departmentalised in which each job falls into one functional department. This is merely known as division on labour based on job needs and skill possessions and requirement.

HRM, on the contrary, encourages organisations to look beyond pay for functional duties. Here, the pay is designed to encourage continuous job performance and improvement which is linked to value-added incentives such as gain sharing schemes, group profit sharing and individual incentive plans.

The job design is no more functional based but teamwork and cyclical based. HRM creates a new approach towards job design such as job rotation which is inter and intra-departmental based and job enlargement which encourages one potential and capable individual to take on more tasks to add value to his/her job and in return enjoy added incentives and benefits.

HRM is more *proactive* than Personnel Management. Whereas personnel management is about the **maintenance** of personnel and administrative systems, HRM is about the **forecasting** of organisational needs, the continual monitoring and adjustment of personnel systems to meet current and future requirements, and the management of change.

Table 1.1: Difference between Personnel Management & HRD

Sr. No.	Dimension	Personnel Management	Human Resource Development
BELIEFS & ASSUMPTIONS			
1.	Contract	Careful delineation of written contracts	Aim to go 'beyond contracts'
2.	Rules	Importance of devising clear rules/mutuality	'Can-do' outlook; impatience with 'rule'
3.	Guide to management Action	Procedures	'Business – need'
4.	Behaviour Referent	Norms/custom & practice	Values/Mission
5.	Managerial Task *vis-à-vis* Labour	Monitoring	Nurturing
6.	Nature of Relations	Pluralist	Unitarist
7.	Conflict	Institutionalised	De-emphasised

contd.

STRATEGIC ASPECTS			
8.	Key Relations	Labour Management	Customer
9.	Initiatives	Piecemeal	Integrated
10.	Corporate Plan	Marginal to	Central to
11.	Speed of Decision	Slow	Fast
LINE MANAGEMENT			
12.	Management Role	Transactional	Transformational leadership
13.	Key Managers	Personnel/IR Specialists	General/business/line managers
14.	Communication	Indirect	Direct
15.	Standardisation	High (e.g. 'parity' an issue)	Low (e.g. 'parity' not seen as relevant)
16.	Prized management skills	Negotiation	Facilitation
KEY LEVERS			
17.	Selection	Separate, marginal task	Integrated, key task
18.	Pay	Job Evaluation (fixed grades)	Performance – related
19.	Conditions	Separately negotiated	Harmonisation
20.	Labour Management	Collective bargaining contracts	Towards individual contracts
21.	Key Relations	Regularized through facilities & training	Marginalized (with exception of some bargaining for change models)
22.	Job categories & grades	Many	Few
23.	Communication	Restricted flow	Increased flow
24.	Job Design	Division of Labour	Teamwork
25.	Conflict Handling	Reach temporary truces	Manage climate & culture
26.	Training & Development	Controlled access to courses	Learning companies
27.	Focus of attention of interventions	Personnel procedures	Wide ranging cultural, structural & personnel strategies

1.19

1.7 Role of HR Professional/Manager

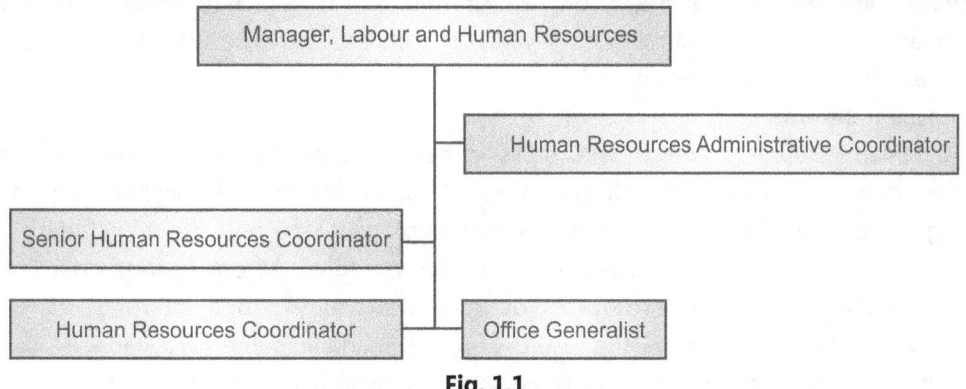

Fig. 1.1

> *The goal of a human resource manager is to strengthen the employer-employee relationship.*

The goal of a human resource manager is to strengthen the employer-employee relationship. This goal is supported by a variety of functions within the human resources department and throughout the organisation. In a small business, the human resource manager may have a great degree of latitude, as well as the time to devote to employee interaction with a small workforce. Both of these are key elements of an effective human resources leader, although she must accomplish a number of functions to achieve this goal.

Manage HR Department

The manager of the human resources department is responsible for ensuring that department employees are well-versed in their areas of expertise. The various disciplines of HR require expertise in compensation, benefits, safety, payroll, recruiting and training. Ideally, the human resource manager is a generalist, which means his expertise is cross-discipline.

Knowledge of Laws

Managing the human resources department also requires knowledge of federal and state employment and labour laws and regulations that apply to human resources professionals. For example, the human resource manager will designate the HIPAA (Health Insurance Portability and Accountability Act) officer in charge of all medical and health-related records for the workplace.

Interaction with Executive Leadership

An effective human resource manager is in constant communication with executive leadership. The HR department is not a revenue-generating source. Consequently, it is important for the leaders of an organisation to understand the return on investment (ROI) in human resources activities as a contribution to the company's bottom line. In a small business, the ROI may be more readily seen than in a large conglomerate. The human resource manager for a small business, which has a smaller workforce, can easily implement methods and strategies that may show faster results. The bureaucratic hierarchy of a large organisation often puts many more layers of authority between the human resource manager and executive leadership.

Employee Relations

A human resource manager who stays in her office all day will not be effective at building strong relationships with employees. Another function of the human resource manager is to gain the trust and confidence of employees--the best way to establish trust and confidence is through daily interaction with the workforce. According to the U.S. Bureau of Labour Statistics, "Human resources occupations require strong interpersonal skills." Again, with a smaller workforce, the results of an HR manager's interpersonal skills may be seen more quickly than in a large organisation. Employee relations are a large part of the human resources manager's job function, because employee concerns encompass a wide range of issues over which the manager has influence. The human resource manager is the "face of HR" and therefore relied upon to be both human resources expert and employee advocate.

1.8 Qualities of Successful HR

Analytical and critical thinking skills, the ability to lead individuals and groups, and clear communication are qualities important for successful HR managers. Equally important are characteristics that enable HR managers to strike a balance between being professional yet approachable, because they have a responsibility to support the entire workforce.

1. Expertise: The ability to manage HR functions is partly based on a generalist's knowledge of HR disciplines: compensation and benefits, safety and risk management, employee relations, recruitment and selection, and training and development.

To supervise HR specialists in each of the disciplines, an HR manager must have extensive knowledge of these areas. The HR manager typically is the expert in both HR management and HR processes.

2. Communication: HR managers have strong communication skills regardless of the audience, interacting effectively with a wide range of people, executives, staff, suppliers, colleagues and applicants. Another, equally important element of an HR manager's role is to listen, the most important aspect of communication. Employees' comments about the workplace should be given as much serious consideration and respect as the chief executives' speeches about organisational strategy.

3. Compassion: Terminating employees is probably an HR manager's least favoured task, but she must balance professionalism with compassion to handle employee terminations in the best possible way.

An HR manager's empathy is also welcomed by employees who share information about medical-related issues requiring a leave of absence or need to discuss sensitive matters, such as complaints about workplace harassment.

4. Integrity: HR managers count on their integrity to uphold equal employment opportunity.

Basic business principles such as fairness and equity are the foundation for fair employment practices, and it takes clear understanding of employment and labour law to support compliance with laws that regulate the workplace. In addition, HR managers have access to employment data, organisational strategy and the company's proprietary information, and depend on their sense of integrity to maintain strict confidentiality.

5. Leadership: In addition to understanding human behaviour, HR managers must exhibit leadership skills.

As managers of the department that recruits workers and provides recommendations for hiring workers, they are able to lead other department managers by example. For example, an HR manager who is committed to training and development for the company's employees sets an example and demonstrates to other department managers the value of improving skills of existing employees.

HR managers also lead by example when they adhere to the organisation's code of conduct in treating employees with respect.

1.9 Structure of HR Department

HR organisational structure is the framework within a human resources department that divides the decision making functions within HR into specific groups with distinct job functions. Examples of the internal structure may be employee/labour relations, compensation/performance management, training and development, recruiting, benefits, administration, health and safety, payroll/HRIS, time and staffing, records, etc. Some aspects of the HR function may be outsourced or decentralised within the organisation. This may result in specialist HR "Head Office" functions and decentralised (e.g. divisional) generalist HR functions that may not report directly to "Head Office" HR.

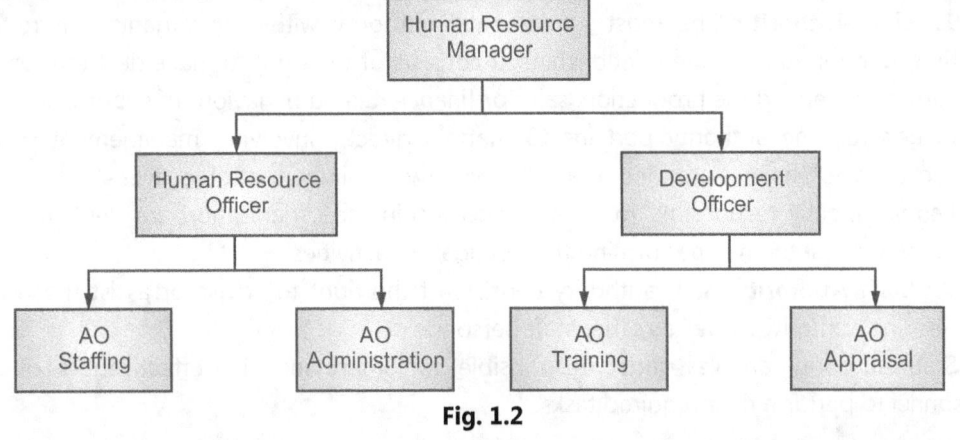

Fig. 1.2

The HR organisational structure establishes specialist groups to work together within their speciality to manage tasks within the HR organisation. Each division may have a manager or team leader depending on the size of the organisation to coordinate efforts and perform reporting tasks.

Major HR projects and activities may require significant overlap and cooperation between HR functions and the ability to temporarily adapt the function to operate on a cross functional team basis. In smaller companies, there may only be a few employees in HR handling multiple tasks.

1.10 Line and Staff Aspects of HRM

All managers are, in a sense, HR managers, since they all get involved in activities like recruiting, interviewing, selecting, and training. Yet most firms also have a human resource department with its own human resource manager.

Authority is the right to make decisions, to direct the work of others, and to give orders. In management, we usually distinguish between line authority and staff authority. Making decisions, Directing work, Giving orders are authorities' characteristics.

Authority means 'the right to perform or command'. It is the power that allows its holder to act in certain designated ways and to directly influence the actions of others through orders.

It also allows its holder to allocate the organisation's resources to achieve organisational objectives.

Types of Authority

Three main types of authority can exist within an organisation:
1. Line Authority
2. Staff Authority
3. Functional Authority

Each type exists only to enable individuals to carry out the different types of responsibilities with which they have been charged.

1. Line Authority: The most fundamental authority within an organisation reflects existing superior-subordinate relationships. It consists of the right to make decisions and to give order concerning the production, sales or finance related behaviour of subordinates.

In general, line authority pertains to matters directly involving management system production, sales, finance etc., and as a result with the attainment of objectives.

People directly responsible for these areas within the organisation are delegated line authority to assist them in performing their obligatory activities.

2. Staff Authority: Staff authority consists of the right to advise or assist those who possess line authority as well as other staff personnel.

Staff authority enables those responsible for improving the effectiveness of line personnel to perform their required tasks.

Line and Staff personnel must work together closely to maintain the efficiency and effectiveness of the organisation. To ensure that line and staff personnel do work together productively, management must make sure both groups understand the organisational mission, have specific objectives, and realise that they are partners in helping the organisation reach its objectives.

Size is perhaps the most significant factor in determining whether or not an organisation will have staff personnel. The larger the organisation, greater is the need and ability, to employ staff personnel.

As an organisation expands, it usually needs employees with expertise in diversified areas. Although small organisations may also require this kind of diverse expertise, they often find it more practical to hire part time consultants to provide as needed, rather than to hire full time staff personnel, who may not always be kept busy.

3. Line – Staff Relationship: A plant manager has line authority over each immediate subordinate, human resource manager, the production manager and the sales manager.

However, the human resource manager has staff authority in relation to the plant manager, meaning the human resource manager possesses the right to advise the plant manager on human resource matters.

Role of Staff Personnel

Harold Stieglitz has pinpointed 3 roles that staff personnel typically perform to assist line personnel:

(i) **The Advisory or Counselling Role**: In this role, staff personnel use their professional expertise to solve organisational problems. The staff personnel are, in effect, internal consultants whose relationship with line personnel is similar to that of a professional and a client.

(ii) **The Service Role**: Staff personnel in this role provide services that can more efficiently and effectively be provided by a single centralised staff group than by many individuals scattered throughout the organisation. This role can probably best be understood if staff personnel are viewed as suppliers and line personnel as customers.

(iii) **The Control Role**: Staff personnel help establish a mechanism for evaluating the effectiveness of organisational plans.

The role of staff in any organisation should be specifically designed to best meet the needs of that organisation.

4. Functional Authority: Functional authority consists of the right to give orders within a segment of the organisation in which this right is normally non-existent.

This authority is usually assigned to individuals to complement the line or staff authority they already possess.

Functional Authority generally covers only specific task areas and is operational only for designated amounts of time. It is given to individuals who, in order to meet responsibilities in their own areas, must be able to exercise some control over organisation members in other areas.

Line Versus Staff Authority: Line managers are authorised to direct the work of subordinates. Staff managers are authorised to assist and advise line managers in accomplishing their basic goals. HR managers are generally staff managers.

Line Managers' HRM Responsibilities: Most line managers are responsible for line functions, coordinative functions, and some staff functions.

Line Manager:

Authorised to direct the work of subordinates, Line managers are in charge of accomplishing the organisation's basic goals.

Line Managers' Human Resource Management responsibilities:

1. Placement
2. Orientation
3. Training
4. Improving job performance
5. Gaining creative cooperation
6. Interpreting policies and procedures
7. Controlling labour costs
8. Developing employee abilities
9. Creating and maintaining departmental morale
10. Protecting employees' health and physical condition

Staff Manager

HR managers are generally staff managers.

Responsibilities of Staff Managers

Staff managers assist and advise line managers in accomplishing these basic goals. They do, however, need to work in partnership with each other to be successful.

Some examples of HR responsibilities of staff managers include assistance in hiring, training, evaluating, rewarding, counselling, promoting, and firing of employees, and the administering of various benefits programmes.

Human Resource Manager

Human resource managers are individuals who normally act in an advisory or staff capacity, working with other managers to help them deal with human resource matters.

HR executives must understand the complex organisational design and be able to determine the capabilities of the company's workforce, both today and in the future.

HR involvement in strategy is necessary to ensure that human resources support the firm's mission.

Difference between human resource executives, generalists, and specialists

(a) **HR Executives:** Executives are top-level managers, who report directly to the corporation's chief executive officer or the head of a major division.

(b) **HR Generalists:** Generalists are people who perform tasks in a wide variety of human resource-related areas. The generalist is involved in several, or all, of the human resource management functions.

(c) **HR Specialist:** Specialist may be a human resource executive, manager, or non-manager who typically is concerned with only one of the functional areas of human resource management.

1.11 HR Relationship and Linkages with other Departments

Human resources departments interact with other department managers in numerous ways. The particular function an HR manager or specialist plays is sometimes contingent upon the department manager's title. A department manager in accounting, for example, may need more numerical statistics from HR than a customer service manager. Whatever the case, the relationship between HR and various department managers is ongoing. Many of the functions performed by HR pertain to employees of department managers.

Selecting and Screening Employees

Department managers in small companies usually ask HR to assist them with selecting and screening job applicants. For example, a marketing manager may need to hire a marketing analyst. Hence, she may ask the human resources manager to find people with specific skills to interview. In turn, the HR manager may help screen candidates who don't meet the qualifications or fail to demonstrate their skills. HR typically screens employees for substance abuse, too, subjecting new hires to drug tests, for example. HR also works with department managers in determining whether to hire permanent employees or independent contractors for certain jobs.

Orientation and Training

HR managers also work with department managers in putting their employees through orientation. The process of orientation may entail introducing new hires to company policies, completing paperwork and signing confidentiality statements. HR may also help department managers introduce new employees to other people in the company with whom they will have a working relationship. Some may also provide training manuals or arrange training sessions for new hires. This helps the department manager better prepare workers for specific job and department tasks.

Determining Compensation Packages

Small company department managers may ask HR to help them determine salaries or wages for various jobs in their department. The department manager may want to determine a low, mid-range and cap on salaries she offers employees. The HR manager may, in turn, research salaries of competitors or comparably sized companies to derive suggested salary ranges. Similarly, HR may work with department managers in deciding which benefits their employees receive, including health, life insurance, paid holidays and vacations, and retirement plans.

Considerations

The relationship between HR and a department manager may also include grievances or sensitivity issues. For example, a finance department manager may need the help of HR to resolve a complaint from a subordinate. The human resources manager may be able to resolve the situation and prevent a possible lawsuit. HR may also assist department managers with employees who violate certain sensitivity policies. These policies can include sexual harassment or conflicts with respect to race, religion or gender.

1.12 Personnel Policies and Principles

Personnel policies help implement a consistent approach to management. According to Gregorio Billikopf at the University of California, Berkeley, "Policies can be a fine tool in reducing perceptions of arbitrary treatment of employees." Everyone from the lowest entry level employees to top level management should fully understand any personnel policies you put in place. Try not to limit your supervisors' individual management style too much, but make sure that everyone knows what is expected of them and how their subordinates or co-workers should be treated in certain situations, including discipline and awards.

1.12.1 Definition

A personnel policy is a pre-planned course of action establishing a guide to work toward acceptable outcomes and objectives. **Personnel policies are the rules that govern how to deal with a human resources or personnel related situation.** They are guidelines to decision making that help keep the system as fair and unbiased as possible. They outline worker conduct within a broad framework that reflects the intentions and goals of top management.

1.12.2 Function

Personnel policies provide a framework for uniform and consistent administration. They help employees understand the reasoning behind decisions and prevent favouritism-real or perceived. Personnel policies outline the hiring procedure, including whether they should be tested first, information about a trial period or other training matters. They also outline pay functions, including salaries, commission and bonuses so that employees have a clear goal and method of reward.

1.12.3 Principles of Personnel Policies

A good personnel policy will help match each employee in the correct position and make your company into an organised and coordinated team. It outlines job training for each position, and following the guidelines should make every employee fully prepared for their work. Personnel policies create security within the opportunity, and provide incentive and recognition. Explicit policies help your employees perform their jobs at their best and work toward career goals and the future.

Policy Contents

Your personnel policies should cover three areas: employer expectations, employee expectations and administrative issues, and should all be included in your employee handbook or other training or procedural materials. Employer expectations include attendance, punctuality, time off, job requirements, and possibly internet or drug policies. Employee expectations include compensation, salary, benefits, sexual harassment, privacy rights, equal opportunity employment and any grievance procedures. Administrative issues include any disclaimers or changes to the handbook or other policies.

Creation and Implementation

"A personnel policy should reflect good practice, be written down, be communicated across the organisation, and should adapt to changing circumstances," advises BNET. Getting your management, supervisors and employees involved is important. Make sure to take into account your past policies, management styles and employee challenges when writing or updating your policy. To be effective, your policies need to be well communicated. Make sure they are available at all times and given to each employee to preclude complaints of ignorance later.

1.13 The HRM Models

The Fomburn/ Michigan/Matching Model
- The Michigan model was propounded by Fombrun Tichy and Devanna (1984) at the Michigan Business School. This model is inclined towards the harder side of HRM. It demands that available human resources must be matched with jobs in the organisation.
- The HR strategy must include the quantity of the human resources required to achieve the objectives in the business strategy.
- Business strategy takes the central stage in this model hence human resources are taken like any other resource which must be fully utilised together with the other resoruces to achieve organisational objectives.

(Evans and Lorange, 1989) argue that the Michigan model is based on the "product market logic" which demands that to gain high profits labour must be obtained cheaply, used sparingly, developed and exploited fully.

Fig. 1.3: The Fomburn Matching Model of HRM

The organisation utilises its resources in the best possible manner to complete the organisational tasks.

Business strategy must be achieved through minimum labour costs enhanced by structural re-organisation, performance related pay and staff reduction.

The Harvard Model

The Harvard Model was postulated by Beer et al (1984) at Harvard University. The authors of the model also coined it the map of HRM territory.

The Harvard model acknowledges the existence of multiple stakeholders within the organisation. These multiple stakeholders include shareholder, groups of employees, government and the community.

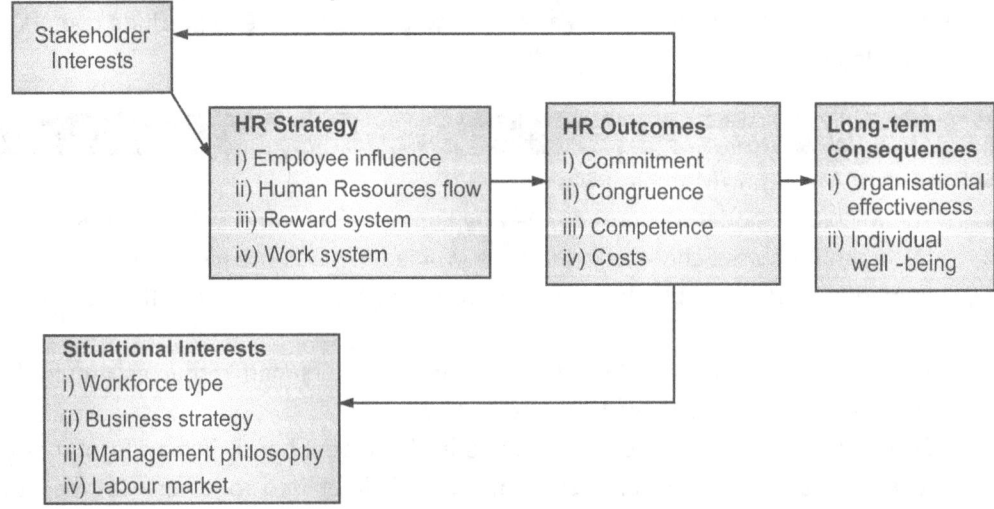

Fig. 1.4

The recognition of the legitimacy of these multiple stakeholders renders this model a neo - pluralist model.

This model emphasises more on the human/soft side of HRM.

Basically this is because this model emphasises more on the fact that employees like any other shareholder are equally important in influencing organisational outcomes.

In fact the interest of the various groups must be fused and factored in the creation of HRM strategies and ultimately the creation of business strategies.

The Guest Model

The Guest model was suggested by David Guest in 1987.

Guest proposes 4 crucial components that support organisational effectiveness.

These 4 crucial components are:

1. **Strategic Integration:** There should be alignment between business strategy and the HR strategy for the organisation to achieve its goals.

   Strategic integration shows the harder side of the Guest Model.

   This is precisely because human resources are treated like any other resource with the objective of achieving business goals.

2. **Flexibility:** Flexibility is basically concerned with the ability adapt to the changing business and work environment.

   Flexibility relates to hard and soft HRM.

   Hard HRM for example: layoff during economic slowdown.

   Flexibility in this case is not only concerned with the need to achieve business objectives but also the need to treat its employees as fairly as possible.

3. **High Commitment:** This is concerned with the need to have both behavioural commitment and attitudinal commitment.

4. **Quality:** Quality improves with better management.

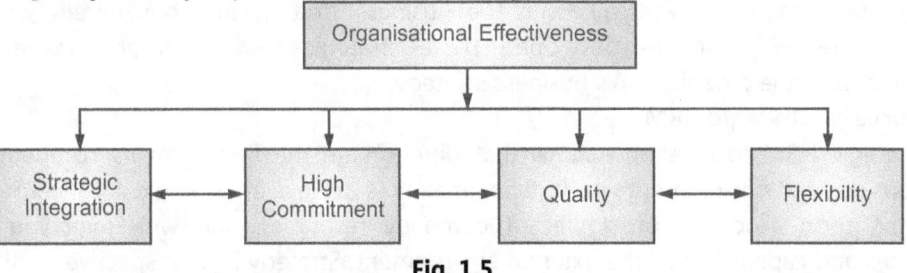

Fig. 1.5

1.14 SHRM

Strategy determines the direction in which the organisation is going in relation to its environment. It is the process of defining intentions (strategic intent) and allocating or matching resources to opportunities and needs (resource-based strategy), thus achieving strategic fit between them. Business strategy is concerned with achieving competitive advantage. The effective development and implementation of strategy depend on the strategic capability of the organisation, which will include the ability not only to formulate strategic goals, but also to develop and implement strategic plans through the process of strategic management. Strategy is about implementation, which includes the management of change, as well as planning.

The concept of strategy is not a straightforward one. There are many different theories about what it is and how it works.

Strategy can have a number of meanings, namely:
- a plan, or something equivalent - a direction, a guide, a course of action;
- a pattern, that is, consistency in behaviour over time;
- a perspective, an organisation's fundamental way of doing things;
- a ploy, a specific 'manoeuvre' intended to outwit an opponent or a competitor.

Strategic HRM defines how an organisation achieves its business goals through its people. Strategic human resource management is the process of linking the human resource function with the strategic objectives of the organisation in order to improve performance.

Strategic human resource management is the proactive management of people. It requires thinking ahead, and planning ways for a company to better meet the needs of its employees, and for the employees to better meet the needs of the company. This can affect the way things are done at a business site, improving everything from hiring practices and employee training programmes to assessment techniques and discipline.

Strategic HRM is an approach to making decisions on the intentions and plans of the organisation concerning the employment relationship and its recruitment, training, development, performance management, reward and employee relations strategies, policies and practices. The key characteristic of strategic HRM is that it is integrated. HR strategies are generally integrated vertically with the business strategy and horizontally with one another. The HR strategies developed by a strategic HRM approach are essential components of the organisation's business strategy.

The Focus of Strategic HRM

Strategic HRM focuses on actions that differentiate the firm from its competitors. It develops declarations of intent which define means to achieve ends, and it is concerned with the long term allocation of significant company resources, and with matching those resources and capabilities to the external environment. Strategy is a perspective on the way in which critical issues or success factors can be addressed, and strategic decisions aim to make a major and long term impact on the behaviour and success of the organisation.

Aims of Strategic HRM

The fundamental aim of strategic HRM is to generate strategic capability by ensuring that the organisation has the skilled, committed and well-motivated employees it needs to achieve sustained competitive advantage. Its objective is to provide a sense of direction in an often turbulent environment, so that the business needs of the organisation, and the individual and collective needs of its employees, can be met by the development and implementation of coherent and practical HR policies and programmes.

An important aspect of strategic human resource management is employee development. This process begins when a company is recruiting and interviewing prospective employees. Improved interviewing techniques can help to weed out applicants that may not be a good match for the company.

Strategic HRM supplies a perspective on the way in which critical issues or success factors related to people can be addressed and strategic decisions are made that have a major and long-term impact on the behaviour and success of the organisation. The fundamental aim of strategic HRM is to generate strategic capability by ensuring that the organisation has the skilled, committed and well-motivated employees it needs to achieve sustained competitive advantage. Its objective is to provide a sense of direction in an often turbulent environment so that the business needs of the organisation, and the individual and collective needs of its employees can be met by the development and implementation of coherent and practical HR policies and programmes.

1.15 HR's Role in Formulating Strategies

Strengthening the employer-employee relationship is the strategic role of a human resources manager. However, there's more than meets the eye to doing this. Human resources managers formulate workforce strategy and determine the functional processes necessary to meet organisational goals. Their job requires expertise as an HR generalist, which means they must be familiar with every human resources discipline.

Workplace Safety

Creating a work environment free from unnecessary hazards is a strategic role of every human resources manager. Strategic development for workplace safety entails risk management and mitigating potential losses from on-the-job injuries and fatalities. Workers' compensation insurance is an area in which a strategic plan helps lower company expense for insurance coverage. Reducing accidents through training employees on the proper use of complex machinery and equipment is one of the functional tasks associated with creating a safe work environment.

Compensation and Benefits

An employer's compensation and benefits structure partly determines the company's business reputation and image. In addition, the decisions that human resources managers make regarding pay scales and employee benefits can impact employee satisfaction, as well as the organisation's ability to recruit talented workers. Job evaluation, labour market conditions, workforce shortages and budget constraints are factors that HR managers consider in a strategic plan for pay and benefits. In addition, a strategy includes weighing an employer's choices between satisfying its workforce and pleasing the company's stakeholders. Pursuant to the health care reform law passed in 2010, human resources managers for companies with more than 50 employees must decide between offering group health coverage and paying fines, beginning in 2014.

Employee Training

Human resources managers' strategic role with respect to employee training and development prepares the workforce for future positions within the company. Succession planning, promotion-from-within policies and performance evaluation factor into the human resources manager's role. Training and development motivate employees, and in some cases, improve employee retention.

Recruitment and Selection

Employee recruitment and selection is as much a part of employee relations as it is a separate discipline unto itself. Therefore, a human resources manager's strategic role is to combine elements of employee relations into the employer's recruitment and selection strategy. Integrating employee recognition programmes into promotion-from-within policies is an effective form of employee motivation that combines the employee relations and recruitment and selection areas of human resources.

Employee Relations

Some human resources managers believe that strengthening the employer-employee relationship rests solely in the employee relations areas of the HR department. This isn't true. Nevertheless, employee relations is such a large part of every discipline -- including salaries, benefits, safety, training and employee development -- that sustaining an employee relations programme is an important element of human resources strategy. Implementing a workplace investigation process and enforcing fair employment practices are two components of an employee relations programme. The strategic role of a human resources manager is to determine how to identify and resolve workplace issues, as well as how best to attract a diverse pool of applicants through effective recruitment and selection processes.

1.16 HR's Role as a Strategic Partner

For several decades, the HR function in corporations has been encouraged to become a strategic partner. An analysis of what HR can do to become a strategic partner shows some clear actions that HR can take. These include talent development in HR, creating corporate centers of excellence, developing the right metrics and analytics, and perhaps most important, understanding how human capital management impacts business results. The results also show that there are a number of strategy activities that HR can be involved in and that to some degree, different factors influence how much HR is involved in each of them.

In the context of strategic human resource management, the HR function and activities are intended to ensure the organisation's financial success.

As partners HR people and employees in the various areas of the organisation's operations must not get in the others' way. Partners do not hinder one another. Instead, they support each other to achieve common objectives with the purpose of attaining the overall objectives, including business objectives.

There are some who are of the opinion that the implementation of HR strategic partnership is not easy. HR people themselves may hinder its implementation.

A strategic plan will ensure that your people will carry out their own specific role in their assigned area of operation in partnership with other employees.

This is part of your HR as strategic partner plan. It incorporates the HR Mission that helps direct HR people in the same direction.

Why make HR an Organisational Strategic Partner:
1. To increase productivity of the labour force and thus, profitability of the organisation.
2. Competency and talent management.
3. Onset of information technology and the vast amount of knowledge used in the course of the activities of organisations.
4. The changing business environment.
5. Effect of globalisation on the business landscape.

Making HR a Strategic Partner
1. Make effective use of your Human Resource Information System (HRIS) to handle daily administrative HR tasks. Employees can make use of the self-service facility online. This saves time and reduces costs.
2. Fully involve your human resource in HR system development that is supportive of business strategy development and implementation. This promotes ownership.
3. Appoint an HR Head who understands well the strategic partnership relationship between organisational strategy and human resource.

   It is said that someone who is an expert in every aspect of the HR function will 'fit the bill'. But, you may not easily find someone of this calibre. You may have to identify someone from within your organisation and groom him or her for this important role.
4. In a knowledge economy, HR has an opportunity to become a strategic partner. Knowledge and information are required to formulate, implement and review strategies. Decide to become a knowledge organisation.

The Human Resource Function and Your Strategic Business Plan

It was shown in a survey that there is a correlation between being strategic business partner and the effectiveness of the HR function.

You require strategic HR management to ensure that your HR function can fully support the achievement of business objectives. Chief executives including general managers need to ensure that this is done.

The administrative reactive approach in people management can no longer support your organisation in an increasingly competitive business environment. Line managers and supervisors resent it and will put the blame on HR when problems arise. And if you do so, it interferes with the effective use of line managers' and supervisors' time in the day-to-day operations of the organisation.

Give line managers and supervisors HR accountability, not responsibility. And give them undivided support in order to make them more proficient in managing their subordinates in the performance of daily tasks.

Strategy Development and Implementation

Full participation of HR people in strategy development and implementation promotes HR as strategic partner.

Ensure that your HR Manager and HR professionals:
- contribute to business decisions,
- develop business acumen to understand how a profitable business is run,
- are customer-oriented,
- learn how to link HR practices to your organisational business strategy.

Measurement-of-HR-Contribution

The things already stated are important. But there is an important matter that needs attention.

You may ask, "How do I know whether my HR function is playing its role?"

Implement an HR performance measurement such as the HR Scorecard. This can show whether your organisation is well on the road to making HR as strategic partner.

Enhancement of Competitive-Advantage

By doing these things, you can increase the competitive advantage of your organisation through the alignment of human resource strategies to your overall business plan.

This goes towards strengthening the importance of HR as strategic partner.

It goes without saying that developing effective leadership skills at various levels in your organisation - including HR-is vital to corporate success. This is the type of leadership that drives the success of organisations.

HR-Budget

In order to ensure that HR truly becomes strategic business partner, adequate financial backing is necessary.

Risks-of-financial-shutdown

Take measures to ward off or minimise risks to HR. Further to this, ensure that HR plays a meaningful role, if not a major role, during financial crises.

Being in HR requires you to know and understand certain things and to do something about them.

You do not have the luxury of experimenting using a trial and error approach. Making HR as strategic partner is an insurance that your organisation will succeed in more ways than one.

1.17 HR's Role in Executing Strategies

For business organisations across the world, strategy execution holds significant priority. Strategy execution is also known as performance management or PM. The entire process of strategy execution or performance management works to define a strategy, to implement it and to interpret it to each individual of an organisation.

HR Role in Strategy Execution

For the previous 10 years, Human Resource has been acting as an outsourcing body. It has been working as consultants to outsource administrative functions. Therefore, consulting in the field of strategy execution is very promising and paying.

Successful projects which act as driving force for strategy execution contain three constituents. These constituents are known as executive sponsorship, project managers and project team members.

Executive Sponsor

Success of a project can be achieved if the executive sponsor makes sure that that the participants of the project are devoted and focused on common aim and vision. The executive sponsor may expand his or her vision and commitment for including bigger support groups and business community.

Human Resources work with particular individuals in order to recognise the roles, which an executive sponsor is expected to play. Other responsibility of HR is to ensure that the executive sponsors accomplish the roles assigned to them. If needed, HR should help the sponsors in this regard. HR professionals should escape the role of leadership development in the execution of strategy.

Role of project team members

Generally, people who are hired as project team members are expected to carry out everyday activities. They are not expected to execute strategic initiatives. These everyday activities include market research, system programmeming, finance and assembling the required items.

The activities of project team members for accomplishing projects require a deep analysis of processes and current systems, planning for the improvement of the performance and challenge-accepting outlook for pursuing non-traditional ideas, actions and activities for best results. Ever thought of why do companies fail to succeed in spite of the great strategies that they have formulated and pursued all along. Most obvious reason being that companies never realise that to pursue a great unique strategy also requires change in the way we carry out work. You cannot expect to reap rich rewards even with a path breaking strategy, without changing the way you work.

People factor differentiates two companies following similar strategy

Classic example quoted in this context are those Wal-Mart, the world biggest retailer and largest business organisation based in The United States, whose low cost strategy during 1980s and 90s was tried by many of its competitors but not with the kind of success that Wal-Mart has achieved. The difference being the people employed who are passionate about lowest prices. The belief that cost advantage gained by the company is passed on ultimately to the customers drives and motivates Wal-Mart employees to generate and implement new ideas of cost cutting. This kind of involvement by people was missing in its competitors.

Key role of HR manager - internal consultant

Though companies realise that culture and more importantly its visible attribute – behaviours – affect strategy implementation and yet not many HR managers know how to act or more precisely do not spare a thought on such an important aspect of strategy implementation. To be able to act, HR managers need to know exactly what changes in working style are required for the company's strategy to be implemented successfully and distinctly in the marketplace.

Knowledge of such subtle change in people behaviours is of little help as the changes in behaviours cannot be brought about until there is an unstinting support from top management team, which comes from their understanding of linkage between behaviours and strategy implementation. In this context HR managers must play the role of internal consultants and work closely with top management to impress upon them the need for subtle changes in organisational culture, gain their support and then create awareness, understanding and systems to reinforce the desired behaviours in the people.

To do this HR managers must involve top management and the people in key roles (which may include people heading key functions, union representatives etc.), preferably in a workshop and can put forth the question how the culture of the company can best be described in terms of most pronounced characteristics. The probable outcome could be identification of characteristics such as innovativeness or status quo, learning or belief of being the best, trust or command structure, customer orientation or product orientation and so on and so forth. Next the team may work on desirable attributes that company must value to pursue the new strategy and that gives the clarity on the need to move from old cultural habits to desired cultural tenets. The team must further work on identification of positive behaviours with respect to each of the values for clear communication to one and all.

From conceptualisation to implementation

After dealing with conceptual part of the exercise to identify and understand the changes required in the way work is conducted to pursue the new strategy, the practical part starts with putting in place the systems and mechanisms to reinforce the identified behaviours.

Changes in systems include incentive and reward schemes for example shift from production volumes and quality to customer satisfaction, or from individual excellence to team excellence and knowledge sharing, organisational structure for example to improve responsiveness to markets and customers, or to provide renewed thrust to new product development or to penetrate new market and customer segments and perhaps people in key positions – to drive the effort through personal traits and abilities. This kind of effort - when it results in desired performance levels - enhances commitment to new set of behaviours which will help in improving the systems further.

Complementary effect of culture and performance

This cycle of culture reinforcing the performance and the performance reinforcing the culture will finally enable HR in establishing a cultural infrastructure of sustained competitive advantage that would become difficult for the competitors to emulate.

HR can thus make a big positive difference by keeping intact the coherence between organisation's strategy and its culture and thus truly be the most important enabler of business results.

Project manager

The roles of project managers revolve round integration and coordination of entire activities, which fulfil the requirements of the business. Some of the additional behavioural skills required for project managers include communication, team merging, casting influence on others, convincing, problem solving and negotiation.

It is very rare that people selected for the positions of project manager are offered training. It is the responsibility of HR to run the operation along with their business partners. HR is also expected to help the business partners in the selection of the appropriate candidate who may lead the project in order to execute strategy.

1.18 HRIS

A Human Resources Management System (HRMS) or Human Resources Information System (HRIS), refers to the systems and processes at the intersection between human resource management (HRM) and information technology. It merges HRM as a discipline and in particular its basic HR activities and processes with the information technology field, whereas the programming of data processing systems evolved into standardised routines and packages of enterprise resource planning (ERP) software. On the whole, these ERP systems have their origin on software that integrates information from different applications into one universal database. The linkage of its financial and human resource modules through one database is the most important distinction to the individually and proprietary developed predecessors, which makes this software application both rigid and flexible.

The function of human resources (HR) departments is generally administrative and common to all organisations. Organisations may have formalised selection, evaluation, and payroll processes. Efficient and effective management of "human capital" progressed to an increasingly imperative and complex process.

The HR function consists of tracking existing employee data which traditionally includes personal histories, skills, capabilities, accomplishments and salary. To reduce the manual workload of these administrative activities, organisations began to electronically automate many of these processes by introducing specialized human resource management systems. HR executives rely on internal or external IT professionals to develop and maintain an integrated HRMS. Before the client–server architecture evolved in the late 1980s, many HR automation processes were relegated to mainframe computers that could handle large amounts of data transactions.

In consequence of the high capital investment necessary to buy or programme proprietary software, these internally developed HRMS were limited to organisations that possessed a large amount of capital. The advent of client–server, application service provider, and software as a service (SaaS) or human resource management systems enabled increasingly higher administrative control of such systems.

Currently, human resource management systems encompass:
1. Payroll
2. Time and attendance
3. Performance appraisal
4. Benefits administration
5. HR management information system
6. Recruiting/Learning management
7. Performance record
8. Employee self-service
9. Scheduling
10. Absence management
11. Analytics

- The **payroll module** automates the pay process by gathering data on employee time and attendance, calculating various deductions and taxes, and generating periodic pay cheques and employee tax reports. Data is generally fed from the human resources and time keeping modules to calculate automatic deposit and manual cheque writing capabilities. This module can encompass all employee-related transactions as well as integrate with existing financial management systems.
- The **time and attendance module** gathers standardized time and work related efforts. The most advanced modules provide broad flexibility in data collection methods, labour distribution capabilities and data analysis features. Cost analysis and efficiency metrics are the primary functions.
- The **benefits administration module** provides a system for organisations to administer and track employee participation in benefits programmes. These typically encompass insurance, compensation, profit sharing and retirement.
- The **HR management module** is a component covering many other HR aspects from application to retirement. The system records basic demographic and address data, selection, training and development, capabilities and skills management, compensation planning records and other related activities. Leading edge systems provide the ability to "read" applications and enter relevant data to applicable database fields, notify employers and provide position management and position control.

Human resource management function involves the recruitment, placement, evaluation, compensation and development of the employees of an organisation.

Initially, businesses used computer based information systems to:
- produce pay checks and payroll reports;
- maintain personnel records;
- pursue talent management.

Online **recruiting** has become one of the primary methods employed by HR departments to garner potential candidates for available positions within an organisation.

Talent management systems typically encompass:
- Analysing personnel usage within an organisation;
- Identifying potential applicants;
- Recruiting through company-facing listings;
- Recruiting through online recruiting sites or publications that market to both recruiters and applicants.

The significant cost incurred in maintaining an organised recruitment effort, cross-posting within and across general or industry-specific job boards and maintaining a competitive exposure of availabilities has given rise to the development of a dedicated applicant tracking system, or 'ATS', module.

The **training module** provides a system for organisations to administer and track employee training and development efforts. The system, normally called a "learning management system" (LMS) if a standalone product, allows HR to track education, qualifications and skills of the employees, as well as outlining what training courses, books, CDs, web based learning or materials are available to develop which skills. Courses can then be offered in date specific sessions, with delegates and training resources being mapped and managed within the same system. Sophisticated LMS allow managers to approve training, budgets and calendars alongside performance management and appraisal metrics.

The **employee self-service module** allows employees to query HR related data and perform some HR transactions over the system. Employees may query their attendance record from the system without asking the information from HR personnel. The module also lets supervisors approve O.T. requests from their subordinates through the system without overloading the task on HR department.

Many organisations have gone beyond the traditional functions and developed human resource management information systems, which support recruitment, selection, hiring, job placement, performance appraisals, employee benefit analysis, health, safety and security, while others integrate an outsourced applicant tracking system that encompasses a subset of the above.

Assigning Responsibilities Communication between the Employees

The **Analytics** module enables organisations to extend the value of an HRMS implementation by extracting HR related data for use with other business intelligence platforms. For example, organisations combine HR metrics with other business data to identify trends and anomalies in headcount in order to better predict the impact of employee turnover on future output.

1.19 Human Capital Management

Human capital is the stock of competencies, knowledge, social and personality attributes, including creativity, embodied in the ability to perform labour so as to produce economic value. It is an aggregate economic view of the human being acting within economies, which is an attempt to capture the social, biological, cultural and psychological complexity as they interact in explicit and/or economic transactions. Many theories explicitly connect investment in human capital development to education, and the role of human capital in economic development, productivity growth, and innovation has frequently been cited as a justification for government subsidies for education and job skills training.

HR world has changed its name from Human Resources, Benefits, and Payroll to something that includes those business processes and MORE. It's branching into the areas of automated, web-based, self-service, analytics and efficient talent management as a whole; coining the new name: Human Capital Management (HCM).

The Human Capital Management department of the 21st century and beyond is a crucial business partner for each department (Financials, Supply Chain, and Customer Relations) in reaching its annual, short-term and long-term goals. HR helps the other departments obtain and retain the right talent, the right people, and the right resources in this mobile and global society, to achieve the organisation's business goals and objectives. In addition, HCM departments ensure that the people that are retained are staying up to date with their skills, training, and their competencies are aligned appropriately to be productive and fruitful for their departments.

The Function of Human Capital Management

Human Capital Management is the mindset that your workforce is your most valuable asset, and more care should go into managing that asset than any other company asset. Caring for and making the most of your Human Capital requires a tightly integrated suite of systems to manage Payroll, HR, Benefits and Time and Labour.

True human capital management is more than just an HR function. It requires strategic analysis of the entire organisation. The more proactive an organisation is, the more the organisation will have the necessary human capital on hand rather than having to "build" or "buy".

The strategic management of human capital requires comprehensive planning and analysis in order to develop, implement, and evaluate programmes that support every facet of employee work life.

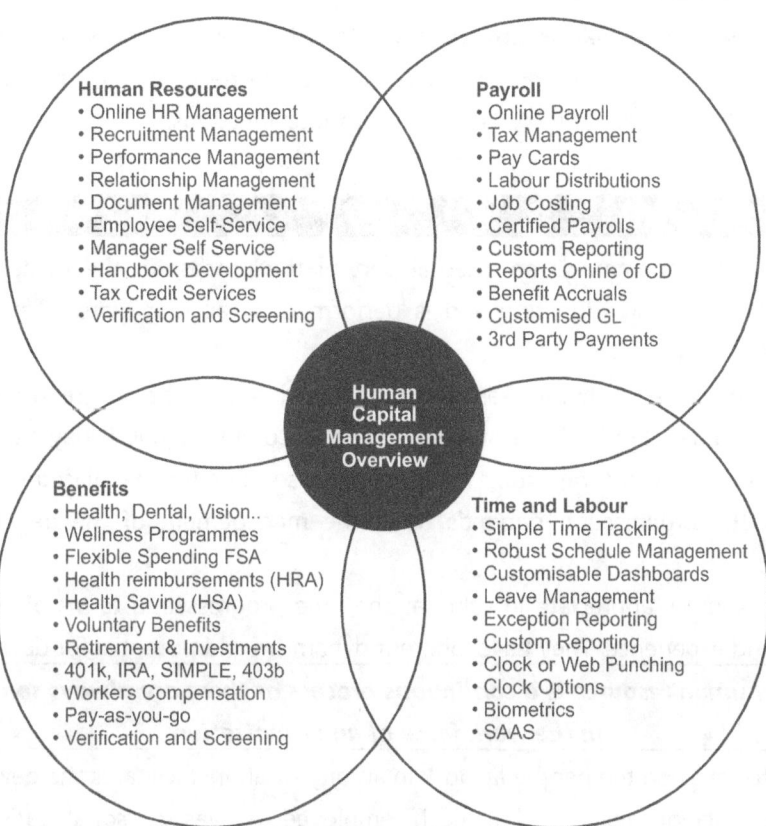

Fig. 1.6

1.20 HR And Employee Performance and Commitment

According to **Scarlett Surveys**, "*Employee Engagement is a measurable degree of an employee's positive or negative emotional attachment to their job, colleagues and organisation that profoundly influences their willingness to learn and perform at work*". Thus engagement is distinctively different from employee satisfaction, motivation and organisational culture.

Some of the initiatives commonly undertaken by HR departments towards employee engagement are:

- **On-boarding**: When an employee joins the organisations he needs to be exposed to the organisations policies and culture. There may be some fresh out of campuses that need to know the basics of communication skills and job related skills. During the induction programme itself, they can be given an exposure about these aspects, skills sets and the expectations. The on-boarding event experience itself leaves a mark on the minds of the new recruits about the company's desire to enhance their skills.

- **Learning and development events**: When business practices and processes are changing. In this environment, there is an acute necessity for enhancing the skill levels of employees already discharging various functions.

1.21 Managing HR

Manpower management is an integral part of the process of the management of a business. It is a pervasive function and is performed by all managers at all levels in an organisation.

Personnel managers or human resource managers interpret the progressive needs of the organisation and direct individual potential towards a common goal. Today, human factor is considered to be the most important resource because the effective utilisation of the other resources of the organisation depends upon the management of the personnel of the organisation.

Human resources appreciate in value as the time progresses in terms of acquisition of knowledge and experience. They have inherent dynamism and potential for development.

Managing human resource is a continuous process as there are always some changes in the work force of an organisation.

It seeks to focus on the people at work in an organisation, facilitates the development of such human relationships so that each employee derives personal satisfaction and contributes optimally towards realisation of overall goals of an organisation. The changes in the business environment with increasing globalisation, changing demographics of the workforce, increased focus on profitability as a result of growth, technological changes, intellectual capital and the never-ending changes that organisations are undergoing have led to increased importance for management of human resources. The idea of Human Resource Management strategy is that of development of innovation skills and aptitude, improve quality of performance of employees and to reduce costs in an organisation by motivating workers to work harder, applying their best efforts, skills and knowledge towards their work and organisation.

The specific objectives of personnel management are:
- To build and maintain cordial relations between people working at different levels of the organisation.
- To ensure effective utilisation of the available human resources.
- To provide fair working conditions, wages and amenities to the employees.
- To achieve the development of each individual employee to his/her fullest potential.

Points to Remember

- Effective HRM enables employees to contribute effectively and productively to the overall company direction and the accomplishment of the organisation's goals and objectives.
- Today, HRM is looked up as a prominent department and shares its existence with the top management functions and figures of the organisation.
- HRM aligns the employee's skills with the present and future needs of the organisation and utilises it towards the achievement of the desired goal.
- Changes in the external environment have a profound impact on the personnel.
- Historically, it is believed that PM preceded HRM.
- Human resource management involves all management decisions and practices that directly affect or influence the people, or human resources, who work for the organisation.
- The goal of a human resource manager is to strengthen the employer-employee relationship.
- Managing human resource is a continuous process as there are always some changes in the work force of an organisation.

The specific objectives of personnel management are:-

- To build and maintain cordial relations between people working at different levels of the organisation.
- To ensure effective utilisation of the available human resources.
- To provide fair working conditions, wages and amenities to the employees.
- To achieve the development of each individual employee to his/her fullest potential

Questions for Discussion

1. Define Human Resource Management.
2. Explain the nature, scope and importance of HRM.
3. Describe evolution of HRM.
4. Enumerate objectives and functions of HRM.
5. Define Personnel Management (PM).
6. Differentiate between PM and HRM.
7. Explain the role of HR professional/manager.
8. Enumerate qualities of successful HR.
9. Identify and describe HRM and its environment.
10. List the different Models of HRM.
11. Explain the Fombrun model.

12. Describe the following models of HRM: Harvard model, Guest model, and Warwick model.
13. Explain HR's Strategic Role.
14. Define SHRM.
15. Identify HR's role as a Strategic Partner.
16. Describe HR's role in executing strategies.
17. What is the HR's role in formulating strategies?
18. Illustrate HRI's.
19. Define Human Capital Management.
20. Describe HR and employee performance and commitment.
21. Describe managing HR.

Objective Questions

Fill in the blanks:
1. Effective HRM enables employees to contribute _____ and _____ to the overall company direction and the accomplishment of the organisation's goals and objectives.
2. HRM is looked up as a _____ and shares its existence with the top management functions and figures of the organisation.
3. HRM aligns the employee's skills with the present and future needs of _____ and utilises it towards the achievement of the desired goal.
4. Changes in the external _____ have a profound impact on the personnel.
5. Historically, it is believed that PM _____ HRM
6. Human resource management involves all management _____ and practices that directly affect or influence the people, or human resources, who work for the organisation.
7. The goal of a human resource manager is to _____ the employer-employee relationship.
8. Staff managers assist and advise _____ in accomplishing these basic goals.

Answers:
1. Effectively and productively
2. Prominent department
3. The organisation
4. Environment
5. Preceded
6. Decisions
7. Strengthen
8. Line managers

Case Study

The president has called a meeting to get your feedback on Rohan, a department manager. Rohan is what some people call "from the old school" of management. He is gruff, bossy and is about five years from retirement.

Rohan is a brilliantly talented person who adds a vast amount of needed knowledge and experience to the company. He is extremely dedicated to the company and lets people know this by his arrival each day at 6:30 a.m. and his departure at 6:00 p.m. He has been with the company for 32 years and he reports directly to the president.

Rohan has a high turnover rate in his department. There have been several complaints on company surveys about him from his department and from outside his department. People have commented on the fact that Rohan is "rude" during meetings and doesn't let others contribute. There are times when he has belittled people in meetings and in the hallway. He also talks about his staff "critically" or "negatively" to other managers.

Rohan has gone to the HR department and complained that the people his supervisors hire are not a good fit for the company. The new employees don't listen and they have a poor work ethic. Rohan feels that HR should do a better job screening people.

Questions:

What suggestions do you have for the President on how to coach Rohan and develop a personal improvement plan?

Activity

Visit an organisation in your vicinity and find the HR tasks that have been outsourced.

References and Web Links

Reference Books
1. Personnel Management by C.B Mamoria.
2. Human Resource Management by Garry Dessler.
3. Human Resource Management by Aswathappa.

Web Links
1. www.smallbusiness.chron.com >Human Resources
2. http://www.bukisa.com/articles
3. www.msu.ac.zw/elearning/material
4. http://en.wikipedia.org/wiki/Human_resource_management_system

Chapter **2**...

Procurement of Human Resources

Contents ...
- 2.1 Job Analysis
- 2.2 Job Description
- 2.3 Job Specification
- 2.4 Human Resource Planning (HRP)
- 2.5 Recruitment
- 2.6 Selection
- 2.7 Interview
- 2.8 Induction
- 2.9 Placement
  - Points to Remember
  - Questions for Discussion
  - Multiple Choice Questions
  - Case Study

Objectives ...
- ➤ To understand the concept of job analysis, job description, job specification, meaning, need and importance.
- ➤ Human Resource Planning, meaning, objectives, importance, and the process of HRP.
- ➤ Recruitment, meaning, need of recruitment, methods, recruitment yield pyramid, concept of succession planning, Selection, meaning and types.
- ➤ Interview, types of interview, induction and placement.

2.1 Job Analysis

Job analysis is the important process of identifying the content of a job in terms of activities involved and attributes needed to perform the work and identifies major job requirements. In other words, Job analysis is a primary tool in personnel management. In this method, a personnel manager tries to gather, synthesise and implement the information available regarding the workforce in the concern. A personnel manager has to undertake job analysis so as to put the right man on the right job.

Job analysis provide information to organisations which helps to determine which employees are best fit for specific jobs. Through job analysis, the analyst needs to understand what the important tasks of the job are, how they are carried out, and the necessary human qualities needed to complete the job successfully.

Job analysis aims to answer questions such as:

- Why does the job exist?
- What physical and mental activities does the worker undertake?
- When is the job to be performed?
- Where is the job to be performed?
- How does the worker do the job?
- What qualifications are needed to perform the job?
- What are the working conditions (such as levels of temperature, noise, offensive fumes, light)?
- What machinery or equipment is used in the job?
- What constitutes a successful performance?

Need of Job Analysis

Job analysis is an essential ingredient in designing a sound personnel programme. Job information gathered from job analysis may be used for the following purposes-

1. **Organisation and Manpower Planning:** Job analysis is helpful in organisational planning, for it defines labour needs in clear terms. It coordinates the activities of the work force and facilitates the division of work, duties and responsibilities. Thus, it is an essential element of manpower planning because it matches jobs with them.

2. **Recruitment and Selection:** Job analysis indicates the specific job requirements of each job i.e. skills and knowledge. In this way, job analysis provides a realistic base for hiring, training, placement, transfer and promotion of personnel. Basically, the goal of job analysis is to match the job requirements with a worker's aptitude, abilities and interests.

3. **Training and Development:** Job analysis determines the levels of standard of job performance. Job analysis provides the necessary information to the management of training and development programmes. It helps to determine the content and subject matter of training courses. It also helps in checking application information, interviewing, weighing test results and checking references.

4. **Wage and Salary Administration:** Job analysis is the foundation for job evaluation. By indicating the qualifications required for doing a specified job and the risks and hazards involved in its performance, it helps in salary and wage administration.

5. **Performance Appraisal:** Job analysis helps in establishing clear cut standards which may be compared with the actual contribution of each individual. Job analysis data provide a clear cut performance for every job.

6. **Job Re-engineering:** Job analysis provides information which enables the management to change jobs in order to provide with the personnel with specific characteristics and qualifications. This takes two forms - industrial engineering activity and human engineering activity. Industrial engineers may use the job analysis information in designing the job by making the comprehensive study. It helps in time study and motion study and work measurement. Human engineering activities such as physical, mental and psychological are studied with the help of job analysis.

7. **Health and Safety:** Job analysis provides an opportunity for identifying hazardous and unhealthy conditions so that corrective measures may be taken to minimise the possibility of accidents and sickness.

Who should Conduct the Job Analysis?

It is always better to use supervisors, job incumbent or combinations of these to obtain information about jobs in an organisation. The job incumbents offer a clear view of what work is actually done as against what work is supposed to be done. Further, involving job incumbents in the job analysis process might increase their acceptance of any work changes stemming from the result of analysis. However, in the negative side job incumbents might exaggerate the responsibilities and importance of their work and, in the process, the whole effort might suffer due to lack of objectivity. External analysts help avoid such biased opinions. They tend to base their write ups on a realistic view of people, jobs and the total organisation system as a whole. To be effective, external analysts should have considerable knowledge about how work is actually processed within the organisation while offering a "snapshot" of the job, present requirements and expected changes in future must also be taken into account. The choice of who should analyse the job depends on many factors, including the location and complexity of jobs to be analysed, how receptive incumbents might be to an external analyst and the ultimate purpose of the results of analysis.

Steps in Job Analysis

The process of job analysis must be conducted in a logical manner, following appropriate management and professional psychometric practices. Therefore, a multistage process usually is followed, regardless of the job analysis methods used. The stages for a typical job analysis are outlined here, but they may vary with the methods used and the number of jobs included.

1. **Doing Organisational Analysis and Planning for Job Analysis:** It is crucial to study the organisation as a whole to establish a link between the organisational objectives and the jobs. Organisation charts can be used for this purpose. Planning for job analysis helps in following ways:
   - It helps to update job descriptions.
   - It may include as an outcome revising the compensation programs in the organisation.
   - It helps to redesign the jobs in a department or division of the organisation.
   - It could be used to change the structure in parts of the organisation to align it better with business strategies.

2. **Collection of Job Analysis Data:** This step involves collection of data based on characteristics of jobs. For example, are the jobs to be analysed hourly, clerical jobs, all jobs in one division, or all jobs in the entire organisation? There are several techniques available for collecting such data. In this phase, those who will be involved in conducting the job analysis and the methods to be used are identified.

3. **Conducting the Job Analysis:** Once the relevant job data is collected, the job analysis can be conducted. The methods selected will determine the time line for the project. Sufficient time should be allotted for obtaining the information from employees and managers. The data also should be reviewed for completeness, and follow-up may be needed in the form of additional interviews or questions to be answered by managers and employees.

4. **Preparing Job Descriptions and Job Specifications:** At this stage the draft of job descriptions and job specifications are prepared by job analysts. Job description includes functions, duties, responsibilities, operations and so on. The job holder is expected to carry out the duties and responsibilities mentioned in the job description. Job specification is a written statement of personal attributes required to carry out the job like traits, skills, training etc.

5. **Maintaining and Updating Job Descriptions and Job Specifications:** Once job descriptions and specifications have been completed and reviewed by all appropriate individuals, a system must be developed for keeping them current. Otherwise, the entire process, beginning with job analysis, may have to be repeated in several years. Because organisations are dynamic and evolving entities, rarely do all jobs stay the same for years.

Stages in the Job Analysis Process

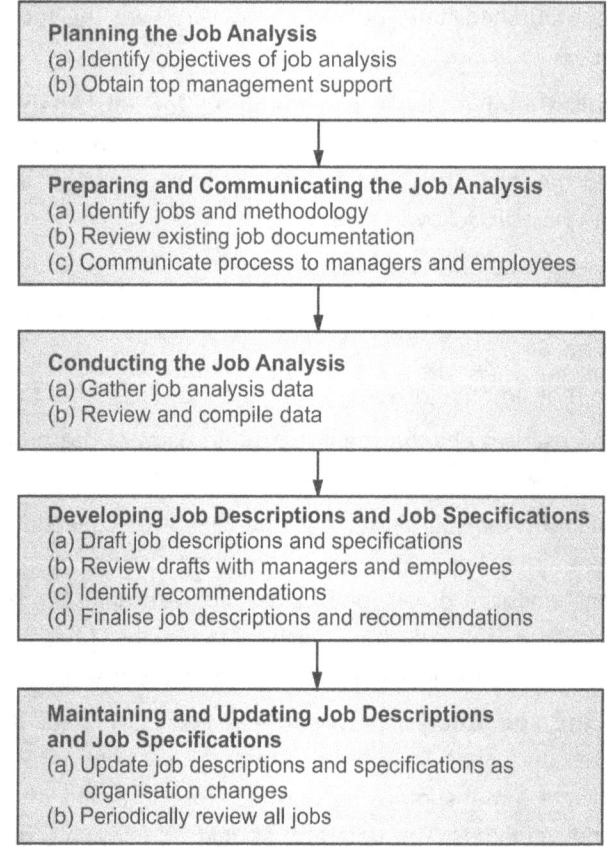

Fig. 2.1: Stages in Job Analysis Process

What to Collect during Job Analysis?

Before starting to conduct a job analysis process, it is very necessary to decide what type of content or information is to be collected and why. The purpose of this process may range from uncovering hidden dangers to the organisation or creating a right job-person fit, establishing effective hiring practices, analysing training needs, evaluating a job, analysing the performance of an employee, setting organisational standards and so on. Each one of these objectives requires different type of information or content.

While gathering job-related content, a job analyst or the dedicated person should know the purpose of the action and try to collect data as accurate as possible. Though the data collected is later on divided in to two sets (job description and job specification) but the information falls in three different categories during the process of analysing a specific job - job content, job context and job requirements.

1. **Job Content:** It contains information about various job activities included in a specific job. It is a detailed account of actions which an employee needs to perform during his tenure. The following information needs to be collected by a job analyst:
   - Duties of an employee.
   - What actually an employee does.
   - Machines, tools and equipments to be used while performing a specific job.
   - Additional tasks involved in a job.
   - Desired output level (What is expected of an employee?)
   - Type of training required.

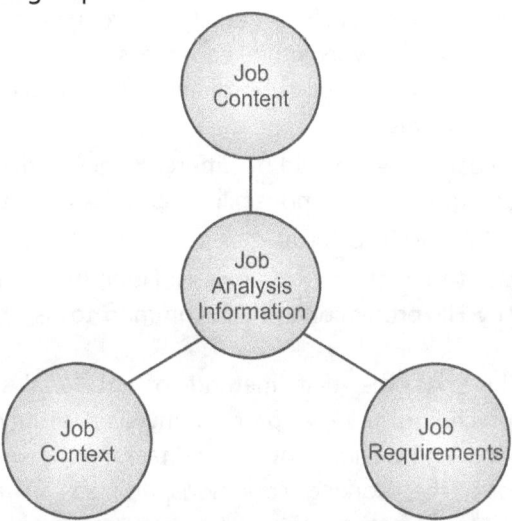

Fig. 2.2: Categorisation of Job Analysis Information

The content depends upon the type of job in a particular division or department. For example, job content of a factory-line worker would be entirely different from that of a marketing executive or HR personnel.

2. **Job Context:** Job context refers to the situation or condition under which an employee performs a particular job. The information collection will include:
   - Working Conditions
   - Risks involved
   - Whom to report
   - Who all will report to him / her
   - Hazards
   - Physical and mental demands
   - Judgment

The data collected under this category are also subjected to change according to the type of job in a specific division or department.

3. **Job Requirements:** These include basic but specific requirements which make a candidate eligible for a particular job. The collected data includes:
   - Knowledge or basic information required to perform a job successfully.
   - Specific skills such as communication skills, IT skills, operational skills, motor skills, processing skills and so on.
   - Personal ability including aptitude, reasoning, manipulative abilities, handling sudden and unexpected situations, problem-solving ability, mathematical abilities and so on.
   - Educational Qualifications including degree, diploma, certification or license.
   - Personal characteristics such as ability to adapt to different environment, endurance, willingness, work ethic, eagerness to learn and understand things, behaviour towards colleagues, subordinates and seniors, sense of belongingness to the organisation, etc .

For different jobs, the parameters would be different. They depend upon the type of job, designation, compensation grade and responsibilities and risks involved in a job.

Methods for Collecting Job Analysis Data

There are several ways to conduct a job analysis. None of them however is perfect. In job analysis conducted by HR professionals, it is common to use more than one of these methods:

1. **Observation:** This was the first method of job analysis used by industrial-organisational psychologists. The process involves simply watching incumbents perform their jobs and taking notes. The tasks performed, the pace at which activities are done, the working conditions and so on, are observed during a complete work cycle. Sometimes they ask questions while watching, and commonly they even perform job tasks themselves. The more jobs one seriously observes, the better one's understanding becomes of both the jobs in question and work in general.
2. **Interviews:** The interview method consists of asking questions to both incumbents and supervisors in either an individual or group setting. It is essential to supplement observation by talking with incumbents. These interviews are most effective when structured with a specific set of questions based on observations, other analysis of the types of jobs in question, or prior discussions with human resources representatives, trainers, or managers knowledgeable about jobs.
3. **Critical incidents and work diaries:** The critical incident technique (CIT) asks subject matter experts to identify critical aspects of behaviour or performance in a particular job that led to success or failure.
   For example, if a shoe salesman comments on the size of a customer's feet and the customer leaves the store in a huff, the behaviour of the salesman may be judged ineffective in terms of the result it produced. Critical incidents are recorded after the events have already taken place- both routine and non routine.

The second method, a work diary, asks workers and/or supervisors to keep a log of activities over a prescribed period of time. They may be asked to simply write down what they were doing at 15 minutes after the hour for each hour of the work day. Or, they may list everything they have done up to a break.

4. **Questionnaires and Surveys:** Expert incumbents or supervisors often respond to questionnaires or surveys as a part of job analysis. These questionnaires include task statements in the form of worker behaviours. Subject matter experts are asked to rate each statement from their experience on a number of different dimensions like importance to overall job success, frequency performance and whether the task must be performed on the first day of work or can be learned gradually on the job. After completion the questionnaires are handed over to supervisors. The supervisor can seek further clarifications on various items by talking to the job holders directly after everything is finalised; the data is given to the job analyst. Unlike the results of observations and interviews, the questionnaire responses can be statistically analysed to provide a more objective record of the components of the job.

   The Questionnaire method is highly economical as it covers a large number of job holders at a time. The collected data can be quantified and processed through a computer. The participants can complete the items leisurely.

5. **Checklists:** Checklists are also used as a job analysis method, specifically in areas like the Air Force. In the checklist method, the incumbent checks the tasks he or she performs from a list of task statements that describe the job. The checklist is preceded by some sort of job analysis and is usually followed by the development of work activity compilations or job descriptions.

Quantitative Job Analysis Techniques

Qualitative approaches like interviews and questionnaires are not always suitable. For example, if aim is to compare jobs for pay purposes, then there is a need to assign quantitative values to each job. The position analysis questionnaire, the Management Position Description Questionnaire, and functional job analysis are three popular quantitative methods.

1. **The Position Analysis Questionnaire (PAQ)** is a well-known job analysis instrument. The PAQ was designed to measure job component validity of attributes presented in aptitude tests. Job component validity is the relationship between test scores and skills required for good job performance. There are 195 behaviour-related statements in the PAQ divided into six major sections: information input, mental process, work output, relationships with others, job context, and other job characteristics.

   The advantage of the PAQ is that it provides a quantitative score or profile of any job in terms of how that job rates on five basic activities:
   (i) Having decision-making/communication/social responsibilities,
   (ii) Performing skilled activities,

(iii) Being physically active,

(iv) Operating vehicles/equipment, and

(v) Processing information.

The PAQ's real strength is thus in classifying jobs. In other words, it lets you assign a quantitative score to each job based on its decision-making, skilled activity, physical activity, vehicle/equipment operation, and information-processing characteristics.

2. **Management Position Description Questionnaire (MPQD):** MPQD is a standardise instrument designed especially for the use in analysing managerial jobs. The 274 item questionnaire contains 15 sections. It would take two and a half hours to complete the questionnaire. In most cases the respondents are asked to state how important each item is to the position.

3. **Functional Job Analysis (FJA):** Functional job analysis is a worker-oriented job analysis approach that attempts to describe the whole person on the job. It rates the job not just on data, people, and things, but also on four more dimensions: the extent to which specific instructions are necessary to perform the task; the extent to which reasoning and judgment are required to perform the task; the mathematical ability required to perform the task; and the verbal and language facilities required to perform the task. Second, functional job analysis also identifies performance standards and training requirements. It therefore lets you answer the question, "To do this task and meet these standards, what training does the worker require?"

FJA is frequently used for government jobs. It provides a quantitative score of each job as a function of its complexity in relationship with people, data, and things. The results are helpful in fixing wage rates and in developing employee succession plans. On the negative side FJA takes a lot of time. Training in it use may mean considerable investment of money.

Advantages of Job Analysis

1. Job analysis helps the personnel manager at the time of recruitment and selection of right man on right job.
2. It helps him to understand the extent and scope of training required in that field.
3. It helps in evaluating the job in which the worth of the job has to be evaluated.
4. In those instances where smooth work force is required in concern.
5. When he has to avoid overlapping of authority- responsibility relationship so that distortion in chain of command doesn't exist.
6. It also helps to chalk out the compensation plans for the employees.
7. It also helps the personnel manager to undertake performance appraisal effectively in a concern.

2.2 Job Description

Job descriptions are written statements that describe the:
- Duties,
- Responsibilities,
- Most important contributions and outcomes needed from a position,
- Required qualifications of candidates, and
- Reporting relationship and coworkers of a particular job.

Job Description is an organised factual statement of job contents in the form of duties and responsibilities of a specific job. The preparation of job description is very important before a vacancy is advertised. It tells in brief the nature and type of job. This type of document is descriptive in nature and it constitutes all those facts which are related to a job such as:

1. Title/ Designation of job and location.
2. The nature of duties and operations to be performed in that job.
3. The nature of authority- responsibility relationships.
4. Necessary qualifications that is required for the job.
5. Relationship of that job with other jobs.
6. The provision of physical and working conditions or the work environment required in performance of that job.

Writing Job Description

According to Ernst Dale, the following guidelines should be kept in mind while writing job descriptions:

1. The JD should indicate the nature and scope of the job including all important relationships.
2. It should be brief, factual, and precise, use active verbs such as collect mail, sort out "mail", "distribute" mail, etc. Avoid statements of opinion. Give a clear picture of the job; explain all the duties and responsibilities of job in greater detail.
3. More specific words be chosen to show: (i) the kind of work, (ii) the degree of complexity, (iii) the degree of skill required, (iv) the extent to which problems are standardised and (v) the degree and type of accountability.
4. The extent of supervision available should also be clearly stated.
5. The reporting relationship must also be clearly indicated (e.g., who reports to whom, frequency etc.)

There is no standard format for writing a job description. However, most descriptions contain sections that cover:

1. Job identification,
2. Job summary,

3. Responsibilities and duties,
4. Authority of incumbent,
5. Standards of performance,
6. Working conditions,
7. Job specifications.

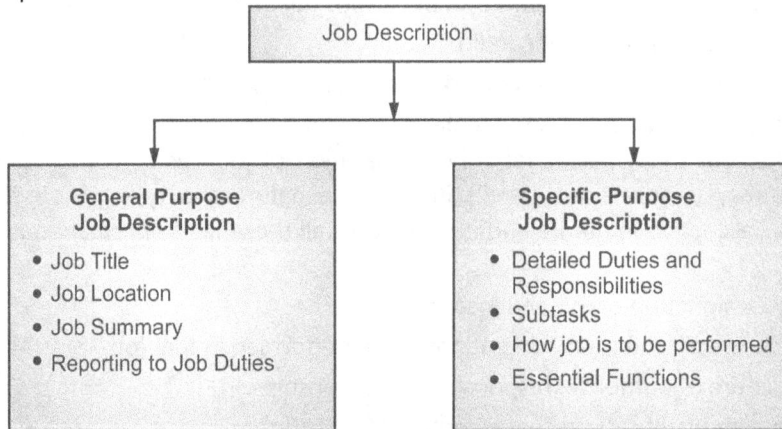

Fig. 2.3: Job Description

Advantages of Job Description
1. It helps the supervisors in assigning work to the subordinates so that he can guide and monitor their performances.
2. It helps in recruitment and selection procedures.
3. It assists in manpower planning.
4. It is also helpful in performance appraisal.
5. It is helpful in job evaluation in order to decide about rate of remuneration for a specific job.
6. It also helps in chalking out training and development programmes.

2.3 Job Specification

A job specification describes the knowledge, skills, education, experience, and abilities one believe are essential in performing a particular job. It is prepared on the basis of Job Description. Job specification translates the job description into human qualifications so that a job can be performed in a better manner. Job specification helps in hiring an appropriate person for an appropriate position. The contents are:
1. Job title and designation,
2. Educational qualifications for that title,
3. Physical and other related attributes,
4. Special attributes and abilities,
5. Maturity and dependability,
6. Relationship of that job with other jobs in a concern.

Advantages of Job Specification
1. It is helpful in preliminary screening in the selection procedure.
2. It helps in giving due justification to each job.
3. It also helps in designing training and development programmes.
4. It helps the supervisors for counseling and monitoring performance of employees.
5. It helps in job evaluation.
6. It helps the management to take decisions regarding promotion, transfers and giving extra benefits to the employees.

2.4 Human Resource Planning (HRP)

Human Resource Planning essentially is the process of getting the right number of qualified people into the right job at the right time so that an organisation can meet its objectives. It is a system of matching the supply of people (existing employees and those to be hired or searched for) with the openings the organisation expect over a given period of time. It is a continuous process of developing and determining objectives, policies that will procure, develop and utilise human resources to achieve the goal of the organisation.

Human Resource Planning is a forward looking function. It tries to assess human resource requirements in future keeping the production schedules, market fluctuations, demand forecasts, etc., in the background. Human Resource plans are prepared for varying time periods, i.e., short term plans covering a time frame of 2 years and long term plans encompassing a period of 5 or more years.

Objectives of Human Resource Planning/ Manpower Planning
1. To recruit and maintain the HR of requisite quantity and quality.
2. To predict the employee turnover and make the arrangements for minimising turnover and filing up of consequent vacancies.
3. To meet the requirements of the programmes of expansion, diversification etc.
4. To anticipate the impact of technology on work, existing employees and future human resource requirements.
5. To check the development of the employees for the achievement of the organisation goal.
6. To provide proper control measures whenever required.
7. To progress the knowledge, skill, standards, ability and discipline etc.
8. To maintain pleasant industrial relations by maintaining optimum level and structure of human resource.
9. To minimize imbalances caused due to non-availability of human resources of right kind, right number in right time and right place.
10. To ensure proper utilisation of human resources.
11. To provide proper control measures whenever required.

Importance of HRP

Forecast future personnel needs: To avoid the situations of surplus or deficiency of manpower in future, it is important to plan the manpower in advance. For this purpose a proper forecasting of futures business needs help to ascertain organisation's future manpower needs. From this angle, HRP plays an important role to predict the right size of manpower in the organisation.

Cope with change: HRP enables an enterprise to cope with changes in competitive forces, markets, technology, products and government regulations. Such changes generate changes in job content, skills demands and number of human resources required.

Creating reservoir of talent: Since jobs are becoming highly intellectual and incumbents getting immensely professionalised, HRP helps prevent shortages of labour caused by attritions. Further technology changes would further upgrade or degrade jobs and create manpower shortages. In these situations only accurate human resource planning can help to meet the resource requirements. Further HRP is also an answer to the problems of succession planning.

International strategies: International expansion strategies largely depend upon effective HRP. With growing trends towards global operations, the need for HRP further becomes more important as the need to integrate HRP more closely into the organisation keeps growing. This is also because the process of meeting staffing needs from foreign countries grows in a complex manner.

Increasing investments in HR: Another importance is the investment that an organisation makes in human capital. It is important that employees are used effectively throughout their careers, because human assets can increase the organisation value tremendously as opposed to physical assets.

Succession planning: HRP prepares people to meet future needs and challenges. The top performers can be selected and trained for further promotions.

Other benefits: Following are the other benefits of HRP.
1. Upper management has a better view of HR dimensions of business.
2. Management can anticipate imbalances before they become unmanageable and expensive.
3. More time is provided to locate talent.
4. Better opportunities exists to include women and minorities in future growth plans.
5. Better planning of assignments to develop managers.
6. Major and successful demands on local labour markets can be made.

The Process of Human Resource Planning

The process of HRP consists of following steps:
1. **Analysing the Corporate Level Strategies:** Human Resource Planning should start with analysing corporate level strategies which include expansion, diversification, mergers, acquisitions, reduction in operations, technology to be used, method of production etc. Therefore Human Resource Planning should begin with analysing the corporate plans of the organisation before setting out on fulfilling its tasks.

2. **Demand forecasting:** Forecasting the overall human resource requirement in accordance with the organisational plans is one of the key aspects of demand forecasting. Forecasting of quality of human resources like skills, knowledge, values and capabilities needed in addition to quantity of human resources is done through the following method:

   Executive or Managerial Judgment: Here the managers decide the number of employees in the future. They adopt one of the three approaches mentioned below:
   - **Bottom-Up approach:** Here the concerned supervisors send their proposals to the top officials who compare these with the organisational plans, make necessary adjustments and finalise them.
   - **Top-Down approach:** Here the management prepares the requirements and sends the information downwards to the supervisory –level who finalise the draft and approves it.
   - **Participative Approach:** Here the supervisors and the management sit together and projections are made after joint consultations.

3. **Analysing Human Resource Supply:** Every organisation has two sources of supply of Human Resources: Internal and External. Internally, human resources can be obtained for certain posts through promotions and transfers. In order to judge the internal supply of human resources in future human resource inventory or human resource audit is necessary. Human resource inventory helps in determining and evaluating the quantity of internal human resources available. Once the future internal supply is estimated, supply of external human resources is analysed.

4. **Estimating manpower gaps:** Manpower gaps can be identified by comparing demand and supply forecasts. Such comparison will reveal either deficit or surplus of Human Resources in the future. Deficit suggests the number of persons to be recruited from outside, whereas surplus implies unneeded employees to be re-deployed or terminated. Employees estimated to be deficient can be trained while employees with higher, better skills may be given more enriched jobs.

5. **Action Planning:** Once the manpower gaps are identified, plans are prepared to bridge these gaps. Plans to meet the surplus manpower may be redeployment in other departments and retrenchment. People may be persuaded to quit voluntarily through a golden handshake. Deficit can be met through recruitment, selection, transfer and promotion. In view of shortage of certain skilled employees, the organisation has to take care not only of recruitment but also retention of existing employees. Hence, the organisation has to plan for retaining of existing employees.

6. **Modify the Organisational plans:** If future supply of human resources form all the external sources is estimated to be inadequate or less than the requirement, the manpower planner has to suggest to the management regarding the alterations or modifications in the organisational plans.

7. **Controlling and Review:** After the action plans are implemented, human resource structure and the processes should be controlled and reviewed with a view to keep them in accordance with action plans.

Factors Affecting Human Resource Planning in an Organisation

1. **Employment:** HRP is affected by the employment situation in the country i.e. in countries where there is greater unemployment; there may be more pressure on the company, from the government to appoint more people. Similarly, some company may force shortage of skilled labour and they may have to appoint people from other countries.
2. **Technical changes in the society:** Technology changes at a very fast speed and new people having the required knowledge are required for the company. In some cases, company may retain existing employees and teach them the new technology and in some cases, the company has to remove existing people and appoint new.
3. **Organisational changes:** Changes take place within the organisation from time to time i.e. the company diversify into new products or close down business in some areas etc. in such cases the HRP process that includes appointing or removing people will change according to situation.
4. **Demographic changes:** Demographic changes refer to things referring to age, population, composition of work force etc. A number of people retire every year. A new batch of graduates with specialisation turns out every year. This can change the appointment or the removal in the company.
5. **Shortage of skill due to labour turnover:** Industries where labour turnover rate is high, the HRP will change constantly to meet the needs of organisation in terms of adequate supply of human resource. This also affects the way HRP is implemented.
6. **Multicultural workforce:** Workers from different countries travel to other countries in search of job. When a company plans it's HRP it needs to take into account this factor also.
7. **Pressure groups:** The Company has to keep in mind certain groups like human rights activist, woman activist, media etc. as they are very capable for creating problems for the company. When issues concerning these groups arise, appointment or retrenchment becomes difficult.

HR Estimation – HR Demand Forecast

Forecasting human resource demand is the process of estimating the future human resource requirement of the right quality and the right number. As discussed earlier, potential human resource requirement is to be estimated keeping in view the organisation's plans over a given period of time. Analysis of employment trends; replacement needs of employees due to death, resignations, retirement, termination; productivity of employees; growth and expansion of the organisation; absenteeism and labour turnover are the relevant factors for human resource forecasting. Demand forecasting is affected by a number of external and internal factors.

Job analysis and forecasting about the quality of potential human resource facilitates demand forecasting. So, existing job design must be thoroughly evaluated taking into consideration the future capabilities of the present employees.

Factors Affecting HR Demand Forecasting

Human Resource Demand Forecasting depends on several factors, some of which are given below:

- Employment trends,
- Replacement needs,
- Productivity,
- Absenteeism, and
- Expansion and growth.

There are number of techniques of estimating/forecasting human resources demand:

(a) Managerial Judgment
(b) Work Study Technique
(c) Ratio-trend Analysis
(d) Econometric Models
(e) Delphi Model
(f) Other Techniques

(a) **Managerial Judgement:** Managerial judgement technique is a very common technique of demand forecasting. This approach is applied by small as well as large scale organisations. This technique involves two types of approaches i.e. 'bottom-up approach' and 'top-down approach'. Under the 'bottom-up approach', line managers send their departmental requirement of human resources to top management. Top management ultimately forecasts the human resource requirement for the overall organisation on the basis of proposals of departmental heads. Under the Top-down approach', top management forecasts the human resource requirement for the entire organisation and various departments. This information is supplied to various departmental heads for their review and approval. However, a combination of both the approaches i.e. 'Participative Approach' should be applied for demand forecasting. Under this approach, top management and departmental heads meet and decide about the future human resource requirement. So, demand of human resources can be forecasted with unanimity under this approach.

(b) **Work-Study Technique:** This technique is also known as 'work-load analysis'. This technique is suitable where the estimated work-load is easily measureable. Under this method, estimated total production and activities for a specific future period are predicted. This information is translated into number of man-hours required to produce per units taking into consideration the capability of the workforce. Past-experience of the management can help in translating the work-loads into number of man-hours required. Thus, demand of human resources is forecasted on the basis of estimated total production and contribution of each employee in producing each unit items.

(c) **Ratio-Trend Analysis:** Demand for manpower/human resources is also estimated on the basis of ratio of production level and number of workers available. This ratio will be used to estimate demand of human resources. The following example will help in clearly understanding this technique.

(d) **Econometrics Models:** These models are based on mathematical and statistical techniques for estimating future demand. Under these models relationship is established between the dependent variable to be predicted (e.g. manpower/human resources) and the independent variables (e.g., sales, total production, work-load, etc.). Using these models, estimated demand of human resources can be predicted.

(e) **Delphi Technique:** Delphi technique is also very important technique used for estimating demand of human resources. This technique takes into consideration human resources requirements given by a group of experts i.e. managers. The human resource experts collect the manpower needs, summarise the various responses and prepare a report. This process is continued until all experts agree on estimated human resources requirement.

(f) **Other Techniques:** The other techniques of Human Resources demand forecasting are specified as under:
  (i) Following the techniques of demand forecasting of human resources used by other similar organisations.
  (ii) Organisation-cum-succession-charts.
  (iii) Estimation based on techniques of production.
  (iv) Estimates based on historical records.
  (v) Statistical techniques e.g. co-relation and regression analysis.

2.5 Recruitment

Recruitment is the process of attracting, evaluating, and hiring employees for an organisation. It is the process of attracting individuals on a timely basis, in sufficient numbers and with appropriate qualifications, to apply for jobs with an organisation.

Recruitment is the process of creating pool of qualified applicants for a specific job. The process begins when applications are brought in and ends when the same is finished. The result is a pool of applicants, from where the appropriate candidate can be selected.

Objectives of Recruitment

Recruitment fulfills the following objectives:
1. It reviews the list of objectives of the company and tries to achieve them by promoting the company in the minds of public.

2. It forecasts how many people will be required in the company.
3. It enables the company to advertise itself and attract talented people.
4. It provides different opportunities to procure human resource.

Recruitment Process:

The Recruitment process involves a systematic procedure from sourcing the candidates to arranging and conducting the interviews and requires many resources and time.

A general recruitment process is as follows:

1. Identifying the vacancy: The recruitment process begins with the human resource department receiving requisitions for recruitment from any department of the company.

    These contain:
    (a) Posts to be filled,
    (b) Number of persons,
    (c) Duties to be performed,
    (d) Qualifications required.
2. Preparing the job description and person specification.
3. Locating and developing the sources of required number and type of employees (Advertising etc).
4. Short-listing and identifying the prospective employee with required characteristics.
5. Arranging the interviews with the selected candidates.

Methods of Recruitment

Recruitment is a process of searching for prospective employees and stimulating them to apply for jobs.

Companies can adopt different methods of recruitment for selecting people in the company. These methods are:

1. Internal sources
2. External sources

The sources can be further explained with the help of the following diagram:

Sources of Recruitment (Manpower Supply)

Internal Sources	External Sources
1. Promotion	1. Management consultant
2. Department exam	2. Employment agency
3. Transfer	3. Campus recruitment
4. Retirement	4. Newspaper advertisement
5. Internal advertisement	5. Internal advertisement
6. Employee recommendations	6. Walk in interview

Fig. 2.4: Sources of Recruitment

Internal Sources of Recruitment

Internal sources of recruitment refer to obtaining people for the job from inside the company. There are different methods of internal recruitment:

1. **Promotion:** Companies can give promotion to existing employees. This method of recruitment saves a lot of time, money and efforts because the company does not have to train the existing employee, since the employee has already worked with the company. He/She is familiar with the working culture and working style. It is a method of encouraging efficient workers.
2. **Departmental examination:** This method is used by government departments to select employees for higher level posts. The advertisement is put up on the notice board of the department. People who are interested must send their application to the HR department and appear for the exam. Successful candidates are given the higher level job. The method ensures proper selection and impartiality.
3. **Transfer:** Many companies adopt transfer as a method of recruitment. The idea is to select talented personnel from other branches of the company and transfer them to branches where there is shortage of people.
4. **Retirement:** Many companies call back personnel who have already retired from the organisation. This is a temporary measure. The method is beneficial because it gives a sense of pride to the retired when he is called back and helps the organisation to reduce recruitment, selection and training cost.
5. **Internal advertisement:** In this method vacancies in a particular branch are advertised in the notice board. People who are interested are asked to apply for the job. The method helps in obtaining people who are ready to shift to another branch of the same company and it is also beneficial to people who want to shift to another branch.
6. **Employee recommendation:** In this method employees are asked to recommend people for jobs. Since the employee is aware of the working conditions inside the company he will suggest people who can adjust to the situation. The company is benefited because it will obtain:

Advantages of Internal Recruitment

1. Internal methods are time saving.
2. No separate induction programme is required.
3. The method increases loyalty and reduces labour turnover.
4. This method is less expensive.

Disadvantages of Internal Recruitment

1. There is no opportunity to get new talent in this method.
2. The method involves selecting people from those available in the company so there is limited scope for selection.
3. There are chances of being biased and partiality.
4. Chances of employee discontent are very high.

External Methods/Sources of Recruitment

External sources of recruitment refer to methods of recruitment to obtain people from outside the company. These methods are:

1. **Management consultant:** Management consultant helps the company by providing them with managerial personnel, when the company is on the lookout for entry level management trainees and middle level managers. They generally approach management consultants.
2. **Employment agencies:** Companies may give a contract to employment agencies that search, interview and obtain the required number of people. The method can be used to obtain lower level and middle level staff.
3. **Campus recruitment:** When companies are in search of fresh graduates or new talent they opt for campus recruitment. Companies approach colleges, management, technical institutes, make a presentation about the company and the job and invite applications. Interested candidates who have applied are made to go through a series of selection test and interview before final selection.
4. **Newspaper advertisement:** This is one of the oldest and most popular methods of recruitment. Advertisements for the job are given in leading newspapers; the details of the job and salary are also mentioned. Candidates are given a contact address where their applications must be sent and are asked to send their applications within a specified time limit. The method has maximum reach and most preferred among all other methods of recruitment.
5. **Internet advertisement:** With increasing importance given to internet, companies and candidates have started using the internet as medium of advertisement and search for jobs. There are various job sites like naukri.com and monster.com etc. Candidates can also post their profiles on these sites. This method is growing in popularity.
6. **Walk in interviews:** Another method of recruitment which is gaining importance is the walk in interview method. An advertisement about the location and time of walk in interview is given in the newspaper. Candidates are required to directly appear for the interview and bring a copy of their C.V. with them. This method is very popular among B.P.Os and call centers.

Advantages of External Recruitment

1. There is influx of new talent in the method.
2. The method encourages more and more competition.
3. There is lesser chance of partiality through this method.
4. If options like campus recruitment have been exercised we get a chance to employ fresh graduates, thus increasing employment.

Disadvantages of External Recruitment

1. The method is costly because it involves recruitment cost, selection, training cost.
2. The method is time consuming.
3. The method reduces loyalty to the company.

Recruiting Yield Pyramid

Some employers use recruitment yield pyramid to calculate the number of applicants they must generate to hire the required number of new employees.

For example, if a company needs 10 management trainees in the next six months, it has to monitor past yield ratios in order to find out the number of candidates to be contacted for this purpose. On the basis of past experience, to continue the same example, the company finds that to hire 10 trainees, it has to extend 20 offers. If the interview-to offer is 3:2, then 30 interviews must be conducted. If the invites to interview ratios are 4:3 then, as many as 40 candidates must be invited. Lastly, if contacts or leads needed to identify suitable Trainees, to be invite are in 5:1 ratio, and then 200 contacts are made.

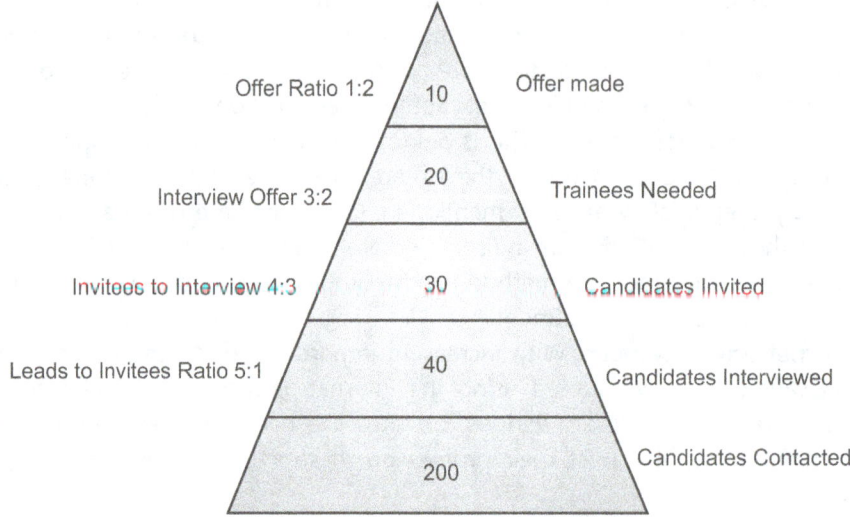

Fig. 2.5: Recruiting Yield Pyramid

Expectation of organisations from New Trainees: Some Examples

Pepsi: Pepsi is a flat organisation. There are a maximum of four reporting levels. Executives here emphasise achievement, motivation, the ability to deliver come what may. As the Personnel Manager of Pepsi Foods remarked "we hire people who are capable of growing the business rather than just growing with the business" recruitees must be capable of thinking out of the box, cutting the cake of conventional barriers whenever and wherever necessary.

Indian Hotels: The Taj group expects the job aspirants to stay with the organisation patiently and rise with the company. Employees should be willing to say "yes sir" to anybody. Other criteria include communication skills, the ability to work long and stressful hours, mobility, attention to personal appearance and assertiveness without aggression.

Succession Planning

Succession planning is a process for identifying and developing internal people with the potential to fill key business leadership positions in the company. Succession planning increases the availability of experienced and capable employees that are prepared to assume these roles as they become available.

Succession planning is a process whereby an organisation ensures that employees are recruited and developed to fill each key role within the company. Through succession planning process, a company recruits superior employees, develop their knowledge, skills, and abilities, and prepare them for advancement or promotion into ever more challenging roles.

Succession planning is nothing more than having a systematic process where managers identify, assess and develop their staff to make sure they are ready to assume key roles within the company. Having this process in place is vital to the success of the organisation because the individuals identified in the plan will eventually be responsible for ensuring the company is able to tackle future challenges. These "high potential" candidates must be carefully selected and then provided training and development that gives them skills and competencies needed for tomorrow's business environment.

In an effective succession plan there are a number of key issues that need to be considered:

- The succession planning programme must have the support and backing of the company's senior level management.
- Identify high-performers that are almost ready to step into those critical positions.
- A systematic approach for identifying, nominating and selecting potential successors must be established.
- The training and development requirements of potential successors needs to be determined.
- The skills of potential successors must be developed through work experiences, job rotation, projects and other challenging assignments.

2.6 Selection

Selection is the process of picking up individuals (out of the pool of job applicants) with requisite qualifications and competence to fill jobs in the organisation.

According to **Thomas**, *"Selection is the process of differentiating between applicants in order to identify those with greater likelihood of success in the job."*

Selection is the process of identifying individuals who have relevant qualifications/ experience/ skills and competencies to fill in the jobs. Once there is a pool of applicants for a job, the next step is to select the best candidate for the job. Selecting the right employees is critical because:

- The organisations performance is dependent on its employees. Employees with the right skills and attributes will do a good job.
- It is costly to recruit and hire employees. Hiring and training a new employee costs a lot of money.
- Incompetent hiring could impact the organisation in a big way. The employee may commit a wrongful act that will impact the image of the organisation adversely.

Process/Steps in Selection

1. **Preliminary Interview:** The purpose of preliminary interviews is basically to eliminate unqualified applications based on information supplied in application forms. The basic objective is to reject misfits. On the other hand preliminary interviews is often called a courtesy interview and is a good public relations exercise.

2. **Selection Tests:** Jobseekers who clear the preliminary interviews are called for tests. There are various types of tests conducted depending upon the jobs and the company. These tests can be Aptitude Tests, Personality Tests, and Ability Tests that are conducted to judge how well an individual can perform tasks related to the job. Besides this there are some other tests also like Interest Tests (activity preferences), Graphology Test (Handwriting), Medical Tests, Psychometric Tests etc.

3. **Employment Interview:** The next step in selection is employment interview. Here interview is a formal and in-depth conversation between applicant's acceptability. It is considered to be an excellent selection device. Interviews can be One-to-One, Panel Interview, or Sequential Interviews. Besides there can be Structured and Unstructured interviews, Behavioural Interviews, Stress Interviews also.

4. **Reference and Background Checks:** Reference checks and background checks are conducted to verify the information provided by the candidates hold true or not. Reference checks can be through formal letters or telephone conversations. However it is merely a formality and selections decisions are seldom affected by it.

5. **Selection Decision:** After obtaining all the information, the most critical step is the selection decision is to be made. The final decision has to be made out of the applicants who have passed the preliminary interviews, tests, final interviews and reference checks. The views of line managers are considered generally because it is the line manager who is responsible for the performance of the new employee.

6. **Physical Examination:** After the selection decision is made, the candidate is required to undergo a physical fitness test. A job offer is often contingent upon the candidate passing the physical examination.

7. **Job Offer:** The next step in the selection process is the job offer to those applicants who have crossed all the previous hurdles. It is made by way of letter of appointment.
8. **Contract of Employment:** After the job offer is made and candidates accept the offer, certain documents need to be executed by the employer and the candidate. There is a need to prepare a formal contract of employment, containing written contractual terms of employment etc.

Essentials of a Good Selection Practice
1. Detailed job descriptions and job specifications prepared in advance and endorsed by personnel and line management.
2. Training the selectors.
3. Determine aids to be used for selection process.
4. Check competence of recruitment consultants before retention.
5. Involve line managers at all stages.
6. Attempt to validate the procedure.
7. Help the appointed candidate to succeed by training and management development.

Barriers to Effective Selection
1. **Perception:** We all perceive the world differently. Our limited perceptual ability is obviously a stumbling block to the objective and rational selection of people.
2. **Fairness:** Barriers of fairness includes discrimination against religion, region, race or gender etc.
3. **Validity:** A test that has been validated can differentiate between the employees who can perform well and those who will not. However it does not predict the job success accurately.
4. **Reliability:** A reliable test may fail to predict job performance with precision.
5. **Pressure:** Pressure brought on selectors by politicians, bureaucrats, relatives, friends and peers to select particular candidate are also barriers to selection.

Types of Tests

Tests can be broadly classified into four and they are:
- **Aptitude test:** These tests measure the latent ability or potential of a candidate to learn a new job or skills.
- **Achievement test:** These tests measure what a person can do. These determine the skill or knowledge already acquired through training and on the job experience.
- **Personality test:** These are pen and paper tests used to judge the psychological make-up of a person. These look into deeply to discover clues to an individual's value system, emotional reactions and maturity and his characteristic mood.

- **Interest test:** These tests are inventories of the candidate's likes and dislike in relation to work. These are generally used for vocational guidance.
- **Situational judgement tests (SJTs):** Situational judgment tests present applicants with a description of a work problem or critical situation related to the job they are applying for and ask them to identify how they would handle it.
- **Work samples techniques:** The work sampling technique tries to predict job performance by requiring job candidates to perform one or more samples of the job's basic tasks. With work samples, examinees are given with situations similar to what they will be actually doing in the job for which they're applying and their responses are evaluated.

Tools for Selection

There are several selection tools which can be used in the selection process. They are:

1. **Cognitive Tests:** Cognitive tests or general mental ability assessments differentiate candidates on mental ability that is required for the job. These tests are most commonly used for entry level jobs and for applicants without professional training or advanced degrees.
2. **Structured Interviews:** Structured interviews ensure that questions are Job related, and contributing to the correspondence between selection methods and suitability of the candidates selected.
3. **Unstructured interview:** Involves little planning on the part of the interviewer. As such, interviews tend to vary greatly between interviewees. The common use of unstructured interviews generally lies in the organisation's lack of time and resources to conduct a more structured interview.
4. **Group Discussion:** A group discussion is a structured/ unstructured discussion amongst the applicants on a relevant issue. It can be used only when there is a large pool of applicants. It is used to screen applicants out and tests for communication, confidence, and presence of mind etc.
5. **Assessment Centres:** Candidates attending an assessment centre participate in two to three days of and individual exercises, role plays, managerial simulations, and psychometric tests that assess managerial potential, problem solving and decision making skills. The candidates are watched closely by trained observers who meet and reach a consensus rating of the candidates for a number of variables considered important for effective management. Assessment centres are most widely used for managerial and high level positions.
6. **Reference Checks:** Most organisations ask candidates for Checklists of references that include previous supervisors or co-workers to check whether the candidate is a good worker. As the lists are generated by the candidates, it is important to be able to identify whether the reference being provided is truthful or not.

2.7 Interview

Interview is the oral examination of candidates for employment. This is the most essential step in the selection process. In this step, the interviewer tries to obtain and synthesise information about the abilities of the interviewee and the requirements of the job.

There are several types of interviews which are used by the organisation depending on the nature and importance of the position.

1. **Structured Interview:** The questions to be asked, the order in which the questions will be asked, the time given to each candidate, the information to be collected from each candidate, etc. is all decided in advance. Structured interview is also called Standardised, Patterned, Directed or Guided interview. Structured interviews are preplanned. They are accurate and precise.

2. **Unstructured Interview:** This interview is not planned in detail. Hence it is also called as Non-Directed interview. The question to be asked, the information to be collected from the candidates and so on are not decided in advance. These interviews are non-planned and therefore, more flexible. Candidates are more relaxed in such interviews. They are encouraged to express themselves about different subjects, based on their expectations, motivations, background, interests, etc. Here the interviewer can make a better judgement of the candidate's personality, potentials, strengths and weaknesses.

3. **Group Interview:** Here, all the candidates or small groups of candidates are interviewed together. The time of the interviewer is saved. A group interview is similar to a group discussion. A topic is given to the group, and they are asked to discuss it. The interviewer carefully watches the candidates. He tries to find out which candidate influences others, who clarifies issues, who summarises the discussion, who speaks effectively, etc. He tries to judge the behaviour of each candidate in a group situation.

4. **Stress Interview:** The purpose of this interview is to find out how the candidate behaves in a stressful situation. The interviewer tries to create a stressful situation during the interview. This is done purposely by asking the candidate rapid questions, criticising his answers, interrupting him repeatedly, etc

5. **Panel Interview:** Panel means a selection committee or interview committee that is appointed for interviewing the candidates. The panel may include three or five members. They ask questions to the candidates about different aspects. They give marks to each candidate. The final decision will be taken by all members collectively by rating the candidates. Such an interview could limit the impact of personal biases of any individual interviewer. A panel interview may make the candidate more stressed than usual.

Designing and Conducting an Effective Interview

Step 1 : Job Analysis: Write a job description with a list of job duties, required knowledge, skills, abilities, and other worker qualifications.

Step 2 : Rate the Job's Duties: Identify the job's main duties. To do so, rate each job duty, based on its importance to job success and on the time required to perform it compared to other tasks.

Step 3 : Create Interview: Questions that are based on actual job duties, with more questions for the important duties.

Step 4 : Create Benchmark Answers: Next, develop answers and a five point rating scale for each, with ideal answers for good (a 5 rating), marginal (a 3 rating), and poor (a 1 rating). Consider the preceding situational

Step 5 : Appoint the Interview Panel and Conduct Interviews: Companies generally conduct structured situational interviews using a panel, rather than sequentially. The panel usually consists of three to six members, preferably the same employees who wrote the questions and answers. It may also include the job's supervisor and/or incumbent, and an HR representative.

The Interview Process

Interview is an art. It demands a positive frame of mind on part of the interviewers. Interviewers must be treated properly so as to leave a good impression about the company in their minds. HR experts have identified certain steps to be followed while conducting interviews:

1. **Preparation:** It involves:
    - Establishing the objective of the interview.
    - Receiving the candidates application and resume.
    - Keeping tests score ready, along with interview assessment forms.
    - Selecting the interview method to be followed.
    - Choosing the panel of experts who would interview the candidates.
    - Identifying proper room for environment.

2. **Reception:** The candidate should be properly received and led into the interview room. Start the interview on time.

3. **Information exchange:**
    - State the purpose of the interview, how the qualifications are going to be matched with skills needed to handle the job.
    - Begin with open ended questions where the candidate gets enough freedom to express himself.
    - Focus on the applicant's education, training, work experience and so on.
    - Find unexplained gaps in applicants past work or college record and elicit facts that are not mentioned in the resume.

4. **Evaluation:** Evaluation is done on basis of answers and justification given by the applicant in the interview.
5. **Physical Examination:** After the selection decision and before the job offer is made, the candidate is required to undergo a physical fitness test. A job offer is often contingent upon the candidate being declared fit after the physical examination.
6. **Medical Examination:** Certain jobs require physical qualities like clear vision, perfect hearing, unusual stamina, tolerance of hard working conditions, clear tone, etc. Medical examination reveals whether or not a candidate possesses these qualities.

2.8 Induction

Induction can be defined as "The HRM function that systematically and formally introduces new employees to the organisation, the jobs, the work groups to which they will belong and the work environment where they will work."

It is a systematic attempt to introduce the new employee to the organisation, the relevant department, the relevant job and the relevant personnel. Also new employee will know who are his/her superiors, subordinators and peers.

Induction serves the following purposes:

(a) **Removes fears:** A newcomer steps into an organisation as a stranger. He is new to the people, workplace and work environment. He is not very sure about what he is supposed to do. Induction helps a new employee overcome such fears and perform better on the job. It assists him in knowing more about:
- The job, its content, policies, rules and regulations.
- The people with whom he is supposed to interact. .
- The terms and conditions of employment.

(b) **Creates a good impression:** Another purpose of induction is to make the newcomer feel at home and develop a sense of pride in the organisation. Induction helps him to:
- Adjust and adapt to new demands of the job.
- Get along with people.
- Get off to a good start.

Through induction, a new recruit is able to see more clearly as to what he is supposed to do, how good the colleagues are, how important is the job, etc. He can pose questions and seek clarifications on issues relating to his job. Induction is a positive step, in the sense; it leaves a good impression about the company and the people working there in the minds of new recruits. They begin to take pride in their work and are more committed to their jobs.

(c) **Act as a valuable source of information:** Induction serves as a valuable source of information to new recruits. It classifies many things through employee manuals/handbook. Informal discussions with colleagues may also clear the fog surrounding certain issues. The basic purpose of induction is to communicate specific job requirements to the employee, put him at ease and make him feel confident about his abilities.

Steps in the Induction Programme

The HR department may initiate the following steps while organising the induction programme:
- Welcome to the organisation
- Explain about the company.
- Show the location, department where the new recruit will work. .
- Give the company's manual to the new recruit.
- Provide details about various work groups and the extent of unionism within the company.
- Give details about pay, benefits, holidays, leave, etc. Emphasise the importance of attendance or punctuality.
- Explain about future training opportunities and career prospects.
- Clarify doubts, by encouraging the employee to come out with questions.
- Take the employee on a guided tour of buildings, facilities, etc. Hand him over to his supervisor.

(a) Content: The areas covered in employee induction programme may be stated as follows:

Induction Programme: Topics

1. **Organisational issues**
   History of company
   - Names and titles of key executives.
   - Employees' title and department.
   - Layout of physical facilities
   - Probationary period
   - Products/services offered
   - Overview of production process
   - Company policy and rules
   - Disciplinary procedures
   - Safety steps
   - Employees' handbook
2. **Employee Benefits**
   - Pay scales, pay days
   - Vacations, holidays
   - Rest pauses
   - Training Avenues
   - Counselling
   - Insurance, medical, recreation, retirement benefit.

3. **Introductions**
   - To supervisors
   - To co-workers
   - To trainers
   - To employee counsellor
4. **Job duties**
   - Job location
   - Job tasks
   - Job safety needs
   - Overview of jobs
   - Job objectives
   - Relationship with other jobs

(b) **Socialisation:** Socialisation is a process through which a new recruit begins to understand and accept the values, norms and beliefs held by others in the organisation. HR department representatives help new recruits to internalise the way things are done in the organisation". Orientation helps the newcomers to interact freely with employees working at various levels and learn behaviours that are acceptable. Through such formal and informal interaction and discussion, newcomers begin to understand how the department/company is run, who holds power and who does not, who is politically active within the department, how to behave in the company, what is expected of them, etc. In short, if the new recruits wish to survive and prosper in their new work home, they must soon come to 'know the ropes'. Orientation programmes are effective socialisation tools because they help the employees to learn about the job and perform things in a desired way.

(c) **Follow up:** Despite the best efforts of supervisors, certain dark areas may still remain in the orientation programme. New hires may not have understood certain things. The supervisors, while covering a large ground, may have ignored certain important matters. To overcome the resultant communication gaps, it is better to use a supervisory checklist and find out whether all aspects have been covered or not. Follow up meetings could be held at fixed intervals, say after every three or six months on a face-to-face basis. The basic purpose of such follow up orientation is to offer guidance to employees on various general as well as job related matters without leaving anything to chance. To improve orientation, the company should make a conscious effort to obtain feedback from everyone involved in the programme. There are several ways to get this kind of feedback: through round table discussions with new hires after their first year on the job, through in-depth interviews with randomly selected employees and superiors and through questionnaires for mass coverage of all recent recruits.

2.9 Placement

Placement is allocation of people to jobs. It is assignment or reassignment of an employee to a new or different job.

The significances of placement are as follows:
- It improves employee morale.
- It helps in reducing employee turnover.
- It helps in reducing absenteeism.
- It helps in reducing accident rates.
- It avoids misfit between the candidate and the job.
- It helps the candidate to work as per the predetermined objectives of the organisation.

Problems in Placement
- Matching the job descriptions with the resumes that have come is a major challenge.
- Candidates need to be accessed in every criteria like technical knowledge, aptitude, attitude, soft skills, communication, etc. due to which reason sometimes there are not enough candidates to fill the available vacancies.
- Deciding the starting pay package for the particular position is also an issue because this is a point where the candidates and companies opinion differs, it needs to be decided based on the type of job.
- There are lots of opportunities but there is a shortage of talent or required skills because of which the recruiters find it difficult to select enough candidates for the number of jobs available.
- Every employee plays an important role in the performance of the company thus the responsibility of selecting the right person for the right job lies with the recruiter and at the same time the candidate should also be satisfied with the job offered to him/her.
- There is a lot for competition for the placement agencies these days as a lot of placement agencies have come up thus companies get lot of applicants which becomes too confusing and chaotic and candidates are confused not knowing where to register themselves

Points to Remember

Job Analysis: A job analysis is the process used to collect information about the duties, responsibilities, necessary skills, outcomes, and work environment of a particular job.

Job descriptions are written statements that describe the:
- Duties,
- Responsibilities,
- Most important contributions and outcomes needed from a position,
- Required qualifications of candidates, and
- Reporting relationship and coworkers of a particular job.

- A job specification describes the knowledge, skills, education, experience, and abilities one believe are essential in performing a particular job.
- **Human Resource Planning** essentially is the process of getting the right number of qualified people into the right job at the right time so that an organisation can meet its objectives. It is a system of matching the supply of people (existing employees and those to be hired or searched for) with the openings the organisation expect over a given period of time.
- **Recruitment** is the process of attracting, evaluating, and hiring employees for an organisation. It is the process of attracting individuals on a timely basis, in sufficient numbers and with appropriate qualifications, to apply for jobs with an organisation.
- **Selection** is the process of picking up individuals (out of the pool of job applicants) with requisite qualifications and competence to fill jobs in the organisation.
- **An interview** is a conversation between two or more people where questions are asked by the interviewer to elicit facts or statements from the interviewee.
- **Induction** is a systematic attempt to introduce the new employee to the organisation, the relevant department, the relevant job and the relevant personnel. Also new employee will know who are his/her superiors, subordinators and peers.
- **Placement** is allocation of people to jobs. It is assignment or reassignment of an employee to a new or different job.

Questions for Discussion

1. Define Job Analysis, Job Description and Job Specification. Discuss the various quantitative techniques used for Job Analysis?
2. Discuss in detail the sources of Recruitment.
3. What do you understand by Human Resource Planning? Describe the process of HRP.
4. Define Interview. Explain the types of interview techniques in detail.
5. Write Short Notes on:
   (a) Selection process.
   (b) Induction.
   (c) Problems in Placement.

Multiple Choice Questions

1. _____ is the important process of identifying the content of a job in terms of activities involved and attributes needed to perform the work and identifies major job requirements.
   (a) job description   (b) job analysis
   (c) job specification   (d) job interview

Human Resource Management   Procurement of Human Resources

2. Job Analysis helps in:
   - (a) training and development
   - (b) performance appraisal
   - c) recruitment and selection
   - (d) all the given

3. The process of attracting individuals on a timely basis, in sufficient numbers and with appropriate qualifications, to apply for jobs with an organisation is:
   - (a) recruitment
   - (b) selection
   - (c) training
   - (d) placement

4. Which among the following is not the internal source of recruitment:
   - (a) promotion
   - (b) transfer
   - (c) employment agencies
   - (d) departmental exam

5. The process of getting the right number of qualified people into the right job at the right time:
   - (a) recruitment
   - (b) selection
   - (c) human resource planning
   - (d) transfer

6. An oral exam conducted for employment is known as:
   - (a) HRP
   - (b) recruitment
   - (c) job analysis
   - (d) interview

7. The HRM function that systematically and formally introduces new employees to the organisation, the jobs, the work groups to which they will belong and the work environment where they will work is known as:
   - (a) job evaluation
   - (b) HRP
   - (c) induction
   - (d) job specification

8. Significance of placement is:
   - (a) It improves employee morale
   - (b) It helps in reducing employee turnover
   - (c) It helps in reducing absenteeism
   - (d) all the given

9. The process whereby an organisation ensures that employees are recruited and developed to fill each key role within the company:
   - (a) HRP
   - (b) succession planning
   - (c) promotion
   - (d) interview

10. A type of interview in which a selection committee or interview committee that is appointed for interviewing the candidates.
    - (a) panel interview
    - (b) stress interview
    - (c) group interview
    - (d) none of the given

Answers

| 1. (b) | 2. (d) | 3. (a) | 4. (c) | 5. (c) | 6. (d) | 7. (c) | 8. (d) | 9. (b) | 10. (a) |

Case Study

Smt. Snehal Ramgade joined Nagesh Bank, Pune in 1999 as a clerk after graduation. She completed her Bank Examination in 2004 and become eligible for promotion. She was aspiring promotion and applied for the post of officer but could not get promotion due to low score in the written test. She was transferred to Solapur, her native place in 2006. Again she applied for the post of officer (from promotion quota), but could not succeed. She started union activities and elected as a president of local unit. She solved number of problems of the members and naturally almost all the employees of the branch joined her union. Since then she was become a problem to management. In 2009, again she was not given promotion, though her score was more than minimum in the written test stating that her score of personal interview was less. In fact promotion was denied on the basis of confidential report of the Branch Manager regarding her trade union activities. Smt. Snehal Ramgade decided later or not to make any application for promotion and devoted more time to the union activities. She also started her own business as well as diverted deposit of business community to other banks. In 2011, Nagesh Bank Management decided to promote Smt. Snehal Ramgade as an officer as per the recommendation of the new Branch Manager and accordingly appointment order was given, but unfortunately she refused to accept the order.

Questions:
   (a) Analyse the above case and give suitable title.
   (b) Why did Smt. Ramgade refused the promotion?

Chapter 3...

Training, Developing and Appraising Employees and Managing Performance

Contents ...
3.1 Training
3.2 Development
3.3 Performance Management System
3.4 Job Evaluation
3.5 Managing Careers
- Points to Remember
- Questions for Discussion
- Multiple Choice Questions
- Case Study

Objectives ...
➢ To understand the concept of Training and Development, Objectives, Need and Importance, Process, Evaluation and Methods of Training
➢ Performance Management, Meaning, Performance Appraisal, Objectives, Methods, Performance Counselling, Mentoring
➢ What is Job evaluation, Definition, Scope, Process and Methods
➢ Career Management Process, Career path, Career Counselling, Types of Promotion and Transfers

3.1 Training

Orientation

An introductory stage in the process of new employee assimilation, and a part of his or her continuous socialisation process in an organisation. Major objectives of orientation are:
1. Gain employee commitment,
2. Reduce his or her anxiety,
3. Help him or her understand organisation's expectations, and
4. Convey what he or she can expect from the job and the organisation

It is commonly followed by training tailored to specific job positions.

Employee orientation is part of a long-term investment in a new employee. It is an initial process that provides easy access to basic information, programmes and services, gives clarification and allows new employees to take an active role in their organisation.

Training

Giving information, knowledge and education in order to develop technical skills, social skills and administrative skills among the employees is defined as training.

According to **Edwin Flippo**, training is *"the act of increasing the knowledge and skill of an employee for doing a particular job."*

Training is next to selection. A worker selected / appointed in an Organisation needs proper training. This enables him to perform the job correctly and also efficiently. Similarly, a manager needs training for promotion and for his self improvement. Employees are now given training immediately after appointment and thereafter from time to time. Training is used as a tool / technique for management/executive development. It is used for the development of human resource working in an organisation.

Objectives of Training

1. **Improving quality of work force:** Training and development help companies to improve the quality of work done by their employees. Training programmes concentrate on specific areas, thereby improving the quality of work in that area.
2. **Enhance employee growth:** Every employee who takes training becomes better at his job. Training provides perfection and the required practice; therefore employee's are able to develop themselves professionally.
3. **Prevents obsolescence:** Through training and development the employee is up to date with new technology and the fear of being thrown out of the job is reduced.
4. **Assisting new employee:** Training and development programmes greatly help new employees to get accustomed to new methods of working, new technology, the work culture of the company etc.
5. **Bridging the gap between planning and implementation:** Plans made by companies, expect people to achieve certain targets, within certain time limits, with certain quality. For this employee performance has to be accurate and perfect. Training helps in achieving accuracy and perfection.
6. **Health and safety measures:** Training and development programmes clearly identifies and teaches employees about the different risks involved in their job, the different problems that can arise and how to prevent such problems. This helps to improve the health and safety measures in the company.

Training Process/ Steps in Training

(a) Organisational Objectives and Strategies

The first step in the training process in an organisation is the assessment of its objectives and strategies. What business are we in? At what level of quality do we wish to provide this product or service? How do we see ourselves in future? Its only after answering these and other related questions, that the organisation must assess the strength and weakness of its human resources.

(b) Needs Assessment

Needs assessment diagnoses present problems and future challenges to be met through training and development. Needs assessment occurs at two levels i.e. group level and individual level. An individual obviously needs training when his or her performance falls short. Inadequate performance may be due to lack of skills or knowledge or any other problem

(c) Training and Development Objectives

Once training needs are assessed, training and development goals must be established. Without clearly-set goals, it is not possible to design a training and development programme and after it has been implemented, there will be no way of measuring its effectiveness. Goals must be tangible, verifiable and measurable. This is easy where skilled training is involved.

(d) Conducting Training Activities

Where is the training going to be conducted and how?
- At the job itself.
- On site but not at the job itself, for example in a training room in the company.
- Off site such as a university, college classroom, hotel, etc.

(e) Designing Training and Development Programme

It includes:
- Who are the trainees?
- Who are the trainers?
- What are the methods and techniques?
- What is the level of training?
- What are the principles of learning?
- Where to conduct the programme?

(f) Implementation of the Training Programme

Program implementation involves actions on the following lines:
- Deciding the location and organising training and other facilities.
- Scheduling the training programme.
- Conducting the programme.
- Monitoring the progress of the trainees.

(g) Evaluation of the Results

The last stage in the training and development process is the evaluation of the results. Since huge sums of money are spent on training and development, how far the programme has been useful must be judge/determined. Evaluation helps determine the results of the training and development programme. In practice, however organisations either overlook or lack facilities for evaluation.

Training Need Assessment

Training needs analysis is a systematic process of understanding training requirements. It is conducted at three stages

1. The level of organisation,
2. Individual,
3. The job.

Each of which is called as the organisational, individual and job analysis. Once these analysis are over, the results are collected to arrive upon the objectives of the training programme.

(i) **Organisational Analysis:** The organisational analysis is aimed at short listing the focus areas for training within the organisation and the factors that may affect the same. Organisational mission, vision, goals, people inventories, processes, performance data are all studied. The study gives cues about the kind of learning environment required for the training. Motorola and IBM for example, conduct surveys every year keeping in view the short term and long term goals of the organisation.

(ii) **Job Analysis:** The job analysis of the needs assessment survey, aims at understanding the 'what' of the training development stage. The kind of intervention that is needed is decided upon, in the job analysis. It is an objective assessment of the job wherein both the worker oriented: approach as well as the task: oriented approach is taken into consideration. The worker approach identifies key behaviours and asks for a certain job, and the task: oriented approach identifies the activities to be performed in a certain job. The former is useful in deciding the intervention and the latter in content development and programme evaluation.

(iii) **Individual Analysis:** As evident from the name itself, the individual analysis is concerned with who in the organisation needs the training and in which particular area. Here performance is taken out from the performance appraisal data and the same is compared with the expected level or standard of performance. The individual analysis is also conducted through questionnaires, 360 feedback, personal interviews etc. Likewise, many organisation use competency ratings to rate their managers; these ratings may come from their subordinates, customers, peers, bosses etc. Apart from the above mentioned, organisations also make use of attitude surveys, critical Incidents and Assessment surveys, to understand training needs which will be discussed in detail in other articles.

Training Evaluation

Evaluation involves the assessment of the effectiveness of the training programmes. This assessment is done by collecting data on whether the participants were satisfied with the deliverables of the training program, whether they learned something from the training and are able to apply those skills at their workplace. There are different tools for assessment of a training programme depending upon the kind of training conducted.

Since organisations spend a large amount of money, it is therefore important for them to understand the usefulness of the same. For example, if a certain technical training was conducted, the organisation would be interested in knowing whether the new skills are being put to use at the workplace or in other words whether the effectiveness of the worker is enhanced. Similarly in case of behavioural training, the same would be evaluated on whether there is change in the behaviour, attitude and learning ability of the participants.

Benefits of Training Evaluation

Evaluation acts as a check to ensure that the training is able to fill the competency gaps within the organisation in a cost effective way. This is specially very important in wake of the fact that the organisations are trying to cut costs and increase globally. Some of the benefits of the training evaluation are as under:

(i) **Evaluation ensures accountability:** Training evaluation ensures that training programmes comply with the competency gaps and that the deliverables are not compromised upon.

(ii) **Check the Cost:** Evaluation ensures that the training programmes are effective in improving the work quality, employee behaviour, attitude and development of new skills within the employee within a certain budget. Since globally companies are trying to cut their costs without compromising upon the quality, evaluation just aims at achieving the same with training.

(iii) **Feedback to the Trainer / Training:** Evaluation also acts as a feedback to the trainer or the facilitator and the entire training process. Since evaluation accesses individuals at the level of their work, it gets easier to understand the loopholes of the training and the changes required in the training methodology.

Not many organisations believe in the process of evaluation or at least do not have an evaluation system in place. Many organisations conduct training programmes year after year only as a matter of faith and not many have a firm evaluation mechanism in place. Organisations like IBM, Motorala have a firm evaluation mechanism in place.

There are many methods and tools available for evaluating the effectiveness of training programmes. Their usability depends on the kind of training programme that is under evaluation. Generally most of the organisations use the Kirk Patrick model for training evaluations which evaluates training at four levels: reactions, learning, behaviour and results.

After it was found out that training costs organisations a lot of money and no evaluation measures the return on investment for training, the fifth level for training evaluation was added to the training evaluation model by Kirk Patrick which is called as the ROI.

Methods and Techniques of Training

Training methods are categorised into two groups-
(i) on-the-job and
(ii) off-the-job methods.

On-the-job methods refer to methods that are applied in the workplace, while the employee is actually working. Off-the-job methods are used away from workplaces.

(i) On the Job Training Methods

1. **Coaching:** On-the-job coaching by a superior is an important and potentially effective approach if superior is properly trained and oriented. The technique involves direct personnel instruction and guidance, usually, with extensive demonstration and continuous critical evaluation and correction. The advantage is increased motivation for the trainee and the minimisation of the problem of learning transfer from theory to practice. The danger in this method lies in the possible neglect of coaching by superior.

2. **Job Rotation:** The major objective of job rotation training is the broadening of the background of trainee in the organisation. If trainee is rotated periodically from one job to another job, he acquires a general background.

   The main advantages are:
   - it provides a general background to the trainee,
   - training takes place in actual situation,
   - competition can be stimulated among the rotating trainees,
   - it stimulates a more co-operative attitude by exposing a man to other fellow's problems and viewpoints.

   There are certain disadvantages of this method-

   The productive work can suffer because of the obvious disruption caused by such changes. Rotations become less useful as specialisation proceeds, for few people have the breadth of technical knowledge and skills to move from one functional area to another.

3. **Apprenticeship:** Apprentice training can be traced back to medieval times when those intended on learning trade skill bound themselves to a master craftsman to learn by doing the work under his guidance. In earlier periods, apprenticeship was not restricted to artisans, but was used in training for the professions, including medicine, law, dentistry, and teaching. Today's industrial organisations require large number of skilled craftsmen who can be trained by this system. Such training is either provided by the organisations or it is also imparted by governmental agencies. Most States now have apprenticeship laws with supervised plans for such training. Arrangements usually provide a mixed programme of classroom and job experience.

4. **Vestibule Schools:** Large organisations frequently provided what are described as vestibule schools, a preliminary to actual shop experience. As far as possible, shop

conditions are duplicated, but instructive, not output, and are major objective, with special instructors provided. Vestibule schools are widely used in training for clerical and office jobs as well as for factory production jobs. Such training is usually shorter and less complex than that adaptable to the apprenticeship system. Vestibule training is relatively expensive, but these costs are justified if the volume of training is large, or if uniform, high-standard results are important.

(ii) Off-the-Job Training Methods

1. **Lecture Method:** Lecturing is the most traditional form of formal training method. The lecture is the traditional and direct method of instructions. First, there are courses which the organisations themselves establish to be taught by members of the organisation. Some organisations have regular instructors assigned to their training and development departments such as Tata and Hindustan Unilever, State Bank of India etc. A second approach to lectures is for organisations to work with universities or institutes in establishing a course or series of courses to be taught by instructors of these institutes. A third approach is for the organisations to send personnel to programmes established by the universities, institutes and other bodies. Such courses are organised for a short period ranging from 2-3 days to a few weeks. In India, such courses are organised frequently by the Institute of Management, Administrative Staff College of India, All India Management Association and some other organisations and universities.

2. **Conferences:** This is also an old method, but still a favourite training method. In order to escape the limitations of straight lecturing, many organisations have adopted guided-discussion type of conferences in their training programmes. In this method, the participants pool their ideas and experience in attempting to arrive at improved methods of dealing with the problems which are common subject of discussion). Conference method allows the trainees to look at the problem from a broader angle. These conferences, however, have certain limitations. Unless the discussion is directed to the fell needs of the participants that may well feel that the whole session is useless.

3. **Case studies:** This technique, which has been developed and popularised by the Harvard Business School, U.S.A., is one of the most common form of training. A case is a written account of a trained reporter or analyst seeking to describe an actual situation. This method increases the trainee's power of observation, helping him to ask better questions and to look for a broader range of problems. A well chosen case may promote objective discussion, but the lack of emotional involvement may make it difficult to effect any basic change in the behaviour and attitude of trainees.

4. **Laboratory Training:** Laboratory training adds to conventional training by providing situations in which the trainees themselves experience through their own interaction some of the conditions they are talking about. In this way, they more or less experiment on themselves. Laboratory training is more concerned about changing

individual behaviour and attitude. It is generally more successful in changing job performance than conventional training methods. There are two methods of laboratory training: simulation and sensitivity training.

(A) Simulation: An increasingly popular technique of management development is simulation of performance. In this method, instead of taking participants into the field, different techniques can be simulated in the training session itself. Simulation is the presentation of real life situation of organisations in the training session. It covers situations of varying complexities and roles for the participants. It creates a whole field organisation, relates participants through key roles in it, and have them deal with specific situations of a kind they encounter in real life. There are two common simulation methods of training: role-playing and business games.

  (i) Role-Playing: Role-Playing is laboratory method which can be used rather easily as a supplement to conventional training methods. Its purpose is to increase the trainee's skill in dealing with other people. It is spontaneous acting of a realistic situation involving two or more persons under class room situations. Dialogue spontaneously grows out of the situation, as it is developed by the trainees assigned to it. Other trainees in the group serve as observers or critics. Since people take roles every day, they are somewhat experienced in the art, and with a certain amount of imagination they can project themselves into roles other than their own.

  (ii) Gaming: Gaming has been devised to simulate the problems of running a company or even a particular department. It has been used for a variety of training objectives, from investment strategy, collective bargaining techniques, to the morale of clerical personnel. It has been used at all levels, from the top executives to the production supervisors. Gaming is a laboratory method in which role-playing exists but its difference is that it focuses attention on administrative problems, while role-playing tends to emphasise mostly on feelings and tone between people who are in interaction.

(B) Sensitivity Training: (T Group) Sensitivity training is a small-group interaction under stress in an unstructured encounter group which requires people to become sensitive to one another's feelings in order to develop reasonable group activity. T-group has several characteristic features: (i) the T-group is generally small, from ten to twenty members; (ii) the group begins its activity with no formal agenda; (iii) the role of trainer is primarily to call attention from time to time to the on going process within the group; (iv) the procedure tends to develop introspection and self-examination, with emotional levels of involvement and behaviour and the possibility of colleagues and some breakdown of established insulation and self-defense on the part of individuals.

The objectives of such training are increased openness with others, more concern for others, increased tolerance for individual differences, less ethnic prejudice, understanding of a group process, enhanced listening skills, and increased trust and support.

3.2 Development

Development means those learning opportunities designed to help employees to grow. Development is not primarily skills oriented. Instead it provides the general knowledge and attitudes, which will be helpful to employers in higher positions. Efforts towards development often depend on personal drive and ambition. Development activities such as those supplied by management development programmes are generally voluntary in nature. Development provides knowledge about business environment, management principles and techniques, human relations, specific industry analysis and the like is useful for better management of a company

In addition to training for operative staff, an organisation has to take steps for training managers. Such training programmes are called 'managerial development/executive development programmes. Managerial talent is the most important asset that a company can possess. Management development ensures that as and when the demand for managers arises, suitably qualified persons are ready to fill the vacancies.

Development consists of all means by which executives learn to improve their performance. It is designed to improve the effectiveness of mangers in their present jobs and to prepare them for higher jobs in future.

Advantages of Development

1. **Making them:**

    Self-starters

    Committed

    Motivated

    Result oriented

    Sensitive to environment

    Understand use of power

2. Creating self awareness
3. Develop inspiring leadership styles
4. Instill zest for excellence
5. Teach them about effective communication
6. To subordinate their functional loyalties to the interests of the organisation

Training versus Development

Training	Development
It's a short term process.	It is a long term educational process.
Refers to instruction in technical and mechanical problems.	Refers to philosophical and theoretical educational concepts.
Targeted in most cases for non-managerial personnel.	Targeted for managerial personnel.
Specific job related purpose.	General knowledge purpose.

Executive Development

Executive development or management development is a systematic process of learning and growth by which managerial personnel gain and apply knowledge, skills, attitudes and insights to manage the work in their organisation effectively and efficiently.

According to P. N. Singh, "Management development is an activity designed to improve the performance of existing managers, provide a supply of managers to meet the need of organisations in future and extend the understanding of the management activity by drawing from the following three resource areas: (a) Knowledge, (b) Experience, and (c) Trainee himself."

Need / Importance of Management Development

According to Edwin Flippo, "No organisation has a choice of whether to develop employees or not, the only choice is that of method." The need for management development is well accepted in the present business, which is fast changing due to technological and social developments.

- **Shortage of trained managers:** Talented and matured managers are not easily available. It is not possible to appoint managers from outside for the key managerial posts. The better alternative is to select talented persons as trainee managers and develop their qualities through special training and wider exposures. In this way, the organisation can create its own team of talented managers to lead the whole organisation.

- **Complexity of management jobs:** The jobs of managers are now complicated and more challenging. They need varied skills for dealing with the complex organisational problems. For this, talented persons should be selected and proper training should be given to them.

- **Technological and social changes:** Rapid technological and social changes are taking place in the business world. In India, such developments are fast taking place along with the liberalisation and globalisation of business. Managers should be given proper training and exposure in computer applications and information technology.

- **Management obsolescence:** Executive obsolescence occurs due to mental deterioration and aging process. This can be corrected by offering self-development opportunities to managers. In fact, self-development must continue throughout the career of an executive.

- **Complexity of business management:** Business management is becoming very complicated due to government legislations, market competition, social pressures and consciousness among consumers. Well-trained and matured managers are therefore required. Such managers are not available easily. The best way is to train existing managers through management development programmes.

3.3 Performance Management System

Performance management is the process of identifying, measuring, managing, and developing the performance of the human resources in an organisation. Basically it emphasises on finding out how well employees perform and then to ultimately improve their performance level. When used correctly, performance management is a systematic analysis and measurement of worker performance (including communication of that assessment to the individual) that is used to improve performance over time.

A performance management system includes the following actions.

- Developing clear job descriptions and employee performance plans which includes the key result areas (KRA) and performance indicators.
- Selection of right set of people by implementing an appropriate selection process.
- Negotiating requirements and performance standards for measuring the outcome and overall productivity against the predefined benchmarks.
- Providing continuous coaching and feedback during the period of delivery of performance.
- Identifying the training and development needs by measuring the outcomes achieved against the set standards and implementing effective development programmes for improvement.
- Holding quarterly performance development discussions and evaluating employee performance on the basis of performance plans.
- Designing effective compensation and reward systems for recognising those employees who excel in their jobs by achieving the set standards in accordance with the performance plans or rather exceed the performance benchmarks.
- Providing promotional/career development support and guidance to the employees.
- Performing exit interviews for understanding the cause of employee discontentment and thereafter exit from an organisation.

By establishing clear performance expectations which includes results, actions and behaviours, it helps the employees in understanding what exactly is expected out of their jobs and setting of standards help in eliminating those jobs which are of no use any longer. Through regular feedback and coaching, it provides an advantage of diagnosing the problems at an early stage and taking corrective actions.

Performance Appraisal

Performance Appraisal is the ongoing process of evaluating employee performance. Performance appraisals are reviews of employee performance over time, so appraisal is just one piece of performance management.

Performance appraisal may be conducted once in every 6 months or once in a year. The basic idea of the appraisal is to evaluate the performance of the employee, and giving him a feedback. Identify areas where improvement is required so that training can be provided. Give incentives and bonus to encourage employees etc.

Objectives of Performance Appraisal

The major objectives of performance appraisal are discussed below:

- To enable the employees towards achievement of superior standards of work performance.
- To help the employees in identifying the knowledge and skills required for performing the job efficiently as this would drive their focus towards performing the right task in the right way.
- Boosting the performance of the employees by encouraging employee empowerment, motivation and implementation of an effective reward mechanism.
- Promoting a two way system of communication between the supervisors and the employees for clarifying expectations about the roles and accountabilities, communicating the functional and organisational goals, providing a regular and a transparent feedback for improving employee performance and continuous coaching.
- Identifying the barriers to effective performance and resolving those barriers through constant monitoring, coaching and development interventions.
- Creating a basis for several administrative decisions, strategic planning, succession planning, promotions and performance based payment.
- Promoting personal growth and advancement in the career of the employees by helping them in acquiring the desired knowledge and skills.

Some additional objectives are:

- To review the performance of the employees over a given period of time.
- To judge the gap between the actual and the desired performance.
- To help the management in exercising organisational control.
- Helps to strengthen the relationship and communication between superior – subordinates and management – employees.
- To diagnose the strengths and weaknesses of the individuals so as to identify the training and development needs of the future.
- Provide clarity of the expectations and responsibilities of the functions to be performed by the employees.
- To reduce the grievances of the employees.

Methods of Performance Appraisal

(I) Traditional Methods of Performance Appraisal

1. Rating Scales Method: Rating Scales Method is a commonly used method for assessing the performance of the employees and a well-known traditional method of performance appraisal of employees. Many corporations and companies like Airtel and Dell Corporation are using this method for evaluating the employees and subsequently taking decisions on the concerned employee.

Depending upon the job of the employee under this method of appraisal, traits like attitude, performance, regularity, accountability and sincerity etc. are rated with a scale from 1 to 10. Here, 1 indicates negative feedback and 10 indicates positive feedback as shown below.

Attitude of employee towards his superiors, colleagues and customers

1	2	3	4	5	6	7	8	9	10

Extremely poor   **Excellent**

Regularity in the job

1	2	3	4	5	6	7	8	9	10

Extremely poor   **Outstanding**

An employee who scored more points will be treated as the top performer and an employee who scored less following descending will be treated as a low performer and the least scored employee will be treated as non-performers.

2. Ranking method: In this method ranks are given to employees based on their performance. There are different methods of ranking employees:

   (i) **Simple ranking method:** Simple ranking method refers to ranks in serial order starting from the best employee. For example: If we have to rank 10 best employees we start with the first best employee and give him the first rank this is followed by the 2nd best and so on until all 10 have been given ranks.

   (ii) **Alternate ranking:** In this method the serial alternates between the best and the worst employee. The best employee is given rank 1 and then we move to the worst employee and give him rank 10 again to 2nd best employee and give him rank 2 and so on.

   (iii) **Paired comparison:** In this method each and every person in the group, department or team is compared with every other person in the team/group/department. The comparison is made on certain criteria and finally ranks are given. This method is superior because it compares each and every person on certain qualities and provides a ranking on that basis.

3. Critical Incidents Methods: This technique of performance appraisal was developed by Flanagan and Burns. The manager prepares a list of points for very effective and ineffective behaviour of an employee. These critical incidents or events represent the outstanding or poor behaviour of employees on the job. The manager maintains a log on each employee, whereby he periodically records critical incidents of the workers behaviour. At the end of the rating period, these recorded critical incidents are used in the evaluation of the workers' performance. An example of a good critical incident of a sales assistant is given as following:

July 20: The sales clerk patiently attended to the customer's complaint. He is polite, prompt, and enthusiastic in solving the customers' problem.

On the other hand the bad critical incident may appear as under:

July 20: The sales assistant stayed 45 minutes over on his break during the busiest part of the day. He failed to answer the store manager's call thrice. He is lazy, negligent, stubborn and disinterested in work.

This method provides an objective basis for conducting a thorough discussion of an employee's performance. This method avoids recency bias (most recent incidents get too much emphasis). This method suffers however from the following limitations:

Negative incidents may be more noticeable than positive incidents.

The supervisors have a tendency to unload a series of complaints about incidents during an annual performance review session.

It results in very close supervision which may not be liked by the employee.

The recording of incidents may be a chore for the manager concerned, who may be too busy or forgets to do it.

4. Graphic Rating Scale: Graphic rating scale refers to using specific factors to appraise people. The entire appraisal is presented in the form of a chart. The chart contains certain columns which indicate qualities which are being appraised and other columns which specify the rank to be given. The senior has to put a tick mark for a particular quality along with the ranking. Such charts are prepared for every employee, according to the department in which they work. Sometimes the qualities which are judged may change depending upon the department.

Table 3.1: Example of Graphic Rating Scale Method

Performance Trait	Excellent	Good	Average	Fair	Poor
Attitude	5	4	3	2	1
Knowledge of Work	5	4	3	2	1
Managerial Skills	5	4	3	2	1
Team Work	5	4	3	2	1
Honesty	5	4	3	2	1
Regularity	5	4	3	2	1
Accountability	5	4	3	2	1
Interpersonal relationships	5	4	3	2	1
Creativity	5	4	3	2	1
Discipline	5	4	3	2	1

This method is popular because it is simple and does not require any writing ability. The method is easy to understand and use. Comparison among pairs is possible. This is necessary for decisions on salary increases, promotion, etc.

5. Forced Distribution: A rating system is used by companies to evaluate their employees. The system requires the managers to evaluate each individual, and rank them typically into one of the three categories (excellent, good, poor). The system is thought to be relatively widely-used, but remains somewhat controversial due to the competition it creates, and also in reality not all employees will fit perfectly into one of the categories and might end up in a category that does not reflect their true performance. One of the first companies to use this system was General Electric, in the 1980s.

Forced ranking is a method of performance appraisal to rank employee but in order of forced distribution, where managers are required to distribute ratings for those being evaluated, into a pre-specified performance distribution ranking

For example, the distribution requested with 10 or 20 percent in the top category, 70 or 80 percent in the middle, and 10 percent in the bottom.

The top-ranked employees are considered "high-potential" employees and are often targeted for a more rapid career and leadership development programmes.

In contrast, those ranked at the bottom are denied bonuses and pay increases. They may be given a probationary period to improve their performance.

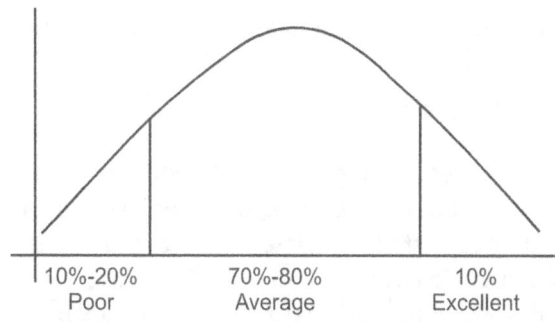

Fig. 3.1

General Electric Company, Ford Motor, Conoco, Sun Microsystems, Cisco Systems, EDS, Enron and a host of other U.S. corporations have adopted similar policies of this method.

6. Narrated essay: In this method the senior or the boss is supposed to write a narrative essay describing the qualities of his junior. He may describe the employee's strength and weakness, analytical abilities etc. The narrative essay ends with a recommendation for future promotion or for future incentives.

7. Check list method: In this method the senior, or the boss is given a list of questions about the junior. These questions are followed by check boxes. The superior has to put a tick mark in any one of the boxes. This method can be explained with the following example:

	Y	N
Does the employee have leadership qualities?	☐	☐
Is the employee capable of group efforts?	☐	☐
Has the employee shown analytical skills?	☐	☐

on the job.

Modern Methods of Performance Appraisal

1. Role analysis: In this method of appraisal the person who is being appraised is called the focal point and the members of his group who are appraising him are called role set members.

These role set members identify key result areas (KRA 2 marks) (areas where you want improvement are called KRA) which have to be achieved by the employee. The KRA and their improvement will determine the amount of incentives and benefits which the employee will receive in future. The appraisal depends upon what role set members have to say about the employee.

2. Assessment centers: Assessment centers (AC) are places where the employee's are assessed on certain qualities, talents and skills which they possess. This method is used for selection as well as for appraisal. The people who attend assessment centers are given management games, psychological test, puzzles, questionnaires about different management related situations etc. based on their performance in these test and games appraisal is done.

3. Behaviourally Anchored Rating Scales (BARS): Behaviourally Anchored Rating Scales (BARS) is a relatively new technique which combines the graphic rating scale and critical incidents method. It consists of predetermined critical areas of job performance or sets of behavioural statements describing important job performance qualities as good or bad (for e.g. the qualities like inter-personal relationships, adaptability and reliability, job knowledge etc). These statements are developed from critical incidents.

In this method, an employee's actual job behaviour is judged against the desired behaviour by recording and comparing the behaviour with BARS. Developing and practicing BARS requires expert knowledge.

A behaviourally anchored rating scale is an employee appraisal system where raters distinguish between successful and unsuccessful job performance by collecting and listing critical job factors. These critical behaviours are categorised and appointed a numerical value which is used as the basis for rating performance.

Table 3.2: Example of Behaviourally Anchored Rating Scales

Performance	Points	Behaviour
Extremely good	7	Can expect trainee to make valuable suggestions for increased sales and to have positive relationships with customers all over the country.
Good	6	Can expect to initiate create ideas for improved sales.
Above average	5	Can expect to keep to touch with the customers throughout the year.
Average	4	Can manage, with difficulty to deliver the goods in time.
Below average	3	Can expect to unload the trucks when asked by the supervisor.
Poor	2	Can expect to inform only a part of the customers.
Extremely poor	1	Can expect to take extended coffee breaks and roam around purposelessly.

4. Management by objective: This method was given by Peter Drucker in 1974. It was intended to be a method of group decision making. It can be use for performance appraisal also. In this method all members of the of the department starting from the lowest level employee to the highest level employee together discus, fix target goals to be achieved, plan for achieving these goals and work together to achieve them. The seniors in the department get an opportunity to observe their junior- group efforts, communication skills, knowledge levels, interest levels etc. based on this appraisal is done.

The key features of management by objectives are as under:

1. Superior and subordinates get together and jointly agree upon the list, the principal duties and areas of responsibility of the individual's job.
2. The subordinate sets his own short-term performance goals or targets in cooperation with his superior.
3. They agree upon criteria for measuring and evaluating performance.
4. From time to time, as decided upon, the superior and subordinate get together to evaluate progress towards the agreed-upon goals. At those meetings, new or modified goals are set for the ensuing period.
5. The superior plays a supportive role. He tries, on a day-to-.day basis, to help the subordinate achieve the agreed upon goals. He counsels and coaches.
6. In the appraisal process, the superior plays less of the role of a judge and more of the role of one who helps the subordinate attain the organisation's goals or targets.

The MBO Process

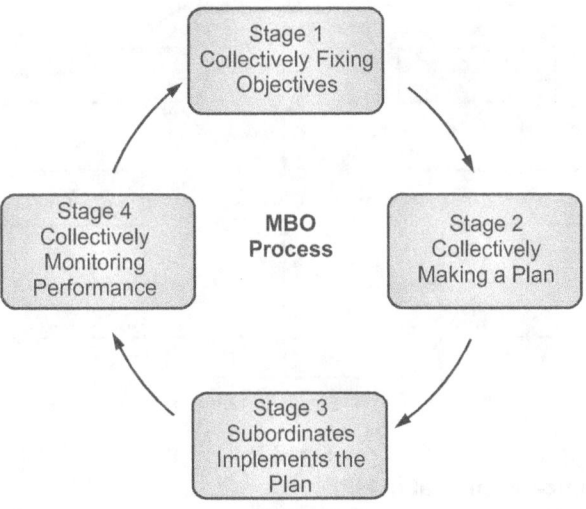

Fig. 3.2

5. 360 degree appraisal: In this method of appraisal an all round approach is adopted. Feedback about the employee is taken from the employee himself, his superiors, his juniors, his colleagues, customers he deals with, financial institutions and other people he deals with. Based on all these observations an appraisal is made and feedback is given. This is one of the most popular methods.

Usually, this tool is used for employees at middle and senior level. The complexity of their roles enables the organisation to generate sufficient data from all stakeholders for a meaningful assessment.

Advantages of 360 Degree Appraisal
1. Offers a more comprehensive view towards the performance of employees.
2. Improves credibility of performance appraisal.
3. Increases responsibilities of employees to their customers.
4. The mix of ideas can give a more accurate assessment.
5. Opinions gathered from lots of staff are sure to be more persuasive.
6. People who undervalue themselves are often motivated by feedback from others.

Disadvantages of 360 Degree Appraisal
- Taking a lot of time, and being complex in administration
- Extension of exchange feedback can cause troubles and tensions to several staff.
- There is requirement for training and important effort in order to achieve efficient working.
- Feedback can be useless if it is not carefully and smoothly dealt.
- Can impose an environment of suspicion if the information is not openly and honestly managed.

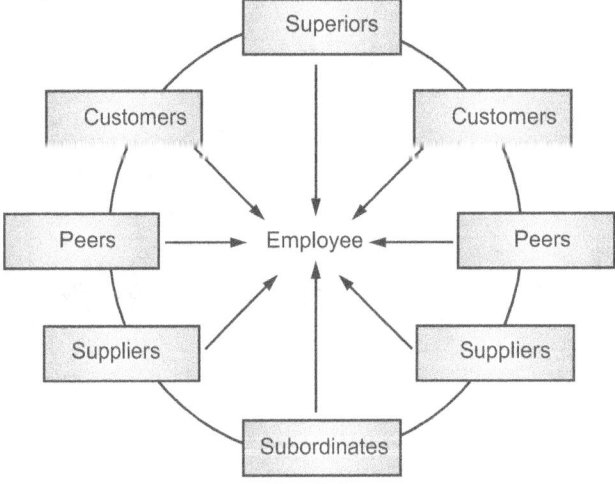

Fig. 3.3

Process of Performance Appraisal in HRM

Performance Appraisal consists of the following steps:
1. **Setting performance standards:** In this very first step in performance appraisal, the HR department decides the standards of performance i.e. they decide what exactly is expected from the employee for each and every job. Sometimes certain marking scheme may be adopted e.g. A score of 90/100 = excellent performance, a score of 80/100 = good, and so on.
2. **Communication standard set to the employee:** Standards of performance appraisal decided in 1st step are now conveyed to the employee so that the employee will know what is expected from him and will be able to improve his performance.

3. **Measuring performance:** The performance of the employee is now measured by the HR department, different methods can be used to measure performance i.e. traditional and modern method. The method used depends upon the company's convenience.

4. **Comparing performance with standard:** The performance of the employee is now judged against the standard, to understand the score achieved by him. Accordingly we come to know which category of performance the employee falls into i.e. excellent, very good, good, satisfactory etc.

5. **Discussing results:** The results obtained by the employee after performance appraisal are informed or conveyed to him by the HR department. A feedback is given to the employee asking him to change certain aspects of his performance and improve them.

6. **Collective action:** The employee is given a chance or opportunity to improve himself in the areas specified by the HR department. The HR department constantly receives or keeps a check on the employee's performance and notes down improvements in performance.

7. **Implementation and review:** The performance appraisal policy is to be implemented on a regular basis. A review must be done from time to time to check whether any change in policy is required. Necessary changes are made from time to time.

Performance Appraisal Process

Process of performance appraisal
↓
Setting performance standards
↓
Communicating standards set to the employee
↓
Measuring performance
↓
Comparing performance with standard
↓
Discussing result
↓
Collective action
↓
Implementation and review

Self Appraisal

Self appraisal is an important part of the performance appraisal process where the employee himself gives the feedback or his views and points regarding his performance. Usually this is done with the help of a self appraisal form where the employee rates himself on various parameters, tells about his training needs, if any, talks about his accomplishments, strengths, weaknesses, problems faced etc.

Points to Remember while doing Self Appraisal

- **Be honest:** Always be truthful and honest while telling your accomplishments or failures. Don't exaggerate your strengths and don't hide your weaknesses. Don't make personal judgments for anybody.
- **Do the preparation:** It's always better to prepare oneself before the meeting. Get all the lists in place; prepare all the evidences and references.
- **Positive attitude:** Have a positive attitude towards the whole appraisal process. Be co-operative. Don't hesitate from taking the responsibility of your failures as well as the achievements. Demonstrate enthusiasm to improve in future and take all his suggestions calmly. Don't complain or demonstrate a negative attitude.
- **Cover all the aspects:** Apart from one's strengths, weaknesses, accomplishments and failures, one should also express the opportunities he/she would like to have for their development and improvement. One should suggest ways to overcome the problems faced and also assess capabilities, behaviours skills and competence they posses.

Self appraisal should ideally include the accomplishments, the goals achieved, the failures, and the personal growth (i.e. new skills acquired, preparation for the future etc.), the obstacles faced during the period, the efforts for removing them, the suggestions, and the areas of training and development felt by the employee.

Performance Counselling

Performance Counselling is a very important activity that helps employees to know themselves better. Performance Counselling refers to the help provided by a manager to his subordinates in objectively analysing their performance. It attempts to help the employee in:

1. Understanding themselves: their strengths and weaknesses.
2. Improving their professional and interpersonal competence by giving them feedback about their behaviour.
3. Setting goals and formulating action plans for further improvement.

Features of Performance Counselling

1. Conditions for effective counselling

- A climate of trust, confidence and openness is essential for effective counselling. Counselling cannot be effective if the subordinate does not trust his boss.

- It is necessary that the subordinate should feel free to participate without fear or inhibition as it is a dialogue between supervisor and subordinate and hence should be a two way communication.
- The main purpose of counselling is employee development.

2. **Performance Counselling Phases**

   (a) **Rapport Building:** In the rapport building phase, a good counsellor attempts to establish a climate of acceptance, warmth, support, openness and mutuality. This phase involves generating confidence in the employee to open up frankly, share his perceptions, problems, concerns, feelings etc. The subordinate must be made to feel wanted and that his superior is genuinely interested in his development.

   (b) **Exploration:** In this phase, the counsellor should attempt to help the employee understand and appreciate his strengths and weaknesses. He should also understand his own situation, problems and needs. Questions should be asked which help the employee focus on his problem.

   (c) **Action Planning:** Counselling interviews should end with specific plans of action for development of the employee. The main contribution of the superior in this phase is in helping the employee think of alternative ways of dealing with a problem.

Finally the superior may render some assistance in helping the employee implement the agreed upon action plan. Often good counselling sessions fail to produce effective results due to lack of follow:

Processes in Performance Counselling

1. **Feedback**

It is extremely important that the feedback is communicated in a manner that produces a constructive response in the subordinate. Given below are some guidelines that could be followed in giving feedback:

- Feedback should be descriptive and non- evaluative. Rather than putting the employee in a defensive position by telling him *"Your coming in late convinces me that you are not serious about your work"*, a manager may say, *"I notice that you have been regularly coming late and I am deeply concerned about this"*.

- It should be focused on the behaviour of the person rather than on the person himself. It is necessary to distinguish between the individual and his behaviour in conveying the negative feedback. It should be clear to the employee that what is being rejected or criticized is some specific behaviour of his. The intent is not to condemn the employee as an individual.

- When conveying feedback, it is generally desirable to back it up with few examples of actual events. Care must be exercised not to overdo this as the subordinate may misinterpret it that the superior is systematically building up a well-documented case against him.

- Feedback should be given timely. It should be given at the first opportunity when the employee is in the receptive mood.
- Feedback should be continuous. It should become a regular practice so that the subordinate develops an ability to accept and act upon the feedback.
- Feedback should be checked and verified. This will ensure that the subordinate has not misinterpreted the feedback received from his superior.

2. **Pre-Interview Preparation**
   - Review the employee's background, education, training and experience.
   - Determine the strengths and development needs to be discussed with the employee.
   - Identify areas that need attention during the next review period.
   - Make sure that the employee has sufficient advance notice for the interview so that he has time to do his own preparation.
   - It is always useful to note down the key points on a piece of paper.

3. **Interview**
   - Be sincere, informal and friendly. Explain the purpose of the discussion and make it clear to the subordinate that the interview is a two way communication.
   - Encourage the employee to discuss how he appraises his own performance.
   - Before discussing suggestions interviewer should also encourage the employee to tell his own plans.
   - Make a record of plans the manager and the employee have made, points requiring follow-up.

Performance Coaching

Performance coaching can be described as a series of guided conversations that enable the "coachee" to discover and implement personal solutions to challenging issues or areas of performance. These solutions, because they are intrinsic to the "coachee," are more likely to succeed and endure than solutions imposed externally.

Performance coaching is:
- A series of conversations that are designed and conducted to enhance someone's well being or performance.
- A process that both parties enter into willingly with clear expectations and agreements on how the process will work.
- A relationship, or partnership, that allows anything to be asked, said or considered.
- Based on the premise that performance in any field can be enhanced by creating a partnership and setting aside time to explore in conversation how performance might be taken to a new level.

Coaching is not ...
- Giving advice, being the expert or having the answers,
- Counselling,
- Fixing people,
- Doing it for them,
- Policing or getting people to work harder,
- A close, personal relationship,
- A replacement for supervision or management.

Coaching is ...
- Listening in a profound way,
- Asking questions that cause new thinking and possible actions,
- Hearing limitations in the other person's speaking,
- A place where people can think out loud,
- Getting the most value and learning from an experience,
- Acknowledging people for who they are and what they produce,
- Generating possibility and keeping it alive,
- A way of allowing people to change how they are relating to something,
- A place to vent, experiment and play with ideas,
- Confidential,
- A supportive relationship,
- A structure for making things happen.

Performance Mentoring
- Performance mentoring is a structured coaching course for individuals or small groups. With performance mentoring you and your company have available an external sounding board who can introduce effective techniques to achieve specific goals.
- The goal may be to create more economic growth, increasing sales or other concrete results. It may also be that a particular department needs to find more motivation and job satisfaction going forward in everyday life.
- Starting with the individual's resources and motivation both identifies the potential for success and directs a new trend from which both individuals and business can benefit.

Performance Based Interviewing (PBI)

Performance Based Interviewing (PBI) is a method to increase the effectiveness of the interviewing process in selecting and promoting quality staff. With PBI, the interviewer carefully defines the skills needed for the job and structures the interview process to elicit behavioural examples of past performance.

Performance Based Interviewing (PBI) is a selection process that uses interviewing techniques to ask job applicants questions about the knowledge, skills, abilities, and other characteristics (KSAOs) they have, that are important in order for them to do a good job. Studies show that the way people behave in the past is probably the way they will behave in the future. PBI questions ask job applicants to tell about what they did (their behaviour) in the past. When deciding who the best applicant is, the interviewer will look at the degree to which each applicant possesses the important knowledge, skills, abilities and other characteristics necessary for a successful job performance.

Performance Based Interview Questions

Following are some of the examples of the performance based interview questions:
- Describe a situation in which you had to use your communication skills in presenting complex information. How did you determine whether your message was received? (With the original question you are assuming the person did understand.)
- Share with me an example of an important personal goal that you set, and explain how you accomplished it.
- Lead me through a decision-making process on a major project you've completed.
- Have you ever had many different tasks given to you at the same time? How did you manage these?
- Give an example of a time you had to make a difficult decision.

Edward Deming's view on Performance Appraisal

William Edwards Deming (October 14, 1900 – December 20, 1993) was an American statistician, professor, author, lecturer and consultant. His views were as follows:

Deming is opposed to employee's assessment, because it:
1. Rewards people for manipulating the system rather than improving it,
2. Is often self-defining,
3. Is consistent with team-work,
4. Acts as a substitute for proper management
5. Is inherently unfair.

His alternatives to performance appraisal are:
1. Meticulous selection of leaders,
2. Educating workers about their obligations, & improved training &education after selection,
3. Getting leaders to function as colleagues rather than as judges,
4. Subordinate performance to be assessed using statistical data,
5. Three to four interviews annually, with subordinates aimed at support and encouragement,
6. Accommodation to lone workers.

Legal issues Associated with Performance Appraisal

Performance appraisal data is used to make many important HR decisions (e.g. Pay, promotion, training, transfer and termination). The appraisal system is a common target of legal disputes by employees involving charges of unfairness and bias. An employee may seek the legal recourse to obtain relief from a discriminatory performance appraisal.

1. Performance appraisals should not be used as only disciplinary or corrective method. It is grossly unprofessional for a manager or supervisor to use the appraisal process to 'get even' with an employee who has displeased or upset them in some way.
2. Appraisals should not be used to discriminate against employees on the basis of race, religion, age, gender, disability, marital status, pregnancy, or sexual preference.
3. Performance appraisal results should be fair, accurate and be supported by evidence and examples. For instance, if an employee has poor interpersonal skills and is harming morale and group performance, the supervisor might keep a log of incidents. Co-workers may be interviewed and their views and reactions recorded. The nature and effects of the employee's behaviour should be documented.
4. An employee should have the opportunity to comment on their appraisal result, to express their agreement or otherwise, and to appeal the result or at least request a review by upline supervisors.
5. Appraisals should be balanced, recording information on both the good and the bad aspects of an employee's performance as far as possible.
6. Appraisals results should not be used as the sole basis for promotion, remuneration or termination decisions. A broad range of information should be considered, in which the employee's appraisal results may be significant but not necessarily conclusive.
7. Employees who receive a poor performance appraisal result should be given a reasonable chance to improve. It is a bad idea to dismiss, demote or penalize an employee because of a single adverse appraisal result (depending of course on the nature and seriousness of the conduct that underlies the poor result).
8. Provide timely feedback, especially to marginal or poor performers. It is not fair to offer zero feedback to a poor performer for twelve months and then present them with a bad appraisal. Be willing, especially with employees who are having trouble, to offer more frequent feedback and guidance. Tell them if something is wrong and give them a chance to correct the problem in a timely manner.
9. Retain records. If an employee believes they have been dealt with unfairly, they may have rights to instigate legal action years later. In the case of poor performers, or persons dismissed or demoted, or those who resign or leave in less than happy circumstances, it is suggested that their appraisal records, together with critical incident logs and other relevant documents, should be maintained. Check with local legal specialists as to required periods of record retention and time limits on the rights of potential litigants, as these vary from one jurisdiction to the next.

10. If an appraisal result is poor (or in any way likely to be controversial or provocative), an organisation should ask an objective third party for their views on whether the appraisal result seems fair and reasonable. Organisations should be prepared to modify their position if the second opinion is not supportive of the result.
11. Managers and supervisors required to conduct staff appraisals should be trained in appraisal principles and techniques. Conducting performance appraisals is one of the most demanding of all supervisory activities. It is a sensitive and sometimes controversial task which, if mishandled, can cause serious damage to employee relations and morale.
12. Appraisal results should be treated as private and confidential information. Record storage should be secure and controlled. Only people with an approved need to know should have access to an employee's performance appraisal information.

1.4 Job Evaluation

A **job evaluation** is a systematic way of determining the value/worth of a job in relation to other jobs in an organisation. It tries to make a systematic comparison between jobs to assess their relative worth for the purpose of establishing a rational pay structure. Its aim is to evaluate the job, not the jobholder, and to provide a relatively objective means of assessing the demands of a job.

Organisations use job evaluation to:
- Establish a rational, consistent job structure based on value to the organisation in terms of each job's complexity, importance and/or other factors (with or without reference to market valuation).
- Help provide a basis for pay-for-performance.
- Assist in establishing pay rates and structures that are competitive.
- Job evaluation helps provide salary equity among all.

When is an evaluation done?

Jobs are evaluated when:
- A new position is established, prior to recruitment.
- When an existing position has changed 10-15% (up or down).

The process of job evaluation involves the following steps:
- **Gaining acceptance:** Before undertaking job evaluation, top management must explain the aims) and uses of the programme to the employees and unions. To elaborate the programme further, oral presentations could be made. Letters, booklets could be used to classify all relevant aspects of the job evaluation programme.

- **Creating job evaluation committee:** It is not possible for a single person to evaluate all the key jobs in an organisation. Usually a job evaluation committee consisting of experienced employees, union representatives and HR experts is created to set the ball rolling.
- **Finding the jobs to be evaluated:** Every job need not be evaluated. This may be too taxing and costly. Certain key jobs in each department may be identified. While picking up the jobs, care must be taken to ensure that they represent the type of work performed in that department.
- **Analysing and preparing job description:** This requires the preparation of a job description and also an analysis of job needs for successful performance.
- **Selecting the method of evaluation:** The most important method of evaluating the jobs must be identified now, keeping the job factors as well as organisational demands in mind.
- **Classifying jobs:** The relative worth of various jobs in an organisation may be found out after arranging jobs in order of importance using criteria such as skill requirements, experience needed, under which conditions job is performed, type of responsibilities to be shouldered, degree of supervision needed, the amount of stress caused by the job, etc. Weights can be assigned to each such factor. When finally all the weights are added, the worth of a job is determined. The points may then be converted into monetary values.
- **Installing the programme:** Once the evaluation process is over and a plan of action is ready, management must explain it to the employees and put it into operation.
- **Reviewing periodically:** Due to the changes in environmental conditions (technology, products, services, etc.) jobs need to be examined closely. For example, the traditional clerical functions have undergone a rapid change in sectors like banking, insurance and railways, after computerisation. New job descriptions need to be written and the skill required for the new jobs need to be duly incorporated in the evaluation process. Otherwise, employees may feel that all the relevant job factors: based on which their pay has been determined: have not been evaluated properly.

For job evaluation to be practicable it is necessary:
- That jobs can be easily identified,
- That there are sufficient difference between different jobs, and
- Agreements on the relative importance or worth of different jobs can be negotiated between the enterprise and its employees and/or their representatives.

Job Evaluation Methods

There are four basic methods of job evaluation:
- Ranking,
- Classification,
- Factor comparison,
- Point method

(I) Ranking method

According to this method, jobs are arranged from highest to lowest, in order of their value or merit to the organisation. Jobs can also be arranged according to the relative difficulty in performing them. The jobs are examined as a whole rather than on the basis of important factors in the job; the job at the top of the list has the highest value and obviously the job at the bottom of the list will have the lowest value. Jobs are usually ranked in each department and then the department rankings are combined to develop an organisational ranking. The variation in payment of salaries depends on the variation of the nature of the job performed by the employees.

Advantage
- The ranking method is simple to understand and practice and it is best suited for a small organisation.

Disadvantage
- Not suitable for big organisations

(II) Classification method

According to this method, a predetermined number of job groups or job classes are established and jobs are assigned to these classifications. Following is a brief description of such a classification in an office.

- **Class I: Executives:** Further classification under this category may be Office Manager, Deputy Office Manager, Office Superintendent, Departmental Supervisor, etc.
- **Class II: Skilled workers:** Under this category the classification may be the Purchasing assistant, Cashier, Receipts clerk, etc.
- **Class III: Semiskilled workers:** Under this category the classification can be done as Steno typists, Machine-operators, Switchboard operator etc.
- **Class IV: Unskilled workers:** This category comprises of File clerks, Office boys, etc.

Advantages
- The job classification method is less subjective when compared to the earlier ranking method.
- The system is very easy to understand and acceptable to almost all employees.
- It takes into account all the factors that a job comprises. This system can be effectively used for a variety of jobs.

Disadvantages
- Even when the requirements of different jobs differ, they may be combined into a single category, depending on the status a job carries.
- It is difficult to write all-inclusive descriptions of a grade.
- When individual job descriptions and grade descriptions do not match well, the evaluators have the tendency to classify the job using their subjective judgements.

(III) Factor comparison method

A more systematic and scientific method of job evaluation is the factor comparison method. Though it is the most complex method of all, it is consistent and appreciable. Under this method, instead of ranking complete jobs, each job is ranked according to a series of factors.

These factors include mental effort, physical effort, skill needed, responsibility, supervisory responsibility, working conditions and other such factors (for instance, know-how, problem solving abilities, accountability, etc.).

Pay will be assigned in this method by comparing the weights of the factors required for each job, i.e., the present wages paid for key jobs may be divided among the factors weighted by importance (the most important factor, for instance, mental effort, receives the highest weight). In other words, wages are assigned to the job in comparison to its ranking on each job factor.

The steps involved in factor comparison method may be briefly stated thus:

- Select key jobs (say 15 to 20), representing wage/salary levels across the organisation. The selected jobs must represent as many departments as possible.
- Find the factors in terms of which the jobs are evaluated (such as skill, mental effort, responsibility, physical effort, working conditions, etc.).
- Rank the selected jobs under each factor (by each and every member of the job evaluation committee) independently.
- Assign money value to each level of each factor (example: consider problem solving is one of the factors, what level of problem solving is required (basic, intermediate or advance) and determine the wage rates for each key job.
- The wage rate for a job is apportioned along the identified factors.
- All other jobs are compared with the list of key jobs and wage rates are determined.

(IV) Point method

This method is widely used today in many organisations. Here, jobs are expressed in terms of key factors. Points are assigned to each factor after prioritising each factor in order of importance. The points are summed up to determine the wage rate for the job. Jobs with similar point totals are placed in similar pay grades. The procedure involved may be explained thus:

1. **Select key jobs:** Identify all the common factors to the jobs such as skill, effort, responsibility, etc.
2. **Divide each major factor into a number of sub factors:** Each sub factor is defined and expressed clearly in the order of importance, preferably along a scale.

    The most frequent factors employed in point systems are:

    (i) **Skill (key factor):** Education and training required, Breadth/depth of experience required, Social skills required, Problem-solving skills, Degree of discretion/use of judgment, Creative thinking.

(ii) **Responsibility/Accountability:** Breadth of responsibility, Specialized responsibility, Complexity of the work, Degree of freedom to act, Number and nature of subordinate staff, Extent of accountability for equipment/plant, Extent of accountability for product/materials.

(iii) **Effort:** Mental demands of a job, Physical demands of a job, Degree of potential stress.

The educational requirements (sub factor) under the skill (key factor) may be expressed thus in the order of importance.

3. Find the maximum number of points assigned to each job (after adding up the point values of all sub-factors of such a job).

This would help in finding the relative worth of a job. For instance, the maximum point assigned to an officer's job in a bank comes to 540. The manager's job, after adding up key factors and sub factors points, may be getting a point value of say 650 from the job evaluation committee. This job is now priced at a higher level.

4. Once the worth of a job in terms of total points is expressed, the points are converted into money values keeping in view the hourly/daily wage rates. A wage survey is usually undertaken to collect wage rates of certain key jobs in the organisation.

Advantages
- Superior to all other methods
- Reliable.

Disadvantages
- Complex
- Time consuming process.

Limitations of job evaluation
1. Job evaluation is not exactly scientific.
2. Most of the techniques are difficult to understand, even for the supervisors.
3. The factors taken by the programme are not exhaustive.
4. There may be wide fluctuations in compensable factors in view of the changes in technology, values and aspirations of employers, etc.

Employees, trade union leaders, management and the programme operators may assign different weight to different factors, thus creating grounds for dispute.

3.5 Managing Careers

Career management is a process by which individuals can guide, direct and influence the course of their careers. The process for enabling employees to better understand, develop and use their career skills and interests, more effectively.

Career management calls for an approach that explicitly takes into account both organisational needs and employee interests. It calls for creativity in identifying ways to provide development opportunities. Career management policies and practices are best based on an understanding of the stages through which careers progresses in organisations.

Career Management - The Process

1. The first step in career management involves clearly determining and establishing one's career goals.
2. The next step in the process is to determine the best course to be taken to achieve the goals set out. It is also essential to clearly map out where one is now and where he/she would like to be at the end of his/her professional career. It is crucial to put on paper the long term career goals and think strategically.
3. Once the goals and path to achieve these are determined, the next critical step is to continuously monitor progress. Career management involves routinely checking the movement made towards your established goals.
4. The fourth step is to get involved in training and acquiring new skills.
5. Over a passage of time, career goals and objectives are also bound to grow and change. This brings us to the final crucial step involved in career management. It involves monitoring, modifying and adjusting goals as and when needed. The map set out in the beginning is only a guide and does not require the individual to remain unchanged. As the person grows and develops a better understanding of who they are and what they want to be, these goals can be suitably altered to identify new paths and destinations that will turn out to be fulfilling.

Career Management Practices

1. Postings regarding internal job openings.
2. Formal education as part of career development.
3. Performance appraisal as a basis for career planning.
4. Career counselling by manager.
5. Lateral moves to create cross-functional experience.
6. Career counselling by HR department.
7. Retirement preparation programmes.
8. Succession planning.
9. Formal mentoring.
10. Common career paths.

CAREER PLANNING

Career planning is the process by which one selects career goals and the path to these goals. The major focus of career planning is on assisting the employees achieve a better match between personal goals and the opportunities that are realistically available in the organisation. Career programmers should not concentrate only on career growth opportunities. Practically speaking, there may not be enough high level positions to make upward mobility a reality for a large number of employees. Hence, career-planning efforts need to pin-point and highlight those areas that offer psychological success instead of vertical growth.

Career planning is not an event or end in itself, but a continuous process of developing human resources for achieving optimum results. It must, however, be noted that individual and organisational careers are not separate and distinct. A person who is not able to translate his career plan into action within the organisation may probably quit the job, if he has a choice. Organisations, therefore, should help employees in career planning so that both can satisfy each other's needs.

Career planning seeks to meet the following objectives:

(i) Attract and retain talent by offering careers, not jobs.
(ii) Use human resources effectively and achieve greater productivity.
(iii) Reduce employee turnover.
(iv) Improve employee morale and motivation.
(v) Meet the immediate and future human resource needs of the organisation on a timely basis.

CAREER PATH

Career path refers to the growth of the employee in an organisation. It refers to the various positions an employee moves to as he grows in an organisation. The employee may move vertically most of the time but also move laterally or cross functionally to move to a different type of job role.

Career path is used interchangeably with career ladder.

Most successful companies chalk out a career path/career ladder for the employees in order to provide them with a realistic picture of their position in the coming years in order to retain them. Having a clear idea about future positions and job responsibilities, the employee and the company can work to identify areas where relevant training is required for the employee to build his competencies to fulfil future job requirements.

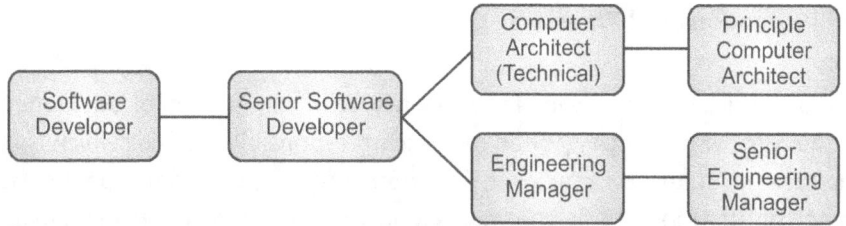

Fig. 3.4: Example of career path

Roles in Career Development

Individual
1. Accept responsibility for your own career.
2. Assess your interests, skills, and values.
3. Seek out career information and resources.
4. Establish goals and career plans.
5. Utilize development opportunities.
6. Talk with your manager about your career.
7. Follow through on realistic career plans.

Manager
1. Provide timely and accurate performance feedback.
2. Provide development assignments and support.
3. Participate in career development discussions with subordinates.
4. Support employee development plans.

Employer
1. Communicate mission, policies and procedures.
2. Provide training and development opportunities including workshops.
3. Provide career information and career programmes.
4. Offer a variety of career paths.
5. Provide career oriented performance feedback.
6. Provide mentoring opportunities to support growth and self direction.
7. Provide employees with individual development plans.
8. Provide academic learning assistance programmes.

The Employee's Role

For the individual employee, career planning means matching individual strengths and weaknesses with occupational opportunities and threats. In other words, the person wants to pursue occupation, jobs, and a career that capitalise on his or her interests, aptitude, values and skills. He or she wants to choose occupations, jobs, and a career that makes sense in terms of projected future demand for various types of occupations. The consequences of a bad choice (or of no choice) are too severe to level such decisions to others.

Managing Promotions and Transfers

Promotion

Promotion basically is a reward for efficiency. It is conferment of additional benefits, usually in the form of higher pay, for an increase in responsibility or skill which is formalised by an increase in status or rank. Yet, in another way, promotion can be defined as advancement of an employee in an organisation to another job, which commands better pay/wages, better status/prestige and higher opportunities/challenges and responsibilities, a better working environment, hours of work and facilities etc.

Types of Promotion

(i) Merit-based promotions: Merit based promotions occur when an employee is promoted because of superior performance in the current job. Merit here denotes an individual's knowledge, skills, abilities and efficiency as measured from his educational qualifications, experience, training and past employment record. The advantages of this system are fairly obvious:

Advantages

- It motivates employees to work hard, improve their knowledge, acquire new skills and contribute to organisational efficiency.
- It helps the employer to focus attention on talented people, recognise and reward their meritorious contributions in an appropriate way.
- It also inspires other employees to improve their standards of performance through active participation in all developmental initiatives undertaken by the employer (training, executive development, etc.)

Disadvantages

- It is not easy to measure merit. Personal prejudices, biases and union pressures may come in the way of promoting the best performer.
- When young employees get ahead of other senior employees in an organisation (based on superior performance), frustration and discontentment may spread among the ranks. They may feel insecure and may even quit the organisation.
- Also, past performance may not guarantee future success of an employee. Good performance in one job (as a Foreman, for example) is no guarantee of good performance in another (as a supervisor).

(ii) Seniority-based promotions: Seniority refers to the relative length of service in the same organisation. Promoting an employee who has the longest length of service is often widely welcomed by unions because it is fairly objective. It is easy to measure the length of service and judge the seniority. There is no scope for favouritism, discrimination and subjective judgement. Everyone is sure of getting the same, one day.

Transfer

Transfer is the lateral movement of employees from one position, division, department or unit to another. Generally transfer does not involve any significant change in compensation, duties, responsibilities or even status.

Purposes of Transfer

Organisations resort to transfers with a view to serve the following purposes:

(i) **To meet the organisational requirements:** Organisations may have to transfer employees due to changes in technology, changes in volume of production, production schedule, product line, quality of products, changes in the job pattern caused by change in organisational structure, fluctuations in the market conditions like demands fluctuations, introduction of new lines and/or dropping of existing lines. All these changes demand the shift in job assignments with a view to place the right man on the right job.

(ii) **To satisfy the employee needs:** Employees may need transfers in order to satisfy their desire to work under a friendly superior, in a department/region where opportunities for advancement are bright, in or near their native place or place of interest, doing a job where the work itself is challenging, etc.

(iii) **To utilise employees better:** An employee may be transferred because management feels that his skills, experience and job knowledge could be put to better use elsewhere.

(iv) **To make the employee more versatile:** Employees may be rolled over different jobs to expand their capabilities. Job rotation may prepare the employee for more challenging assignments in future.

(v) **To adjust the workforce:** Workforce may be transferred from a plant where there is less work to a plant where there is more work.

(vi) **To provide relief:** Transfers may be made to give relief to employees who are overburdened or doing hazardous work for long periods.

(vii) **To reduce conflicts:** Where employees find it difficult to get along with colleagues in a particular section, department or location – they could be shifted to another place to reduce conflicts.

(viii) **To punish employees:** Transfers may be effected as disciplinary measures – to shift employees indulging in undesirable activities to remote, far-flung areas.

Types of Transfers

(i) **Production transfers:** Transfers caused due to changes in production.

(ii) **Replacement transfers:** Transfers caused due to replacement of an employee working on the same job for a long time.

(iii) **Rotation transfers:** Transfers initiated to increase the versatility of employees.

(iv) **Shift transfers:** Transfers of an employee from one shift to another.

(v) **Remedial transfers:** Transfers initiated to correct the wrong placements.

(vi) **Penal transfers:** Transfers initiated as a punishment for indisciplinary behaviour of an employee.

Points to Remember

Giving information, knowledge and education in order to develop technical skills, social skills and administrative skills among the employees is defined as training.

Objectives of Training:
1. Improving quality of work force.
2. Enhance employee growth.
3. Prevents obsolescence.
4. Assisting new employee.
5. Bridging the gap between planning and implementation.
6. Health and safety measures.

Steps in Training:
1. Organisational Objectives and strategies.
2. Needs Assessment.
3. Training and Development Objectives.
4. Conducting Training Activities.
5. Designing training and development programme.
6. Implementation of the training programme.
7. Evaluation of the Results.

Methods of Training:
(i) On-the-job and
(ii) Off-the-job methods.

Development means those learning opportunities designed to help employees to grow. Development is not primarily skills oriented. Instead it provides the general knowledge and attitudes, which will be helpful to employers in higher positions.

Training versus Development

Training	Development
It's a short term process.	It is a long term educational process.
Refers to instruction in technical and mechanical problems.	Refers to philosophical and theoretical educational concepts.
Targeted in most cases for non-managerial personnel.	Targeted for managerial personnel.
Specific job related purpose.	General knowledge purpose.

Performance management is the process of identifying, measuring, managing, and developing the performance of the human resources in an organisation.

Performance Appraisal is the ongoing process of evaluating employee performance. Performance appraisals are reviews of employee performance over time, so appraisal is just one piece of performance management.

Methods of Performance Appraisal
- Rating Scale methods
- Ranking methods
- Critical incidents Methods
- Graphic rating scale
- Forced Distribution
- Narrated essay
- Check list method

Modern Methods of Performance Appraisal
- Role analysis
- Assessment centers
- Behaviourally Anchored Rating Scales (BARS)
- Management by objective
- 360 degree appraisal

Performance Based Interviewing (PBI) is a method to increase the effectiveness of the interviewing process in selecting and promoting quality staff.

A **job evaluation** is a systematic way of determining the value/worth of a job in relation to other jobs in an organisation.

Job Evaluation Methods
Classification method
Factor comparison method
Point method

Career management is a process by which individuals can guide, direct and influence the course of their careers.

Career planning is the process by which one selects career goals and the path to these goals.

Career path refers to the growth of the employee in an organisation.

Questions for Discussion

1. Define "Training". What are various methods adopted by organisations to train the employees.
2. Explain Performance Management System. Explain in detail the modern methods of performance appraisal
3. Define Job Evaluation. Discuss in detail the process of Job Evaluation.
4. Write Short Notes on:
    (a) Types of Promotion
    (b) Executive Development Program
    (c) Carrier Planning
    (d) Types of Transfers

Multiple Choice Questions

1. An introductory stage in the process of new employee assimilation, and a part of his or her continuous socialization process in an organisation is called:
   (a) training
   (b) development
   (c) orientation
   (d) induction

2. Which of the following are off the job methods of training?
   (a) lecture
   (b) conference
   (c) case studies
   (d) all the given

3. _____ provides the general knowledge and attitudes, which will be helpful to employers in higher positions.
   (a) training
   (b) development
   (c) orientation
   (d) none of the given

4. Training evaluation helps in:
   (a) ensuring accountability
   (b) check the Cost
   (c) feedback to the Trainer/Training
   (d) all the given

5. The process of identifying, measuring, managing, and developing the performance of the human resources in an organisation is known as:
   (a) training and development
   (b) human resource planning
   (c) performance management
   (d) induction

6. Which among the following is not the modern method of performance appraisal?
   (a) Behaviourally Anchored Rating Scales (BARS)
   (b) Management by objective
   (c) Checklist method
   (d) 360 degree appraisal

7. A systematic way of determining the value/worth of a job in relation to other jobs in an organisation is known as:
   (a) job evaluation
   (b) job analysis
   (c) job description
   (d) job specification

8. In _____ method, feedback about the employee is taken from the employee himself, his superiors, his juniors, his colleagues, customers he deals with, financial institutions and other people he deals with.
   (a) BARS
   (b) MBO
   (c) 360 degree
   (d) Ranking method

9. The lateral movement of employees from one position, division, department or unit to another is known as:
   (a) promotion
   (b) demotion
   (c) transfer
   (d) none of the given

10. It is the process by which one selects career goals and the path to these goals:
    (a) career path
    (b) career planning
    (c) performance management
    (d) training

Answers

| 1. (c) | 2. (d) | 3. (b) | 4. (d) | 5. (c) | 6. (c) | 7. (a) | 8. (c) | 9. (c) | 10. (b) |

Case Study

Is Rajat in needs of Remedial Training?

Rajat Sharma has been employed for six months in the accounts section of a large manufacturing company in Faridabad. You have been his supervisor for the past three months. Recently you have been asked by the management to find out the contributions of each employee in the Accounts Section and monitor carefully whether they are meeting the standards set by you.

A few days back you have completed your formal investigation and with the exception of Rajat, all seem to be meeting the targets set by you. Along with numerous errors, Rajat's work is characterised by low performance – often he does 20 percent less than the other clerks in the department.

As you look into Rajat's performance review sheets again, you begin to wonder whether some sort of remedial training is needed for people like him.

Questions:

1. As Rajat's supervisor can you find out whether the poor performance is due to poor training or to some other cause?
2. If you find Rajat has been inadequately trained, how do you go about introducing a remedial training programme?
3. If he has been with the company six months, what kind of remedial programme would be best?
4. Should you supervise him more closely? Can you do this without making it obvious to him and his co-workers?
5. Should you discuss the situation with Rajat?

Chapter **4**...

Compensation and Productivity Management

Contents ...

4.1 Wage and Salary Administration
    4.1.1 Meaning of Rewards
    4.1.2 Meaning of Wages
    4.1.3 Meaning of Salary
    4.1.4 Meaning of Increment
4.2 Establishing Pay Rates
4.3 Compensation Trends
4.4 Factors Affecting Employee Remuneration
4.5 Wage and Salary Structure
4.6 Minimum Fair and Living Wage
4.7 Wage Policy in India
4.8 Preparation of Salary/Pay Structure
4.9 Nature and Need of Benefits and Services
    4.9.1 Types of Employee Benefits and Services
    4.9.2 Administration of Benefits and Services
    4.9.3 Insurance - Retirement – Flexible Benefits Programmes
4.10 Nature of Incentive Schemes
    4.10.1 Scope of Incentive Schemes
    4.10.2 Types of Incentive Schemes
    4.10.3 Wage Incentive Schemes and Plans in India
    4.10.4 Incentive Schemes for Operation Employees, Managers and Executives
4.11 Performance Productivity Management
    4.11.1 Total Quality Management (TQM)
    4.11.2 Kaizen
    4.11.3 Quality Circles
    4.11.4 Performance Productivity Management through TQM, Kaizen, Quality Circles
- Points to Remember
- Questions for Discussion
- Multiple Choice Questions
- Case Study
- References and Further Readings

Objectives ...

- Describe Wage and Salary Administration
- Define Reward, Wage, Salary,
- Enumerate methods of establishing Pay Rates
- Learn Compensation Trends
- List factors affecting Employee Remuneration
- Illustrate Wage and Salary Structure
- Describe Minimum Fair and Living Wage
- Define Wage Policy in India
- Learn Preparation of Salary Structure
- Describe Nature and Need of Benefits and Services
- Enumerate Types of Employee Benefits and Services
- Define Fringe Benefits
- Illustrate Administration of Benefits and Services
- Describe Insurance - Retirement – Flexible Benefits Programmes
- Describe Nature of Incentive Schemes
- Enumerate Scope and Types of Incentive Schemes
- Define Wage Incentive Schemes and Plans in India
- Illustrate Team or Group Variable Plans
- Describe Incentive Schemes for Operation Employees, Managers and Executives and Sales People
- Define Performance Productivity Management
- Learn Total Quality Management (TQM)
- Define Kaizen
- Illustrate Quality Circles
- Describe Performance Productivity Management through TQM, Kaizen, Quality Circles

Introduction

Compensation Management is an organised practice that involves balancing the work employee relation by providing monetary and non-monetary benefits to employees.

Compensation includes payments such as bonuses, profit sharing, overtime pay, recognition rewards and sales commission.

Compensation can also include non-monetary perks such as a company-paid car, housing and stock options.

Compensation is an integral part of human resource management which helps in motivating the employees and improving organisational effectiveness.

Compensation administration is a segment of management or human resource management focusing on planning, organising, and controlling the direct and indirect payments employees receive for the work they perform.

Compensation includes direct forms such as base, merit, and incentive pay and indirect forms such as vacation pay, deferred payment, and health insurance.

Compensation does not refer, however, to other kinds of employee rewards such as recognition ceremonies and achievement parties.

The ultimate objectives of compensation administration are:
- Efficient maintenance of a productive workforce,
- Equitable pay, and
- Compliance with federal, state, and local regulations based on what companies can afford.

The basic concept of compensation administration—compensation management—is rather simple: employees perform tasks for employers and so companies pay employees wages for the jobs they do. Consequently, compensation is an exchange or a transaction, from which both parties—employers and employees—benefit: both parties receive something for giving something.

Compensation, however, involves much more than this simple transaction. From the employer's perspective, compensation is an issue of both affordability and employee motivation.

Companies must consider what they can reasonably afford to pay their employees and the ramifications of their decisions: will they affect employee turnover and productivity? In addition, some employers and managers believe pay can influence employee work ethics and behaviour and hence link compensation to performance.

Moreover social, economic, legal, and political forces also exert influence on compensation management, making it a complicated yet important part of managing a business.

Compensation management is a strategic matter.

Importance of Compensation Management

A good compensation is must for every business organisation and helps in the following ways:
- It tries to give proper return to the workers for their contributions to the organisation.
- It imparts a positive control on the efficiency of employees and encourages them to perform better and achieve the specific standards.

- It forms a basis of happiness and satisfaction for the workforce that minimizes the labour turnover and confers a stable organisation.
- It augments the job evaluation process which in turn helps in setting up the more realistic and achievable standards.
- It is designed to comply with the various labour acts and therefore does not result in disputes between the employee union and the management. This builds up a peaceful relationship between the employer and the employees.
- It arouses an environment of morale, efficiency and cooperation among the workers and provides satisfaction to the workers.
- It stimulates the employees to perform better and show their excellence.
- It provides growth and advancement opportunities to the deserving employees.

Types of Compensations

- **Direct Compensation** is normally made up of salary payments and health benefits. The formation of salary ranges and pay scales for different positions within the company are the chief responsibility of compensation management staff.

    Direct compensation that is in line with industry standards gives employees the assurance that they are getting paid reasonably and fairly. This aids the employer in avoiding the costly loss of trained staff to a competitor.

- **Indirect Compensation** focuses on and includes the personal motivations of each employee to work. Even though salary is imperative, employees are most productive in jobs where they share the company's values and priorities.

    These benefits can include things such as free staff development courses, subsidised day care, the prospect for promotion or transfer within the company, public recognition, the ability to effect change in the workplace, and service to others.

Components of Compensation

- **Wages and Salary:** Wages correspond to hourly rates of pay, and salary refers to the monthly rate of pay, irrespective of the number of hours put in by an employee. These are subject to annual increments.
- **Allowances:** Several allowances are paid in addition to basic pay. Some of these allowances are given below:
- **Dearness Allowance:** This allowance is given to protect real income against inflation. Generally, dearness allowance (DA) is paid as a per centage of basic pay.
- **House Rent Allowance:** Employers who do not provide accommodation pay house rent allowance (HRA) to employees. This allowance is calculated as a per centage of basic pay.

- **City Compensatory Allowance:** This allowance is paid usually to employees in metros and other big cities where cost of living is comparatively high. City compensatory allowance (CCA) is generally a fixed amount per month (30 per cent of basic pay in case of government employees).

- **Transport Allowance/Conveyance Allowance:** Some employers pay transport allowance (TA) to their employees. A fixed sum is paid every month to cover a part of travelling charges.

- **Incentives:** Incentive compensation is performance-linked remuneration paid with a view to inspire employees to work hard and do better. Both individual incentives and group incentives are used. Bonus, profit-sharing, commissions on sales are some examples of incentive compensation.

- **Fringe Benefits/Perquisites:** These include employee benefits such as provident fund, gratuity, medical care, hospitalisation, accident relief, health and group insurance, canteen, uniform, recreation and the likes.

4.1 Wage and Salary Administration

Wage and Salary administration is the process of compensating an organisation's employees in accordance with the accepted policy and procedures.

An important component of a successful organisation's Wage and Salary administration policy is monitoring and evaluating all employees' compensation to ensure that they're being paid appropriately, both with respect to others in the same organisation and to the marketplace as a whole.

Wage and Salary administration is often an integral function of the organisation's human resources department, but in general, the larger the organisation, the more likely is that it will be handled by a separate department.

The first element of the Wage and Salary administration, the **periodic payroll** is a critical component of any organisation's functioning.

Employees' personal budgets and plans depend upon getting paid regularly, and if compensation is late, short, or missing any time, morale is severely affected, as is the confidence in the employer's stability.

Whether an employer utilises the services of a third-party payroll service or handles all payroll functions internally, it will usually devote significant resources to making sure that employees are paid on time.

Wages and salary administration is an integral part of the management of the organisation.

> *Wages and salary is a systematic approach to providing monetary value to employees in exchange for work performed*

It may achieve several purposes like assisting in recruitment, job performance, and job satisfaction.

It is the remuneration received by an employee in return for his/her contribution to the organisation.

It is an organised practice that involves balancing the work –employee relation, by providing monetary and non-monetary benefits to employees.

The second element of salary and wage administration — **monitoring and evaluating employees' compensation** — is an ongoing function.

It includes **evaluating** the elements of each job in the organisation and **classifying** them according to a number of different criteria like:

- The nature of the work itself,
- The amount of supervision necessary,
- The physical exertion normally associated with the job, and
- The amount of training necessary to do the job proficiently.

The underlying idea is to determine the value of each job to the employer, and compensate the employees accordingly. From time to time, especially in the absence of collective bargaining, the results of this monitoring and evaluation process will result in adjustments being made to wages and salaries.

In a collective bargaining environment, these evaluations will be important in determining any such adjustments, although other considerations may affect adjustments to wages and salaries.

Employers need to maintain a competitive edge in the marketplace, and one way to do so is to employ the best people.

Employee retention is an important responsibility of those responsible for salary and wage administration.

4.1.1 Meaning of Rewards

Compensation would include rewards when you offer monetary payment such as incentives, various bonuses and performance bonus. Organisations reward their staff when they attain their goals or targets that they have jointly set with the employees.

Rewards can also be non-monetary such as a paid vacation for two.

Rewards are therefore what employees receive for performing well. As mentioned above sometimes these rewards come from the organisation in the form of money, recognition and promotions. Rewards can also consist of feelings from having performed well in work. It can be said that rewards are very powerful motivators of performance.

- These rewards in organisations help employees to be more committed and motivated to their job and working environment.
- System rewards are automatically given to all employees for merely being members of their organisation. System rewards can be defined as being the basic wage rates.
- Individual rewards are given to employees based on the quality and quantity of their performance. Performance related pay (PRP) is seen as an individual reward policy, where pay is rewarded in relation to the volume of output. PRP can cause divisions amongst workers, where employees become more worried about the fact that their colleagues are being paid more than them.
- Growth rewards are received by employees for job innovation, learning and improvement.
- The key to managing performance through rewards is linking the desired performance with the appropriate reward.

Non-Financial Rewards

In an ever more competitive environment, the aim of organisations is now to focus on increasing the added value of their employees. This is achieved, by encouraging employees to increase their effort and performance higher than the average standards. This has been carried out using employee appraisals and motivational methods.

Employers have become increasingly aware of the rich potential for good constructive ideas that exist from the employees on the job experiences. One method for using this knowledge is through suggestion schemes, these are becoming highly recognised, as they allow for improvements in all areas of work. These schemes are very flexible and can be readily adapted to meet all kinds of working conditions. Suggestion schemes can be seen as a means of increasing profit and worker participation.

Suggestion schemes aim to improve employee attitudes by directing their attention to the positive and progressive aspects of their jobs. This helps to boost employee morale and increase job satisfaction. It can be identified that if an employee is unhappy in his/her job it reflects on a negative attitude on his/her performance and also with other people.

Experience in many companies has shown low employee morale reflects on low productivity and increasing costly errors. Suggestion schemes play a useful role in increasing and maintaining morale.

Another method which is not related to pay is the performance appraisal system. This method is used as a means of raising individual performance and identifying development needs. Appraisal systems today are becoming part of the management culture, where managers feel it necessary to appraise and be appraised.

Self Rating, this is a form of appraisal where the employee takes a look at themselves, avoiding any negative feedback from traditional appraisals. Self rating is an effective way of trying to get the employee to look at what their roles are in relation to business needs.

4.1.2 Meaning of Wages

Wages means all remuneration capable of being expressed in terms of money, which would, if the terms of contract of employment, express or implied, were fulfilled, be payable to a person employed in respect of his employment or of work done in such employment.

A Wage is thus the remuneration paid for the service of labour in production periodically to an employee / worker. So payment made to labour is generally referred to as wages. Wages also refer to the hourly rate paid to such groups as production and maintenance.

Wages include basic wage / salary and allowances.

4.1.3 Meaning of Salary

A salary is a form of periodic payment from an employer to an employee, which may be specified in an employment contract. It is contrasted with piece wages, where each job, hour or other unit is paid separately, rather than on a periodic basis.

From the point of a business, salary can also be viewed as the cost of acquiring human resources for running operations, and is then termed personnel expense or salary expense. In accounting, salaries are recorded in payroll accounts.

Salary normally refers to the periodically rates paid to clerical, administrative and professional employees. So money paid periodically to person whose output cannot be measured is generally referred as salary.

4.1.4 Meaning of Increment

An increment is an increase of some amount, either fixed or variable. For example one's salary may have a fixed annual increment or one based on a per centage of its current value.

Salary increment is a very sensitive issue in an organisation. This is usually the job of the Human Resources department, also known as HR.

Salary increases can be a great motivator for the employee. It will inspire an employee to push oneself to perform better and gives the employee a sense of fulfillment.

4.2 Establishing Pay Rates

When establishing pay rates, the interaction between 13 factors affects the actual pay rates employees receive, according to Richard I. Henderson, author of *Compensation Management in a Knowledge-Based World*.

The 13 factors are:

1. Types and levels of skills and knowledge required.
2. Type of business.
3. Union affiliation or no union affiliation.

4. Capital-intensive or labour-intensive.
5. Company size.
6. Management philosophy.
7. Complete compensation package.
8. Geographic location.
9. Labour supply and demand.
10. Company profitability.
11. Employment stability.
12. Gender Difference.
13. Length of employment and job performance.

The process of establishing pay rates while ensuring external, internal and (to some extent) procedural equity consist of five steps:

1. Conduct a salary survey of what other employers are paying for comparable jobs (to help ensure external equity).
2. Determine the worth of each job in your organisations through job evaluation (to ensure internal equity).
3. Group similar jobs into pay grades.
4. Price each pay grade by using wave curves.
5. Fine tune pay rates.

Salary Survey

A survey aimed to determining prevailing wage rates. A good salary survey provides specific wages rates for specific jobs. Formal written questionnaire surveys are the most comprehensive but telephone surveys and newspaper ads are also sources of information.

It's difficult to set pay rates if you don't know what others are paying so salary surveys – surveys of what others are paying – play a big role in pricing jobs. Virtually every employer conducts at least informal telephone, newspaper, or internet salary survey.

Benchmark Job

A job that is used to anchor the employer's pay scale and around which other jobs are arranged in order of relative worth.

Employers use these surveys in three ways:

1. They use survey data to price benchmark jobs. Benchmark jobs are the anchor jobs around which they slot their other job, based on each job's relative worth to the firm. (Job evaluation, explained next, helps determine the relative worth of each job).

2. Employers typically price 20% or more of their positions directly in the marketplace (rather than relative to the firm's benchmark jobs), based on a formal or informal survey of what comparable firms are paying for comparable jobs. (Google might do this for jobs like Web programmer whose salaries fluctuate widely and often).
3. Surveys also collect data on benefits like insurance, sick leave, and vacations to provide a basis for decisions regarding employee benefits.

Salary surveys can be formal or informal. Informal phone or Internet surveys are good for checking specific issues, such as when a bank wants to confirm the salary at which, to advertise a newly opened teller's job.

Some large employers can afford to send out their own formal surveys to collect compensation information from other employers like e.g. number of employee, overtime policies starting salaries and paid vacations.

Commercial, Professional, and Government Salary surveys

Many employers use surveys published by consulting firms, professional associations, or government agencies.

Professional organisations like the Society for Human Resource Management and the financial executives Institute publish surveys of compensation practices among members of their associations.

The following are the most common methods used to establish pay scales:

- **The going rate:** You determine what other businesses in your industry and region are paying for similar jobs, and structure your pay accordingly.
- **Job evaluation and pay grading:** You evaluate each job based on several factors, such as how it affects the bottom line, how difficult or dangerous it is, and what kind of training is necessary, and then you develop an appropriate pay range.
- Job evaluation and pay grading works best for large companies that must have some type of structured approach to pay ranges.
- **Management fit:** You decide the amount of pay for each employee, without using any system. As you may expect, the management-fit approach usually results in inconsistent pay. Resentment, hostility, and a lack of teamwork can result when inequities are discovered.
- You can also look into alternative structures that are based more on what the employee can do rather on what the job description is:
- **Skill-based pay:** Pay scales are determined by skill level, not job title. You create a list of skills necessary for each job and develop the criteria that signify the mastery of each skill. As your employees master the skill, they receive pay increases.

- **Competency-based pay:** This system bases compensation on an employee's traits or characteristics, rather than on specific skills. Salaries and raises are based on how well employees acquire the core competencies needed for their positions.
- **Broad banding:** You group several related jobs, such as office assistant and receptionist, into one band — for example, administrative staff. You assign a pay range to that band, but you don't base it on a job title.
- **Variable pay:** This system links a per centage of an employee's pay to performance and accomplishments. You first establish a base pay rate, and then define group and individual objectives as a variable salary component.

4.3 Compensation Trends

Managers and supervisors play a vital role in the implementation and the ongoing administration of the Compensation Programme. They are most familiar with work performed in their departments and the abilities of the individuals who do the work.

Specifically, managers and supervisors will have the responsibility to regularly and consistently:

- Respond to questions about individual pay and Compensation Programme policies and practices.
- Review, at least annually, with each individual the content of their job.
- Keep Human Resources advised of changes in job content.
- Develop and update job information for jobs in their departments.
- Provide continuous performance feedback and develop goals with staff.
- Managers and supervisors administer the programme within their own departments.
- Human Resource oversees the overall programme.

In order to provide market competitive and reasonable salaries, jobs must be assigned to an appropriate pay grade.

The process of assigning a job to an appropriate pay grade involves:

- Collecting and reviewing job information.
- Comparison with other like jobs.
- Relevant market considerations.

Job Information and Comparison

Job descriptions are available for staff and supervisor reference. The job descriptions found online reflect the major job functions and minimum requirements for the job and is used for job classification across the institution.

Position descriptions are developed at the department level to reflect more specific descriptions of the major job functions and are used for recruiting the best talent for the role, for training, and for performance development and evaluation.

Position descriptions should be reviewed at least annually as a part of the performance evaluation process. Significant changes may be submitted on-line through the job description database unless the job is utilised across numerous departments.

Human Resources will review job changes, make comparisons within relevant market and with other like jobs to recommend appropriate job title and pay level.

Relevant Market Considerations

Relevant competitive market salary studies are conducted by the Office of Compensation, Human Resources in consultation with the appropriate budgetary official(s) to establish and adjust pay levels as necessary.

The market analysis process includes data collection and analysis of:
- Salaries paid to jobs recruited on a local, regional or national basis
- Supply of applicants with specialised or unique skills
- Staffing needs in terms of number of vacancies and length of time to identify qualified applicants

Ongoing Compensation Trends 2013

Economic conditions stagnated or reduced salaries over the past 3 years. As conditions begin to improve, companies are realising that their market competitiveness may have suffered. Many companies are beginning to re-evaluate their existing salaries and the salary structures by undertaking market studies to determine where they stand.

1. Since some employees may be eager to seek other employment as the labour market opens up, it is important to **understand market positioning** in the event that compensation is one of the main drivers for seeking another job, particularly for recent graduates.

2. Employees are only aware of what they are getting (cash compensation, benefits, professional development, etc.) if their employers tell them so. **Total rewards statements are effective in getting that message across.**

3. Concurrent with improvements to the economy is the fact that companies are refocusing on their strategic plans. **Ensuring the total rewards package is properly structured** will enable employees to contribute towards goals that relate to the strategic plan. However, this is a significant effort that needs to be undertaken by HR.

   Incentive compensation provides organisations with another layer of "pay-for-performance" in addition to annual merit increases to base salary, which are relatively modest as compared to the impact incentive compensation can make to total rewards.

4. Many companies also want to refocus on **pay-for-performance** to use their compensation dollars more effectively. While many companies embrace a "pay-for-performance" concept, this was somewhat stalled during the recent economic crisis. However, as the market begins to improve, companies are returning to this concept and looking to reward employees for their performance.

True merit-based pay is most effective when it can be tied to a performance management process that objectively and accurately evaluates individual performance, so that the merit increase is commensurate with the performance contribution of the individual, while recognising company budget and overall performance.

While many companies want to use pay-for-performance systems, there are still organisations who continue to provide employees with across-the-board or cost of living increases, with no relationship to performance. In many of these organisations, this is a cultural issue that has existed for many years, which is difficult to move away from as employees feel a sense of entitlement.

5. While difficult, the culture can shift to **transition to a merit-based process**. Strong communications with a commitment from the top down is the first step to moving away from entitlement, along with effective management training. While turnover may result as part of this transition, most likely it will be from the poorer performers who have hidden behind across-the-board increases.

4.4 Factors Affecting Employee Remuneration

Factors influencing the remuneration payable to employees can be categorised into
(i) External and
(ii) Internal factors.

(i) Internal Factors: These factors include the following:

Ability to pay: This is one of the most significant factors influencing employee compensation. Generally, a firm, which is prosperous and successful, has the ability to pay more than the competitive rate to attract superior personnel or to satisfy the labour unions demand.

Employee Related Factors" Employees related factors influencing compensation include the following:

- **Performance:** Rewards like pay increase to motivate the workers.
- **Experience:** It is proportionate to the number of years of relevant work experience.

    The companies presume that experienced candidate possess leadership skills which influence the behaviour and performance of others. Generally experienced candidates perform the job without need of too much training. Training is time consuming and increases the 'cost to company.' Hence experienced candidates demand more pay than inexperienced candidates.

- **Seniority:** Senior employees expect to be paid a higher compensation as compared to junior employees.

  Today many companies are demanding senior employees for key positions in an organisation e.g. retired personnel for administration work.
- **Potential:** Firms also pay their employees on the basis of their future potential. Software companies are a very good example of this.

Job-requirements

Jobs, which demand more skill, responsibility, efforts and are of hazardous in nature, will be paid a higher pay package.

Job evaluation

Job evaluation establishes a consistent and systematic relationship among base compensation rates for all jobs. It helps establish satisfactory wage differentials.

Organisational strategy

The organisation's strategy regarding wages also influences employee compensation. For example, an organisation, which wants rapid growth, will set higher wages than competitors. On the other hand, organisations that want smooth going and just maintain the current earning will pay average or below average compensation.

(ii) External Factors

These factors include the following:

Laws and Regulations

Laws and regulations impact the remuneration of employees in many areas, such as:
- Working hours and compulsory time-off (paid and unpaid)
- Minimum wages
- Overtime
- Compulsory bonuses
- Employment at will

Labour market
- Official laws on wage and salary, labour contract, payment time, wage payment delay, working insurance, and so on.
- Standard of living of people in the areas where the offices of the company are.
- Peoples' living and consuming customary.
- The average wage rate in the labour market of similar work.

Economy

Economic slowdown affects the salary and wages. Wage rates will be different in a stable economy than in a depressed economy. In case of depressed economy there may be increase in supply of labour and results in the fixation of lower wage rates.

Inflation

Increase in the prices of commodities and decrease in value of the money is called as inflation. The causes of inflation are many which are increasing costs; fall in the currency value in international markets, raising taxes by government and stagnation in the development of economy, etc.

Technological changes

Technological changes also influence the fixation of wage levels. Due to the advancements in the technology there may be shortage of skilled manpower in that area. So, the organisation will provide high wages for skilled personnel.

Academic Institutions

People having good academic qualifications from reputed and standard educational institution influence the compensation of the potential candidate in their recruitment in companies. Example, Indian Top Business schools like Indian Institute of Management, and IIT (Indian Institute of Technology) graduates demands higher pay packages.

4.5 Wage and Salary Structure

The first and the most important problem in wage and salary administration is the establishment of base compensation for the job. This problem is enormously complicated by such factors as Supply and Demand, Labour organisation, the firm's ability to pay, Variations in productivity and Cost of living, Government legislation, Including CIVICS RIGHTS ACT.

In order to attract and retain needed personnel for the organisation, employees must perceive that compensation offered is equitable in relation to their inputs and relative contributions. The most likely to be used method to solve this problem at present would be job evaluation, a systematic and orderly process for establishing the worth of job.

The importance of a pay system to an event of major importance to employees and its effects upon them cannot be ignored. It is a valid system if it results in a structure acceptable to both employee and employer.

In general, structures that are internally and externally consistent have the greatest chances of affecting overall satisfaction. Under reward, Over-reward and inconsistency of reward not only tend to lead to lower satisfaction but encourage behaviour that often proves dysfunctional to organisational objectives.

A sound, systematic, consistent system of compensation determination will do much to promote equity and satisfaction, provided that such a system is understood and accepted by most employees.

Factors Influencing Wage and Salary Structure and Administration

The wage policies vary in different organisation. Marginal units pay the minimum necessary to attract the required number of kind of labour. Often, these units pay minimum wage rates required by labour legislation, and recruit marginal labour.

At the other extreme, some units pay well about going rates in the labour market.

Some units pay high wages because of a combination of a favourable product market demand, higher ability to pay and the bargaining power of trade union. But a large number of them seek to be competitive in their wage programme, i.e., they aim at paying somewhere near the going rate in the labour they employ.

Most units give greater weight to two wage criteria, i.e. job requirements and the prevailing rates of wages in the labour market. Other factors, such as changes in the cost of living the supply and demand of labour, and ability to pay are of secondary importance.

A sound wage policy is to adopt a job evaluation programme in order to establish fair differentials in wages based upon differences in job contents.

Administration of Wages and Salaries

Wage and salary administration should be controlled by some proper agency. This responsibility may be entrusted to the personnel department or to some job executive.

The major functions of such agency/ committee are:

(a) Approval and/or recommendation to management on job evaluation methods and findings;

b) Review and recommendation of basic wage and salary structure;

(b) Help in the formulation of wage policies from time to time;

(c) Co-ordination and review of relative departmental rates to ensure conformity; and

(d) Review of budget estimates for wage and salary adjustments and increases.

This Committee should be supported by the advice of the technical staff. Such staff committees may be for job evolution. Job description, merit rating, wage and salary surveys in an industry, and for a review of present wage rates procedure and policies.

4.6 Minimum Fair and Living Wage

Wages have been classified into three categories:

1. Living wages
2. Minimum wages
3. Fair wages

1. **Living Wages:** Living wages is defined as "Living wage is a wage sufficient to ensure the workman food, shelter, clothing, frugal comfort, provision for evil days etc. as regard for the skill of an artisan, if he is one".

   Thus, living wages means the provision for the bare necessities plus certain amenities considered necessary for the wellbeing of the workers in terms of his social status.

2. **Minimum Wages:** The minimum wage may be defined as the lowest wage necessary to maintain a worker and his family at the minimum level of subsistence, which includes food, clothing and shelter. When the government fixes minimum

wage in a particular trade, the main objective is not to control or determine wages in general but to prevent the employment of workers at a wage below an amount necessary to maintain the worker at the minimum level of subsistence.

Minimum wage in a country is fixed by the government in consultation with business organisations and trade unions.

3. **Fair Wages:** A fair wage is something more than the minimum wages. Fair wage is a mean between the living wage and the minimum wage.

While the lower limit of the fair wage must obviously be the minimum wage, the upper limit is the capacity of the industry to pay fair wage compares reasonably with the average payment of similar task in other trades or occupations requiring the same amount of ability.

Fair wage depends on the present economic position as well as on its future prospects.

Thus the fair wages depends upon the following factors:

1. Minimum Wages.
2. Capacity of the industry to pay.
3. Prevailing rates of wages in the same or similar occupations in the same or neighbouring localities.
4. Productivity of labour.
5. Level of national income and its distribution.
6. The place of the industry in the economy of the country.

4.7 Wage Policy in India

The term 'wage policy' refers to all systematic efforts of the Government in relation to a national wage and salary system, The policy lays down guidelines concerning the level and structure of wages.

The guiding principles of national wage policy are as follows:

1. Subserves the national objective of economic growth with social justice.
2. Promote employment, productivity and capital formation.
3. Remove sectorial imbalances and wage differentials.
4. Promote price stability.
5. Avoid automatic double linkages.
6. Ensure rising real wages consistent with the capacity of the industry and the national economy.
7. Have relationship with national income, state of the industry and prevailing wage rates.

Main Objectives of National Wage Policy in India are discussed below:

One of the objectives of economic planning is the raising of the standard of living of the people. This means that the benefits of planned economic development should be distributed among the different sections of the society.

Therefore, in achieving a socialistic pattern of society, the needs for proper rewards to the working class of the countryman never is over emphasised.

A national wage policy, thus aims at establishing wages at the highest possible level, which the economic conditions of the country permit and ensuring that the wage earner gets a fair share of the increased prosperity of the country as a whole resulting from the economic development.

The term "wage policy" here refers to legislation or government action calculated to affect the level or structure of wages or both, for the purpose of attaining specific objectives of social and economic policy.

1. To eliminate malpractices in the payment of wages.
2. To set minimum wages for workers, whose bargaining position is weak due to the fact that they are either unorganised or inefficiently organised. In other words, to reduce wage differential between the organised and unorganised sectors.
3. To rationalise inter-occupational, inter-industrial and inter-regional wage differentials in such a way that disparities are reduced in a phased manner.
4. To ensure reduction of disparities of wages and salaries between the private sector and public sector in a phased manner.
5. To compensate workers for the raise in the cost of living in such a manner that in the process, the ratio of disparity between the highest paid and the lowest paid worker is reduced.
6. To provide for the promotion and growth of trade unions and collective bargaining.
7. To obtain for the workers a just share in the fruits of economic development.
8. To avoid following a policy of high wages to such an extent that it results in substitution of capital for labour thereby reducing employment.
9. To prevent high profitability units with better capacity to pay a level of wages far in excess of the prevailing level of wages in other sectors.
10. To permit bilateral collective bargaining within national framework so that high wage islands are not created.
11. To encourage the development of incentive systems of payment with a view to raising productivity and the real wages of workers.

12. To bring about a more efficient allocation and utilisation of man-power through wage differentials and appropriate systems of payments. In order to achieve the above objectives under the national wage policy, the following regulations have been adopted by the state:

    (a) **Prescribing minimum rates of wages:** In order to prescribe the minimum rate of wages, the Minimum Wages Act, 1948 was passed. The Act empowers the government to fix minimum rates of wages in respect of certain sweated and unorganised employments. It also provides for the review of these wages at intervals not exceeding 5 years.

    (b) **Compulsory conciliation and arbitration:** With the object of providing for conciliation and arbitration, the Industrial Disputes Act 1947 was passed. It provides for the appointment of Industrial Tribunals and National Industrial Tribunals for settlement of industrial disputes including those relating to wages.

    (c) **Wage Boards:** A wage board is a tripartite body with representatives of management and workers, presided over by a government nominated chairman who can act as an umpire in the event of disagreement among the parties.

Technically, a wage board can make only recommendations, since there is no legal sanction for it, but for all practical purposes, they are awards which if made unanimously, are considered binding upon employers.

4.8 Preparation of Salary/Pay Structure

Pay structure in a company depends upon several factors, e.g., wage settlements, labour market situation, company's nature and size, etc.

Pay structure consists of certain grades, scale and range of pay in each scale. Each scale has a minimum and a maximum limit.

Jobs placed within a particular grade carry the same value though the actual pay in a grade depends upon length of service and or performance of the employee.

Pay structure in India generally consists of the following components:

1. Basic wage/salary.
2. Dearness allowance (D.A.) and other allowances.
3. Bonus and other incentives.
4. Fringe benefits or perquisites.

1. Basic Wage

The basic wage provides the foundation of pay pocket. It is a price for services rendered. It varies according to mental and physical requirements of the job as measured through job evaluation. In India, basic wage has been influenced by statutory minimum wage, wage settlements, and awards of wage boards, tribunals, pay commissions and so on.

Minimum Wage

Minimum wage is that wage which is sufficient to cover the bare physical needs of a worker and his family. But the committee felt that the minimum wage should provide not merely for the base subsistence or sustenance of life but for the preservation of the health, efficiency and well-being of the worker by some measure of education, medical facilities and other amenities. Minimum wage has got to be paid to every worker irrespective of the capacity of the industry to pay. If an enterprise is unable to pay its workers at least a bare minimum, it has no right to exist.

The Fair Wages Committee defined the components of minimum wage but did not quantify them. The Indian Labour Conference at its 15th Session held in July 1957 formally quantified the minimum wage. The Conference laid down the following criterion for the calculation of minimum wage:

- The standard working class family should be taken to consist of 3 consumption units for the one earner, disregarding the earnings of women, children and adolescent.
- Minimum food requirements should be calculated on the basis of a net intake of 2,700 calories, as recommended by Dr. Aykroyed for an average Indian adult of moderate activity.
- Cloth requirements should be 18 yards per consumption unit per annum.
- Rent is to be calculated as per the minimum rent charged by the Government under the subsidised Industrial Housing Scheme for low income groups.
- Fuel, lighting and other miscellaneous expenditure is to constitute 20 per cent of the minimum wage.

Fair Wage

A fair wage is something more than the minimum wage providing the bare necessities of life. While the lower limit of the fair wage is set by the minimum wage, the upper limit should be the capacity of the industry to pay. Between these two limits, fair wage should depend on several factors like:

- The productivity of labour,
- The prevailing rates of wages in the same or similar occupations in the same region or neighbouring regions,
- Level of national income and its distribution,
- The place of the industry in the economy of the country,
- The employer's capacity to pay. Thus, the fair wage should be determined on industry-cum-region basis. Fair wage is a step toward the ideal of living wage.

Living Wage

It is the wage that provides, in addition to the necessities of life, certain amenities considered necessary for the well-being of the worker in a particular society. It should ensure a normal standard of life to the average employee regarded as human beings living in a civilised community. According to the Fair Wages Committee, "the living wage should enable the male earner to provide for himself and his family not merely the bare essentials of food, clothing and shelter but also a measure of frugal comfort including education for children, protection against ill-health, requirements of essential social needs and measure of insurance against the more important misfortunes including old age."

The concept of living wage is dynamic related with the level of economic development in a country. There should be progressive improvement in the wage with improvements in the economic life of the nation. In an underdeveloped country like India, living wage is the ideal or target that is to be achieved through higher productivity.

2. **Dearness Allowance (D.A.) and Other Allowances**

This allowance is given to protect the real wages of workers during inflation. Under Section 3 of the Minimum Wages Act, it is described as cost of living allowance. Dearness allowance has now become an integral part of the wage system in India. The following methods are used to calculate dearness allowance:

- **Flat Rate:** According to this method, D.A. is paid at a flat rate to all workers irrespective of their wage levels and regardless of changes in the consumer price index. This method was used in jute, cotton and engineering industries in West Bengal in the early days of adjudication.

- **Graduated Scale:** Under this method, D.A. increases with each slab of salary. Therefore, D.A. as a per centage of basic pay decreases steadily.

Pay Scale (₹)	Amount of D.A. (₹)	D.A. as Percentage of Maximum of the Pay Scale
0 - 500	100	20
500 - 1000	150	15
1000 - 1500	200	13
1500 - 2000	250	12.54

Types of Allowances Paid to Employees Index Based D.A. In this method, a flat rate per point of index is prescribed so that all workers determine the same amount of D.A. irrespective of their pay scale. For example, if ₹ 1.50 is the rate ₹ 15 will be paid as D.A. whenever the All India Consumer Price Index (AICPP) increases by 10 points. This method is in force in the cotton mills of Mumbai and Chennai and in many Central Government undertakings.

D.A. Linked to Index and Pay Scale. Under this method, a higher rate of D.A. is prescribed for lower pay scales and a lower rate for higher pay scales. This method is used to pay D.A. to employees in Government offices and in many central public sector undertakings.

Types of Allowances Paid to Employees

Acting	House Rent Allowance (HRA)
City Compensatory Allowance (CCA)	Conveyance/Car Allowance
Bank Allowance	Medical Allowance
Education Allowance	Tiffin Allowance

3. Bonus

Bonus is a deferred wage aimed at bridging the gap between actual wage and the need based wage. Bonus is a share of the workers in the prosperity of an enterprise. Bonus may also be regarded as an incentive to higher productivity. According to the Bonus Commission (1961), bonus is "sharing by the workers in the prosperity of the concern in which they are employed. In the case of low paid workers such sharing in the prosperity augments their earnings and helps to bridge the gap between the actual wage and the need based wage." It has little direct incentive effect because it is usually paid to all workers at the same rate irrespective of their individual efficiency and long after the close of the financial year.

Payment of Bonus Act, 1965: The Act provides for the payment of bonus to persons employed in specified establishments. The main provisions of the Act are as follows:

- Every employee in the specified establishments drawing a salary (basic pay plus D.A.) not exceeding ₹ 3,500 per month is entitled to bonus provided he has worked for not less than 30 days in the year.
- Bonus is to be calculate on a salary of ₹ 2,500 per month wherever the actual salary exceeds this amount.
- Every employer is bound to pay a minimum bonus of 8.33 per cent of the salary of an employee or ₹ 100 per year whichever is higher whether or not he has any allocable surplus in the accounting year.
- Where an employee has not worked for all the working days in any accounting year, the minimum bonus of ₹ 100 or 60 as the case may be, shall be proportionately reduced, if such bonus is higher than 8.33 of his salary or wage.
- No minimum bonus is payable by a newly set up establishment in the circumstances prescribed under Section 16 of the Act.
- The bonus is to be paid within 8 months from the close of the accounting year.
- An employee dismissed from service for fraud, theft, misappropriation of sabotage of property and riotous/violent behaviour on the premises or the establishment is not entitled to bonus.

Thus, the Payment of Bonus Act imposes a statutory liability upon an employer to pay bonus. It also defines the principle of bonus payment as per the prescribed formula.

4.9 Nature and Need of Benefits and Services

Benefits are any perks offered to employees in addition to salary. The most common benefits are medical, disability, and life insurance; retirement benefits; paid time off; and fringe benefits.

> *Benefits are any perks offered to employees in addition to salary.*

The phrase "employee benefits" is an umbrella term that includes insurance programmes, fully compensated absences (vacations, holidays, sick leave), pensions, stock ownership plans, and employer-provided services (such as child care) offered by employers to their employees.

Employee benefits and benefits in kind (also called fringe benefits, perquisites, or perks) are various non-wage compensations provided to employees in addition to their normal wages or salaries.

The term perks is often used colloquially to refer to those benefits of a more discretionary nature. Often, perks are given to employees who are doing notably well and/or have seniority. Common perks are take-home vehicles, hotel stays, free refreshments, leisure activities on work time (golf, etc.), stationery, allowances for lunch, and—when multiple choices exist—first choice of such things as job assignments and vacation scheduling. They may also be given first chance at job promotions when vacancies exist.

In some instances, where an employee exchanges (cash) wages for some other form of benefit is generally referred to as a 'salary packaging' or 'salary exchange' arrangement. In most countries, most kinds of employee benefits are taxable to at least some degree.

Employee benefits are also referred to as fringe benefits. Yet other benefits sometimes are treated by government as forms of income for tax purposes. These include bonuses, profit sharing, and the provision of a leased vehicle or housing.

All "fringes" are by definition offered at the employer's option thus, employer contributions to Social Security, Medical aid, basic Medicare, Workers' Compensation, and other programmes are not viewed as fringe benefits; they are required under law.

> *The purpose of employee benefits is to increase the economic security of staff members, and in doing so, improve worker retention across the organisation.*

Certain categories of employee benefits may require that the employee pay a part of the cost of the benefit in order to receive the employer's contribution. For this reason, employees who have *access* to benefits outnumber employees who actually *participate* in the benefits offered. Young employees, for instance, may opt out of retirement programmes. An employee may choose not to participate in a medical insurance programme because he or she may already be covered by the spouse's participation in a family programme elsewhere.

4.9.1 Types of Employee Benefits and Services
- Medical Insurance
- Disability Insurance
- Life Insurance
- Retirement Benefits
- Fringe Benefits

1. **Medical insurance**

    Medical insurance covers the costs of physician and surgeon fees, hospital rooms, and prescription drugs. Dental and optical care might be offered as part of an overall benefits package. It may be offered as separate pieces or not covered at all. Coverage can sometimes include the employee's family (dependents).

    Employers usually pay all or part of the premium for employee medical insurance. Often employees pay a per centage of the monthly cost.

2. **Disability insurance**

    Disability insurance replaces all or part of the income that is lost when a worker is unable to perform their job because of illness or injury. This benefit is not commonly offered. There are two main types of disability insurance:
    - **Short-term disability** insurance begins right away or within a few weeks of an accident, illness, or some other disability. For example, someone hurt in a car accident would be offered a few paid weeks to recover.
    - **Long-term disability** insurance provides benefits to an employee when a long-term or permanent illness, injury, or disability leaves the individual unable to perform his or her job. For example, an employee with spinal injuries could be entitled to long-term disability benefits until retirement age.

3. **Life insurance**

    Life insurance protects your family in case you die. Benefits are paid all at once to the beneficiaries of the policy — usually a spouse or children.

    You can get life insurance through an employer if they sponsor a group plan. Company-sponsored life insurance plans are standard for almost all full-time workers in medium and large firms across the country. You can also buy it privately, but this is usually more expensive.

4. **Retirement benefits**

    Retirement benefits are funds set aside to provide people with an income or pension when they end their careers. Retirement plans fit into two general categories:

    In **defined benefit plans** (sometimes called pension plans), the benefit amount is pre-determined based on salary and the years of service. In these plans, the employer bears the risk of the investment.

    In **defined contribution plans** (such as a 401k plan), employer or employee contributions are specified, but the benefit amount is usually tied to investment returns, which are not guaranteed.

5. **Fringe Benefits**

Fringe benefits are a variety of non-cash payments are used to attract and retain talented employees. They may include tuition assistance, flexible medical or child-care spending accounts (pre-tax accounts to pay qualified expenses), other child-care benefits, and non-production bonuses (bonuses not tied to performance).

Most firms offering tuition assistance require that courses are related to job duties.

4.9.2 Administration of Benefits and Services

Benefits administration involves the creation and management of employee benefits, as well as providing a means for employees to be trained in understanding how the benefits work, and what types of standards employees must meet in order to qualify for the benefits.

Often, benefits administration occurs within the Human Resources department of a larger company, although smaller companies may designate the function of benefits administration to other areas or individuals.

Much of the work of the administrator is devoted to coordinating a benefits plan that is currently in place. Benefits administration involves spending a lot of the day making sure benefit plans are running smoothly. This will often include review of accumulation of personal days, vacation days, and sick days.

The administrator will make sure the process for adding days off to an employee's account is being done according to the company's defined process. In addition, the administrators will work with the payroll department to make sure that the employee is paid for any approved days taken, and that those days are deducted from the appropriate resource.

4.9.3 Insurance - Retirement – Flexible Benefits Programmes

Flexible benefit plans allow employees to choose the benefits they want or need from a package of programmes offered by an employer. Flexible benefit plans may include health insurance, retirement benefits and reimbursement accounts that employees can use to pay for out-of-pocket health or dependent care expenses.

In a flexible benefit plan, employees contribute to the cost of these benefits through a payroll deduction of their before-tax income, reducing the employer's contribution.

In addition, the ability to pay for benefits with pre-tax income lowers an employee's taxable income while raising the amount of their take-home pay—an added "benefit."

In the short term, companies obviously benefit from sharing costs with employees.

Flexible benefit plans have become increasingly popular with employers. Health and child-care costs have risen tremendously over the past several decades. This has had a major effect on a business' ability to offer benefits, yet most employees still expect to receive benefits as a result of employment.

Small businesses in particular are often unable to take advantage of the economies of scale that larger companies can use to their advantage in securing benefits programmes. These companies, as well as larger ones, have subsequently found means by which their employees can contribute to the cost of benefits.

4.10 Nature of Incentive Schemes

An incentive programme is a formal scheme used to promote or encourage specific actions or behaviour by a specific group of people during a defined period of time.

> *Incentive programmes are particularly used in business management to motivate employees, and in sales to attract and retain customers.*

An incentive is something that motivates an individual to perform an action.

Ultimately, incentives aim to provide value for money and contribute to organisational success

The following are some key fundamentals in any successful incentive plan.

1. **Keep it simple and special:** Good plans are easy to implement and to follow. The employees need to know what they can do to earn an incentive and what exactly that incentive will be.

2. **Reward only for surpassing business goals:** Incentive plans should initiate only after average performance is exceeded. This means that management needs to have clear goals and expectations.

   Employees need to have a clear understanding of what is expected for average performance and what actions they can take to help the company exceed the basic business goals and thus earn an incentive.

   A target goal might be to increase productivity by 10 per cent within the year. The CSRs then need to understand that they will need to handle 10 per cent or more commissions by the end of the year in order to earn an incentive. If the service staffs do not increase productivity, then there is no reward.

3. **Reward great individual effort:** If employee is doing something right and make sure everyone in the office sees that management recognises it. If a CSR did a great job handling a difficult account then shower him or her with immediate praise, recognition and a reward. There does not need to be any analytical performance tracking for this incentive plan. This way the staff will know that management appreciates the extra effort they put in. This is one aspect of the first layer of employees' incentives.

4. **Encourage team results:** For service staff and administrative employees there needs to be a fair amount of teamwork. In an effective plan, performance results are also tracked and rewarded based on unit or department results. Tracking individual

performance can be difficult, so this is a good compromise between rewarding great individual effort and excellent overall agency wide results (such as total growth in sales).

5. **Noticeable rewards:** A good rule of thumb is that the total value of incentive rewards that an employee can earn should be around 8 per cent to 12 per cent of his or her base compensation. Anything under 8 per cent will not be appreciated. This does not mean that the employee must earn incentives of 8 per cent or more, but that they can earn up to that amount.

6. **Be creative:** Today's employees look beyond money for other rewards. They are looking for challenges, recognition and empowerment. Non-cash recognition awards are a very effective way to reinforce the agency's values. For example, employees who provide outstanding customer service receive special awards. One way is for employees to be nominated as the top performer of the month or quarter. Management needs to think about the types of awards that make sense for employees.

7. **Long-term incentives:** A good plan will allow employees to earn incentives monthly or quarterly. A great plan will add in a long-term reward system as the third layer of incentives. Think of long-term incentives as golden handcuffs.

4.10.1 Scope of Incentive Schemes

Companies use employee incentive plans for a variety of reasons – to meet or increase sales goals, to meet or increase production goals, to raise employee morale or for extraordinary employee performance, all of which drive the success of the company.

> *Incentive Plans reward employees for their achievement and create a sense of accomplishment.*

Incentives can range from simple rewards, including gifts, plaques or trophies to monetary rewards, such as profit sharing, bonuses or travel incentives.

4.10.2 Types of Incentive Schemes

Incentive awards are a way of rewarding employees and others with cash, goods or holidays rather than increases in pay.

Awards may be linked to sales performance, good timekeeping, safety or production records, or may involve participation in a lottery or prize draw. Schemes may be intended to benefit employees or the self-employed, or both.

Awards may be made by the employee's direct employer or by a third party with an interest in the performance of the employee. For example, a car manufacturer is more likely to give an incentive award to a person employed by a dealership than the direct employer.

Different types of incentive plans are as follows:

Stock Options

A stock option is an incentive offered to employees that want to invest their money into the company's stock by purchasing stock with pre-tax money. Employees that participate in a stock option incentive plan are able to defer paying income tax on the gains realised by their stock purchases until the stock is sold. The company itself does not get any kind of tax break by offering a stock option incentive, but it does reap the benefits of selling more stock.

Profit Sharing

Profit sharing is another incentive plan. The company sets aside a portion of their pre-tax profits and distributes that money to the employees. In most cases, an employee must qualify to receive profit sharing by meeting company performance metrics, and by having a predetermined amount of service in with the company.

Some companies offer to place the pre-tax dollars into the employees' company retirement plans, so it can add to future fund growth. Companies may also develop a profit sharing per centage based on the amount of time worked for the company, the position held within the company or a combination of both conditions.

Performance Units

According to the Society for Human Resource Management, one type of incentive plan for executives is known as the performance unit. In the executive's agreement there is a schedule of financial milestones that the company must achieve for the executive to get awarded a pre-determined amount of units. The amount of a performance unit varies by company. Performance units are paid out based on a schedule agreed to by the executive and the company.

Bonus Pay

The bonus pay structure is common in professions such as sales, marketing and production. When the employees reach a predetermined goal, the company may create an incentive plan that pays a bonus for going beyond that goal. For example, if a manufacturing plant has a goal of 100 units in a month, the company may offer to pay each employee a bonus for each unit manufactured beyond 100 in that month.

4.10.3 Wage Incentive Schemes and Plans in India

The employee benefit package normally contains apart from basic wage, a dearness allowance, overtime payment, annual bonus, incentive systems, and a host of fringe benefits.

Basic Wage

The concept of basic wage is contained in the report of the Fair Wages Committee. According to this Committee, the floor of the basic pay is the "minimum wage" which provides "not merely for the bare sustenance of life but for the preservation of the efficiency of the workers by providing some measure of education, medical requirements and amenities." The basic wage has been the most stable and fixed as compared to dearness allowance and annual bonus which usually change with movements in the cost of living indices and the performance of the industry.

Dearness Allowance

The fixation of wage structure also includes within its compass a fixation of rates of dearness allowance. In the context of a changing pattern of prices and consumption, real wages of the workmen are likely to fluctuate greatly. Ultimately, it is the goods and services that a worker buys with the help of wages that are an important consideration for him. The real wages of the workmen thus require to be protected when there is a rise in prices and a consequent increase in the cost of living by suitable adjustments in these wages. In foreign countries, these adjustments in wages are effected automatically with the rise or fall in the cost of living.

In India, the system of dearness allowance is a special feature of the wage system for adjustment of the wages when there are frequent fluctuations in the cost of living. In our country, at present, there are several systems of paying dearness allowance to the employees to meet the changes in the cost of living. In practice, they differ from place to place and industry to industry.

One of the methods of paying dearness allowance is by a flat rate, under which a fixed amount is paid to all categories of workers, irrespective of their wage scales.

The second method is its linkage with consumer price index numbers published periodically by the government. It indicates the changes in the prices of a fixed basket of goods and services customarily bought by the families of workers. In other words, the index shows the rise or falls in the cost of living due a rise or fall in consumer prices.

The Consumer Price Index (CPI) is a monthly index published by the Bureau of Labour Statistics. The CPI is compiled by price data collected throughout the country for a fixed set of goods, such as food, clothing, shelter, fuels, prescriptions, transportation fares, and medical fees. The CPI is important as a predictor of wage increases and of employees' need for greater income.

The third method of paying dearness allowance is on a graduated scale according to slabs. Under this method, workers are divided into groups according to the slabs of wage scales to whom fixed amounts of dearness allowance are paid on a graduated scale. After a limit, there will not be any increase in the amount of dearness allowance at all, however high the wage rate may be. This method is popular because it is convenient and also considered to be equitable.

Overtime Payment

Working overtime in industry is possibly as old as the industrial revolution. The necessity of the managements' seeking overtime working from employees becomes inevitable mainly to overcome inappropriate allocation of manpower and improper scheduling, absenteeism, unforeseen situations created due to genuine difficulties like breakdown of machines.

In many companies, overtime is necessary to meet urgent delivery dates, sudden upswings in production schedules, or to give management a degree of flexibility in matching labour capacity to production demands. The payment of overtime allowance to the factory and workshop employees is guaranteed by law.

All employees who are deemed to be workers under the Factories Act or under the Minimum Wages Act are entitled to it at twice the ordinary rate of their wages for the work done in excess of 9 hours on any day or for more than 48 hours in any week. The major benefit of overtime working to workers is that it offers an increase in income from work.

Annual Bonus

The bonus component of the industrial compensation system, though a quite old one, had assumed a statutory status only with the enactment of the Payment of Bonus Act, 1965. The Act is applicable to factories and other establishments employing 20 or more employees.

Eligibility: Every employee not drawing salary/wages beyond ₹ 10,000 per month who has worked for not less than 30 days in an accounting year, shall be eligible for bonus for minimum of 8.33% of the salary/wages even if there is loss in the establishment whereas a maximum of 20% of the employee's salary/wages is payable as bonus in an accounting year. However, in case of the employees whose salary/wages range between ₹ 3500 to ₹ 10,000 per month for the purpose of payment of bonus, their salaries/wages would be deemed to be ₹ 3500.

Incentive Systems

The term "incentive" has been used both in the restricted sense of participation and in the widest sense of financial motivation. It is used to signify inducements offered to employees to put forth their best in order to maximise production results. Incentives are classified as financial and non-financial.

Important financial incentives are attractive wages, bonus, dearness allowance, travelling allowance, housing allowance, gratuity, pension, and provident fund contributions. Some of the non-financial incentives are designation, nature of the job, working conditions, status, privileges, job security, opportunity for advancement and participation in decision making.

However, a vast diversity exists in regard to policy and practice of incentive payments. Incentive systems also have been classified into three groups: individual wage incentive plan, group incentive scheme, and organisation-wide incentive system.

> *The individual wage incentive plan is the extra compensation paid to an individual over a specified amount for his production effort.*

Individual incentive systems are based upon certain norms established by work measurement techniques such as past performance, bargaining between union and the management, time study, standard data, predetermined elemental times and work sampling. There are four types of individual incentive systems such as measured day-work, piece-work standard, group plans and gains-sharing plans. Under the measured day-work incentive wage system, an individual receives his regular hourly rate of pay, irrespective of his performance. Piece-work system forms the most simple and frequently used incentive wage. In this, individual's earnings are direct and proportionate to their output. Group plans embody a guaranteed base rate to the workers in which the performance over standard is rewarded by a proportionate premium over base pay. Gains-sharing system involves a disproportionate increase in monetary rewards for increasing output beyond a predetermined standard. As the gains are shared with the entrepreneurs, the worker gets less than one per cent increment in wage for every one per cent increase in output.

The group or area incentive scheme provides for the payment of a bonus either equally or proportionately to individuals within a group or area. The bonus is related to the output achieved over an agreed standard or to the time saved on the job – the difference between allowed time and actual time. Such schemes may be most appropriate where:

(a) People have to work together and teamwork has to be encouraged; and

(b) High levels of production depend a great deal on the cooperation existing among a team of workers as compared with the individual efforts of team members.

The organisation-wide incentive system involves cooperation among employees and the management and purports to accomplish broader organisational objectives such as:

(i) To reduce labour, material and supply costs;

(ii) To strengthen loyalty to the company;

(iii) To promote harmonious labour-management relations; and

(iv) To decrease turnover and absenteeism.

One of the aspects of organisation-wide incentive system is profit sharing under which an employee receives a share of the profit fixed in advance under an agreement freely entered into. The major objective of the profit sharing system is to strengthen the unity of interest and the spirit of cooperation. Some of the advantages of such a scheme are:

(i) It inculcates in employees' a sense of economic discipline as regards wage costs and productivity;

(ii) It engenders improved communication and increased sense of participation;

(iii) It is relatively simple and its cost of administration is low; and

(iv) It is non-inflationary, if properly devised.

One of the essentials of a sound profit sharing system is that it should not be treated as a substitute for adequate wages but provides something extra to the participants. Full support and cooperation of the union is to be obtained in implementing such a scheme.

Fringe Benefits

The remuneration that the employees receive for their contribution cannot be measured by the mere estimation of wages and salaries paid to them. Certain supplementary benefits and services known as "fringe benefits" are also available to them.

4.10.4 Incentive Schemes for Operation Employees, Managers and Executives

Employee achievement, recognition and incentive programmes are mostly designed for non-sales employees for achieving specific sales and non-sales support related corporate goals.

Here are several types of employee incentives:

Program	Reward Vehicle
Sales Support	Travel Programme With Sales Team or Online Reward Catalog
Customer Service	Gift Certificates, Online Reward Catalog
Length of Service	Gift Certificates, Special gift, Plaque
Safety Programmes	Online Reward Catalog, Individual Travel
Attendance	Gift Certificates, Online Reward Catalog, Individual Travel
Employee Performance	Gift Certificates, Online Reward Catalog, Individual Travel
Suggested Systems	Gift Certificates, Online Reward Catalog, Individual Travel

4.11 Performance Productivity Management

'Performance management' is a system of conducting employee performance reviews. The aim of performance management is to align organisational objectives with the skills, performance goals and competencies of employees.

> *The aim of performance management is to align organisational objectives with the skills, performance goals and competencies of employees*

It involves creating a workforce that has an understanding of what is to be achieved at the overall organisational level.

Where it differs from the traditional performance appraisal system is in creating the link between employee objectives and that of the business. Old performance appraisal systems usually involve an annual review meeting, to assess whether an employee is doing their job well or not, and often rely in part on financial incentives and rewards in the process.

Appraisal systems may lack clear objectives for the employee to achieve during the year and development plans for the future.

Performance appraisals assess and evaluate the work of employees, but performance management reflects the continuous nature of performance improvement and recognises the contributions of all levels of the workforce, as well as the importance of effective management and work systems.

4.11.1 Total Quality Management (TQM)

Total Quality Management / TQM is an integrative philosophy of management for continuously improving the quality of products and processes.

Total Quality Management is formally defined as *"management philosophy and company practices that aim to harness the human and material resources of an organisation in the most effective way to achieve the objectives of the organisation."*

Total quality management can be summarised as a management system for a customer-focused organisation that involves all employees in continual improvement. It uses strategy, data, effective communications and involvement of all level employees to integrate the quality discipline into the culture and activities of the organisation.

The basic elements of TQM, as expounded by the American Society for Quality Control, are:

1. Policy, planning, and administration;
2. Product design and design change control;
3. Control of purchased material;
4. Production quality control;
5. User contact and field performance;
6. Corrective action; and
7. Employee selection, training, and motivation.

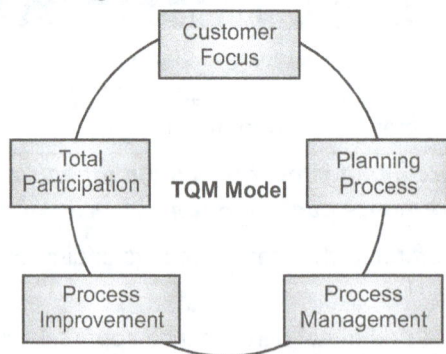

Fig. 4.1: Total Quality Management Model

No two organisations have the same TQM implementation. There is no recipe for organisation success. The simplest model of TQM is shown in this above TQM diagram. The model begins with understanding customer needs. TQM organisations have processes that continuously collect, analyse, and act on customer information.

Activities are often extended to understanding competitor's customers. Developing an intimate understanding of customer needs allows TQM organisations to predict future customer behaviour.

TQM organisations use the techniques of process management to develop cost-controlled processes that are stable and capable of meeting customer expectations.

TQM organisations also understand that exceptional performance today may be unacceptable performance in the future so they use the concepts of process improvement to achieve both breakthrough gains and incremental continuous improvement. Process improvement is even applied to the TQM system itself.

> *TQM organisations understand that all work is performed through people.*

The final element of the TQM model is total participation. TQM organisations understand that all work is performed through people. This begins with leadership.

In TQM organisations, top management takes personal responsibility for implementing, nurturing, and refining all TQM activities. They make sure people are properly trained, capable, and actively participate in achieving organisational success. Management and employees work together to create an empowered environment where people are valued.

All of the TQM model's elements work together to achieve results

4.11.2 Kaizen

Kaizen, Japanese for "improvement", or "change for the better" refers to philosophy or practices that focus upon continuous improvement of processes in manufacturing, engineering, and business management. It has been applied in healthcare, psychotherapy, life-coaching, government, banking, and other industries.

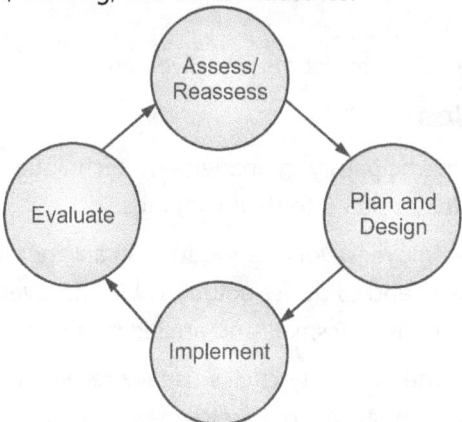

4.2: Cycle of Kaizen

The Toyota Production System is known for Kaizen, where all line personnel are expected to stop their moving production line in case of any abnormality and, along with their supervisor, suggest an improvement to resolve the abnormality which may initiate a kaizen.

The cycle of Kaizen activity can be defined as:
- Standardise an operation and activities.
- Measure the operation (find cycle time and amount of in-process inventory).
- Gauge measurements against requirements.
- Innovate to meet requirements and increase productivity.
- Standardise the new, improved operations.
- Continue cycle *ad infinitum*.

When used in the business sense and applied to the workplace, kaizen refers to activities that continually improve all functions, and involves all employees from the CEO to the assembly line workers.

> *By improving standardised activities and processes, Kaizen aims to eliminate waste.*

It also applies to processes, such as purchasing and logistics that cross organisational boundaries into the supply chain. By improving standardised activities and processes, Kaizen aims to eliminate waste.

The Five Elements of Kaizen:
- Management teamwork
- Increased labour responsibilities
- Increased management morale
- Quality circle
- Management suggestions for labour improvement

4.11.3 Quality Circles

A quality circle is a participatory management technique that enlists the help of employees in solving problems related to their own jobs.

Circles are formed of employees working together in an operation who meet at intervals to discuss problems of quality and to devise solutions for improvements. Quality circles have an autonomous character, are usually small, and are led by a supervisor or a senior worker.

Employees who participate in quality circles usually receive training in formal problem-solving methods—such as brain-storming, Pareto analysis, and cause-and-effect diagrams—and are then encouraged to apply these methods either to specific or general company problems.

After completing an analysis, they often present their findings to management and then handle implementation of approved solutions.

4.11.4 Performance Productivity Management through TQM, Kaizen, Quality Circles

Managers who want to increase motivational levels in employees need to use effective performance management techniques. They need to take into consideration that different human beings have different motivational factors.

By implementing an effective performance management program, a company can positively influence employee productivity and decrease organisational turnover.

Once workers understand their participation and involvement in Total Quality Management is essential to its success, morale and productivity improve. Workers become empowered through participation on quality improvement teams. Businesses can improve morale further by recognising improvement teams that make meaningful changes in the production process to reduce or eliminate waste.

Points to Remember

- **Compensation Management** is an organised practice that involves balancing the work-employee relation by providing monetary and non-monetary benefits to employees.
- **Wage and Salary administration** is the process of compensating an organisation's employees in accordance with accepted policy and procedures.
- Wages and salary is a systematic approach to providing monetary value to employees in exchange for work performed.
- **Bonus** is a share of the workers in the prosperity of an enterprise.
- **Benefits** are any perks offered to employees in addition to salary.
- The purpose of employee benefits is to increase the economic security of staff members, and in doing so, improve worker retention across the organisation.
- In a flexible benefit plan, employees contribute to the cost of these benefits through a payroll deduction of their before-tax income, reducing the employer's contribution
- **Employee incentive** programmes are a very powerful concept when employees can understand and see the connection between their performance and their rewards.
- A great plan can help transform an organisation from an average performer– where people come to work to just do their job and get paid –into one where excellence and outstanding results are the goals.
- In recent years, a great deal of attention has been directed to the development of compensation systems that go beyond just money. In particular there has been a marked increase in the use of pay-for-performance (PrP) for management and professional employees, especially for executive management and senior managers.

- **Compensation** is a primary motivation for most employees. People look for jobs that not only suit their creativity and talents, but compensate them both in terms of salary and other benefits accordingly.
- Adequate rewards and compensations help in attracting a quality workforce, maintaining the satisfaction of existing employees, keeping quality employees from leaving and motivating them for higher productivity.
- **Total Quality Management** is formally defined as "management philosophy and company practices that aim to harness the human and material resources of an organisation in the most effective way to achieve the objectives of the organisation."
- **'Performance management'** is a system of conducting employee performance reviews.
- The aim of performance management is to align organisational objectives with the skills, performance goals and competencies of employees.
- By improving standardised activities and processes, kaizen aims to eliminate waste.
- Managers who want to increase motivational levels in employees need to use effective performance management techniques.

Questions for Discussion

1. Describe Wage and Salary Administration.
2. Define Reward, Wage, Salary.
3. Enumerate methods of establishing Pay Rates.
4. Describe Compensation Trends.
5. List factors affecting Employee Remuneration.
6. Illustrate Wage and Salary Structure.
7. Describe Minimum Fair and Living Wage.
8. Define Wage Policy in India.
9. Illustrate the Preparation of Salary Structure.
    (a) Describe Nature and Need of Benefits and Services.
10. Enumerate Types of Employee Benefits and Services.
11. Define Fringe Benefits.
12. Illustrate Administration of Benefits and Services.
13. Describe Insurance - Retirement – Flexible Benefits Programmes.
14. Describe Nature of Incentive Schemes.
15. Enumerate Scope and Types of Incentive Schemes.

16. Define Wage Incentive Schemes and Plans in India.
17. Illustrate Team or Group Variable plans.
18. Describe Incentive Schemes for Operation Employees, Managers and Executives and Sales People.
19. Define Performance Productivity Management.
20. Learn Total Quality Management (TQM).
21. Define Kaizen.
22. Illustrate Quality Circles.
23. Describe Performance Productivity Management through TQM, Kaizen, Quality Circles.

Multiple Choice Questions

Questions 1-10 Answer True or False

1. **Compensation Management** is an organised practice that involves balancing the work-employee relation by providing monetary and non-monetary benefits to employees.
2. **Wage and Salary administration** is not a process of compensating an organisation's employees in accordance with accepted policy and procedures.
3. Wages and salary is a systematic approach to providing monetary value to employees in exchange for work performed.
4. Bonus is not a share of the workers in the prosperity of an enterprise.
5. Benefits are any perks offered to employees in addition to salary.
6. The purpose of employee benefits is not to increase the economic security of staff members, and in doing so, improve worker retention across the organisation.
7. In a flexible benefit plan, employees contribute to the cost of these benefits through a payroll deduction of their before-tax income, reducing the employer's contribution.
8. Incentive programmes are particularly used in business management to de-motivate employees, and in sales to attract and retain customers.
9. Incentive Plans reward employees for their achievement and create a sense of accomplishment.
10. 'Performance management' is a system of conducting employer's performance reviews.

Questions 11-15 Fill in the Blanks

11. The aim of performance management is to align _____ with the skills, performance goals and competencies of employees.
12. By improving standardised activities and processes, _____ aims to eliminate waste.
13. Managers who want to increase _____ levels in employees need to use effective performance management techniques.
14. TQM organisations understand that all _____ is performed through people.
15. The individual wage incentive plan is the extra _____ paid to an individual over a specified amount for his production effort.

Answers

1. True
2. False
3. True
4. False
5. True
6. False
7. True
8. False
9. True
10. False
11. organisational objectives
12. Kaizen
13. Motivational
14. Work
15. compensation

Case Study

Rishi was troubled while preparing the annual salary budget for his retail chain, Akshay Retail. The company had a presence in all the major metros. It had a 100 per cent growth on year to year basis, making it a good poaching ground for other retail companies, which were also aggressive in their growth plans. Last year, 60 junior marketing executives left to join rival companies. The company has been at a loss to understand what went wrong as it offers competitive salaries and deferrals. The fixed variable ratio of salary was 50:50.

Also, earning the variables did not require an employee to stretch, as the company had already achieved the brand identity. Akshay Retail made the shopping experience so compelling that customers enjoyed visiting their stores again and again.

Rishi was a very innovative compensation administrator, and he designed compensation structure in such a flexible way that an employee could earn twice their average monthly salary, given some initiative in retaining customers. The company's stores were so arranged that each customer care executive (CCE) monitored counters with some common items. They were given training to educate customers about products and why they should buy it. Every CCE got a bonus point for repeat customer purchases. At the end of the year, based on the accumulated bonus points, these employees got surprise incentives.

Rishi's friend Kumar worked for a big multinational company. Kumar advised Rishi to study the work culture and design a compensation package while considering the career development initiatives of employees.

The core advice was to opt for an organisational work culture survey and ensure that employees' morale was high.

Another friend of Rishi, Ravi, had a different story to tell. He advised Rishi not to bow down to employees' pressure for a pay rise. He suggested that employees who wanted to leave should be allowed to do so. Ravi believed in deferrals. He advised Rishi to make deferrals attractive, and employees by default would continue.

Question:

Design an effective compensation package to enable the retention of customer care executives at Akshay Retail.

References and Further Readings

Reference Books
1. Personnel Management by C.B Mamoria
2. Human Resource Management by Garry Dessler
3. Human Resource Management by Aswathappa

Web Links
1. http://EzineArticles.com/1626637
2. http://hrmba.blogspot.in
3. http://www.referenceforbusiness.com/encyclopedia/Clo-Con/Compensation-Administration
4. http://www.inc.com/encyclopedia/quality-circles.html
5. http://www.citeman.com/9947-establishing-pay-rates
6. http://jethr.com/magazine/hr-corporate-strategy/compensation-management

■■■

Chapter **5**...

Industrial Relations, Separations and Safety Management

Contents ...
5.1 Industrial Relations
    5.1.1 Definition of Industrial Relations
    5.1.2 Concepts and Objectives of IR
    5.1.3 Objectives of IR
    5.1.4 Parties to IR
    5.1.5 Theories and Approaches to IR
    5.1.6 Trade Unions and its Role in IR
5.2 Dispute Settlement
    5.2.1 Dispute Settlement
    5.2.2 Machinery to Dispute Settlement
5.3 Define Separation
    5.3.1 VRS/CRS
5.4 Safety and Security
    5.4.1 Employee Safety
    5.4.2 Types of Safety
    5.4.3 Safety and Health Programs
    5.4.4 Statutory Provisions of Safety in India
- Points to Remember
- Questions for Discussion
- Case Study
- Activity
- Objective Questions
- References

Objectives ...
➢ To define IR
➢ To enumerate Concepts and Objectives of IR
➢ To list Parties to IR
➢ To describe Approaches to IR
➢ To illustrate Trade Unions and its Role in IR

- To define the Machinery to Dispute Settlement
- To enumerate Grievance Procedure
- To list the features of Collective Bargaining
- To describe Negotiation, Conciliation, Arbitration, Adjudication
- To illustrate Labour Courts
- To define Separations
- To enumerate VRS/CRS
- To list features of Resignation
- To describe Superannuation, Gratuity
- To illustrate procedures of Discharge, Dismissal, Suspension, Layoff and Retrenchment

Introduction

'Industrial relations' is a multidisciplinary field that studies the employment relationship.

Industrial relations is increasingly being called employment relations or employee relations because of the importance of non-industrial employment relationships; this move is sometimes seen as further broadening of the human resource management trend. Indeed, some authors now define human resource management as synonymous with employee relations. Other authors see employee relations as dealing only with non-unionised workers, whereas labour relations are seen as dealing with unionised workers. Industrial relations examine various employment situations, not just the ones with an unionised workforce.

However, according to Bruce E. Kaufman "To a large degree, most scholars regard trade unionism, collective bargaining and labour-management relations, and the national labour policy and labour law within which they are embedded, as the core subjects of the field."

5.1 Industrial Relations

5.1.1 Definitions of Industrial Relations

Industrial relations has become one of the most delicate and complex problems of modern industrial society. Industrial progress is impossible without co-operation of labours and harmonious relationships. Therefore, it is in the interest of all to create and maintain good relations between employees (labour) and employers (management).

Today, industry is an important part of most societies and nations. A major part of our population is employed in industries. To understand *industrial relations*, we first need to understand the term *industry*. The word industry has its roots in the Latin word *industrius* which means industrious, diligent. Industry can be defined as the manufacturing of a good or a service within a category.

Industrial relations (IR) are used to denote the collective relationships between management and the workers. Traditionally, the term industrial relations is used to cover such aspects of industrial life such as trade unionism, collective bargaining, workers participation in management, discipline and grievance handling, industrial disputes and interpretation of labour laws and rules and code of conduct.

In the words of Lester, "Industrial relations involve attempts at arriving at solutions between the conflicting objectives and values; between the profit motive and social gain; between discipline and freedom; between authority and industrial democracy; between bargaining and co-operation; and between conflicting interests of the individual, the group and the community.

The National Commission on Labour (NCL) also emphasises on the same concept. According to NCL, industrial relations affect not merely the interests of the two participants - labour and management, but also the economic and social goals to which the State addresses itself. To regulate these relations in socially desirable channels is a function, which the State is in the best position to perform.

Definitions: Lester defines industrial relations as, *"Industrial relations involve attempts at arriving at solutions between the conflicting objectives and values; between the profit motive and social gain; between discipline and freedom; between authority and industrial democracy; between bargaining and cooperation and between conflicting interests of the individual, the group and the community"*.

Merriam-Webster defines industrial relations as, *"the dealings or relationships of a usually large business or industrial enterprise with its own workers, with labour in general, with governmental agencies, or with the public"*.

The **National Commission on Labour (NCL)** states that, *"industrial relations affect not merely the interests of the two participants - labour and management, but also the economic and social goals to which the State addresses itself. To regulate these relations in socially desirable channels is a function, which the State is in the best position to perform"*.

According to **Alistair McMillan** industrial relations is the *"Interaction between employers, employees, and the government; and the institutions and associations through which such interactions are mediated. Government has a direct involvement in industrial relations, through its role as an employer; one that is particularly prominent in states where there are high levels of nationalisation. Indirectly, government has a major role through the regulation of the economy and the relationship between employers and trade unions"*.

Some more definitions of Industrial Relations are given below:
1. Industrial Relation is that part of management which is concerned with the manpower of the *enterprise – whether machine operator, skilled worker or manager.*

   – (Bethel, Smith & Group)

2. *Industrial Relation is the relation between employer and employees, employees and trade unions.*

   – Industrial Disputes Act 1947

3. Industrial Relation is viewed as the, *"process by which people and their organisations interact at the place of work to establish the terms and conditions of employment".*

Industrial relations thus is a term which explains the relationship between employees and management which stem directly or indirectly from the union-employer relationship. Industrial relations are the relationships between employees and employers within the organisational settings. The field of industrial relations looks at the relationship between management and workers, particularly groups of workers represented by a union. Industrial relations are basically the interactions between employers, employees and the government, and the institutions and associations through which such interactions are mediated.

In fact, industrial relations encompasses all factors which influence the behaviour of people at work. A few such important factors are:

Institution: It includes government, employers, trade unions, union federations or associations, government bodies, labour courts, tribunals and other organisations which have direct or indirect impact on the industrial relations system.

Characters: It aims to study the role of workers' unions and employers' federations officials, shop stewards, industrial relations officers/ managers, mediators/conciliators / arbitrators, judges of labour court, tribunal etc.

Methods: Methods focus on collective bargaining, workers' participation in the industrial relations schemes, discipline procedure, grievance redressal machinery, dispute settlements machinery, working of closed shops, union reorganisation, organisations of protests through methods like revisions of existing rules, regulations, policies, procedures, hearing of labour courts, tribunals etc.

Contents: It includes matter pertaining to employment conditions like pay, hours of works, leave with wages, health and safety disciplinary actions, lay-offs, dismissals, retirements etc., laws relating to such activities, regulations governing labour welfare, social security, industrial relations, issues concerning workers' participation in management, collective bargaining etc.

Features of Industrial Relations

1. Industrial relations are outcomes of employment relationships in an industrial enterprise. These relations cannot exist without the two parties namely employers and employees.

2. Industrial relations system creates rules and regulations to maintain harmonious relations.

3. The government intervenes to shape the industrial relations through laws, rules, agreements, terms, charters etc.

4. Several parties are involved in the Industrial relations system. The main parties are employers and their associations, employees and their unions and the government. These three parties interact within economic and social environment to shape the Industrial relations structure.

5. Industrial relations are a dynamic and developing concept, not a static one. They undergo changes with changing structure and scenario of the industry as and when change occurs.
6. Industrial relations include both individual relations and collective relationships.

Importance of Industrial Relations

1. **Uninterrupted Production:** The most important benefit of industrial benefits is that it ensures continuity of production. This means continuous employment for all involved right from managers to workers. There is uninterrupted flow of income for all. Smooth running of industries is important for manufacturers, if their products are perishable goods and to consumers if the goods are for mass consumption (essential commodities, food grains etc.). Good industrial relations bring industrial peace which in turn tends to increase production.
2. **Reduction in Industrial Disputes:** Good Industrial relations reduce Industrial disputes. Strikes, grievances and lockouts are some of the reflections of Industrial unrest. Industrial peace helps in promoting co-operation and increasing production. Thus good Industrial relations help in establishing Industrial democracy, discipline and a conducive workplace environment.
3. **High Morale:** Good Industrial relations improve the morale of the employees and motivate the worker workers to work more and better.
4. **Reduced Wastage:** Good Industrial relations are maintained on the basis of co-operation and recognition of each other. It helps to reduce wastage of material, manpower and costs.
5. Contributes to economic growth and development.

Causes of Poor Industrial Relations

1. **Economic causes:** Often poor wages and poor working conditions are the main causes for unhealthy relations between management and labour. Unauthorised deductions from wages, lack of fringe benefits, absence of promotion opportunities, faulty incentive schemes are other economic causes. Other causes for Industrial conflicts are inadequate infrastructure, worn-out plant and machinery, poor layout, unsatisfactory maintenance etc.
2. **Organisational causes:** Faulty communications system, unfair practices, non-recognition of trade unions and labour laws are also some other causes of poor relations in industry.
3. **Social causes:** Uninteresting nature of work is the main social cause of poor industrial relations. Dissatisfaction with job and personal life culminates into industrial conflicts.

4. **Psychological causes:** Lack of job security, non-recognition of merit and performance, poor interpersonal relations are the psychological reasons for unsatisfactory employer-employee relations.//
5. **Political causes:** Multiple unions, inter-union rivalry weaken the trade unions. Defective trade unions system prevailing in the country has been one of the most responsible causes for Industrial disputes in the country.

5.1.2 Concepts and Objectives of IR

The term 'Industrial Relations' comprises two terms: 'Industry' and 'Relations'. "Industry" refers to "any productive activity in which an individual (or a group of individuals) is (are) engaged". By "relations" we mean "the relationships that exist within the industry between the employer and his workmen". The term industrial relations explains the relationship between employees and management which stem directly or indirectly from union-employer relationship.

Industrial relations are the relationships between employees and employers within the organisational settings. The field of industrial relations looks at the relationship between management and workers, particularly groups of workers represented by a union. Industrial relations are basically the interactions between employers, employees and the government and the institutions and associations through which such interactions are mediated.

The term industrial relations has a broad as well as a narrow outlook. Originally, industrial relations was broadly defined to include the relationships and interactions between employers and employees. From this perspective, industrial relations covers all aspects of the employment relationship, including human resource management, employee relations and union-management (or labour) relations. Now its meaning has become more specific and restricted. Accordingly, industrial relations pertains to the study and practice of collective bargaining, trade unionism and labour-management relations, while human resource management is a separate, largely distinct field that deals with non-union employment relationships and the personnel practices and policies of employers.

The relationships which arise at and out of the workplace generally include the relationships between individual workers, the relationships between workers and their employer, the relationships between employers, the relationships employers and workers have with the organisations formed to promote their respective interests, and the relations between those organisations, at all levels. Industrial relations, also includes the processes through which these relationships are expressed (such as collective bargaining, workers' participation in decision-making and grievance and dispute settlement) and the management of conflict between employers, workers and trade unions, when it arises.

Today, industry is a broad term for any kind of economic production and is classified into four sectors. These four key industrial economic sectors are:

1. The *primary sector*, which is largely involved in raw material extraction and includes industries like mining and farming;
2. The *secondary sector*, where refining, construction and manufacturing are involved;
3. The *tertiary sector*, which deals with providing services like law and medicine, distribution of manufactured goods; and
4. The *quaternary sector*, which focuses on technological research, design and development such as computer programming and biochemistry.

The early industries were involved in the manufacture of goods for trade, which included weapons, clothing, pottery etc. Industrial relations can be traced back to medieval Europe, where industry became dominated by the guilds in cities and towns. They supported and looked out for their member's interests, and maintained standards of workmanship and ethical conduct.

The industrial revolution led to the development of factories for large-scale production, with consequent changes in the society. Originally the factories were steam-powered, but later transitioned to electricity. Then came the assembly line and today automation is being used to replace human operators. The industrial revolution brought in its wake the labour/trade union, which is an organisation of workers who band together to achieve common goals in key areas such as wages, working hours and working conditions. This in turn gave rise to the industrial relations system which deals with the relationships between employees and employers, which are managed by the means of conflict and cooperation.

5.1.3 Objectives of IR

The main objectives of industrial relations system are:

1. To safeguard the interest of labour and management by securing the highest level of mutual understanding and good-will among all those sections in the industry which participate in the process of production.
2. To avoid industrial conflict or strife and develop harmonious relations, which are an essential factor in the productivity of workers and the industrial progress of a country.
3. To raise productivity to a higher level in an era of full employment by lessening the tendency to high turnover and frequency absenteeism.
4. To establish and promote the growth of an industrial democracy based on labour partnership in the sharing of profits and of managerial decisions, so that an individual's personality may grow to its full stature for the benefit of the industry and of the country as well.

5. To eliminate or minimise the number of strikes, lockouts and gheraos by providing reasonable wages, improved living and working conditions, and fringe benefits.
6. To improve the economic conditions of workers in the existing state of industrial managements and political government.
7. Socialisation of industries by making the state itself a major employer.
8. Vesting of a proprietary interest of the workers in the industries in which they are employed.

5.1.4 Parties To IR

Industrial relations affect not merely the interests of the two participants- labour and management, but also the economic and social goals to which the State addresses itself. To regulate these relations in socially desirable channels is a function, which the State is in the best position to perform.

The parties involved in industrial relations are:

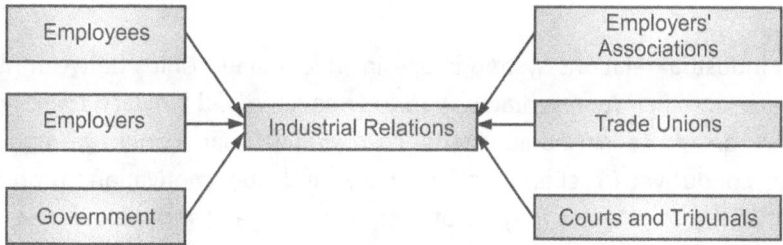

Fig. 5.1: Parties to Industrial Relations

1. **Workers and their Organisations**: The personal characteristics of workers, their culture, educational attainments, qualifications, skills, attitude towards work etc., play an important role in industrial relations. Workers' organisations, known as trade unions, are political institutions. Workers always try to improve the terms and conditions of their employment. They like to be involved in the decision making process of the management. They like to have a platform where they can exchange views and air their grievances. If the management is open and shares a good relationship with their workers it will earn their trust and loyalty; if not, it could lead to labour unions standing up to the management by means of lock-outs and strikes. Workers generally unite to form unions against the management and get support from these unions.

2. **Employers and their Organisations**: The employers are a very important variable in industrial relations and regulate their behaviour for getting high productivity from them. Industrial unrest generally arises when the employers' demands from workers are very high and they offer low economic and other benefits.

The employers have certain rights with respect to the work force. The right to hire or fire rests with them. They have the right to relocate, close or merge the factory or introduce technological changes. These rights affect the workers interest and if not carried out sensitively can lead to conflict.

3. **Government**: The government exerts an important influence on industrial relations through such measures as providing employment, and regulating wages, bonus and working conditions, through various laws relating to labour. The central and state government influences and regulates industrial relations through laws, rules, agreements, awards of court and the like. It also includes third parties and labour and tribunal courts.

The parties involved in industrial relations as given above are important components of the industrial relations system. These should thus be studied in detail.

An industrial relations system consists of the whole gamut of relationships between employees and employees and employers which are managed by the means of conflict and cooperation.

A sound industrial relations system is one in which relationships between management and employees (and their representatives) on the one hand and between them and the State on the other, are more harmonious and co-operative than conflictual and creates an environment conducive to economic efficiency and the motivation, productivity and development of the employee and generates employee loyalty and mutual trust.

1. **Industry:** Industrial Disputes Act 1947 defines an industry as, any systematic activity carried on by cooperation between an employer and his workmen for the production, supply or distribution of goods or services with a view to satisfy human wants or wishes, whether or not any capital has been invested for the purpose of carrying on such activity; or such activity is carried on with a motive to make any gain or profit. Thus, an industry is a whole gamut of activities that are carried on by an employer with the help of his employees and labourers for production and distribution of goods to earn profits.

2. **Employer:** An employer can be defined from different perspectives as:
   - a person or business that pays a wage or fixed payment to other person(s) in exchange for the services of such persons.
   - a person who directly engages a worker/employee in employment.
   - any person who employs, whether directly or through another person or agency, one or more employees in any scheduled employment in respect of which minimum rates of wages have been fixed.

As per Industrial Disputes Act, 1947 an employer means:

- In relation to an industry carried on by or under the authority of any department of [the Central Government or a State Government], the authority prescribed in this behalf, or where no authority is prescribed, the head of the department;
- In relation to an industry carried on by or on behalf of a local authority, the chief executive officer of that authority.

3. **Employee:** Employee is person who is hired by another person or business for a wage or fixed payment in exchange for personal services and who does not provide the services as part of an independent business.
   - An employee is any individual employed by an employer.
   - A person who works for a public or private employer and receives remuneration in wages or salary by his employer while working on a commission basis, piece-rate or time rate.
   - An employee, as per Employee State Insurance Act, 1948, is any person employed for wages in or in connection with work of a factory or establishment to which the act applies.

   In order to qualify to be an employee, under ESI Act, a person should belong to any of the categories:
   - Those who are directly employed for wages by the principal employer within the premises or outside in connection with work of the factory or establishment.
   - Those employed for wages by or through an immediate employer in the premises of the factory or establishment in connection with the work thereof.
   - Those employed for wages by or through an immediate employer in connection with the factory or establishment outside the premises of such factory or establishment under the supervision and control of the principal employer or his agent.
   - Employees whose services are temporarily lent or let on hire to the principal employer by an immediate employer under a contract of service (employees of security contractors, labour contractors, housekeeping contractors etc. come under this category).

4. **Employment:** The state of being employed or having a job. The market in which workers compete for jobs and employers compete for workers. It acts as the external source from which organisations attract employees. These markets occur because different conditions characterise different geographical areas, industries, occupations, and professions at any given time.

5. **Trade union** or **labour union** is an organisation of workers who have banded together to achieve common goals in key areas such as wages, working hours and

working conditions. The trade union, through its leadership, bargains with the employer on behalf of union members (rank and file members) and negotiates labour contracts (collective bargaining) with employers. This may include the negotiation of wages, work rules, complaint procedures, rules governing hiring, firing and promotion of workers, benefits, workplace safety and policies. The agreements negotiated by the union leaders are binding on the rank and file members and the employer and in some cases on other non-member workers.

To conclude, industrial relations can be explained as the relationships which arise at and out of the workplace and generally include the relationships between individual workers, the relationships between workers and their employer, the relationship the employers and workers have with the organisations formed to promote their respective interests and the relations between those organisations, at all levels. Industrial relations also includes the processes through which these relationships are expressed (such as, collective bargaining, workers' participation in decision making, and grievance and dispute settlement), and the management of conflict between employers, workers and trade unions, when it arises. The field of industrial relations (also called labour relations) looks at the relationship between management and workers, particularly groups of workers represented by a union.

A sound industrial relations system is one where a harmonious and cooperative environment is created between the management and employees and the company and the State, as this would lead to economic efficiency. On the other hand, if there is conflict rather than cooperation in the relationship it would lead to lack of motivation, productivity and loyalty, which in turn would have a negative impact on economic efficiency.

Industrial relations encompasses all such factors that influence behaviour of people at work.

5.1.5 Theories and Approaches to IR

There are many theories regarding industrial relations. The most important ones are:

- Unitary perspective
- Pluralistic perspective
- Marxist/Radical perspective
- Dunlop's theory.

1. Unitary Perspective: The unitary perspective visualises the organisation to be an integrated and harmonious whole, where the management and the workforce have a common goal. It's ideal is that of one big happy family, where mutual cooperation is the key. Unitarism is predominantly managerial in its emphasis and application and it demands unstinting loyalty from all its employees. Also, trade unions are believed to be unnecessary and conflict is seen to be disruptive.

Unitary approach from the *employees'* perspective:
- Working practices should be flexible. Individuals should be oriented towards business process improvement, they should have multiple skills and be ready to tackle any task with efficiency.
- If a union is recognised, its role is to further improve communication between groups of staff and the company.
- The emphasis is on good relationships and sound terms and conditions of employment.
- Employee participation in workplace decisions is encouraged. This helps in empowering individuals in their roles and emphasises teamwork, innovation, creativity, discretion in problem-solving, quality and improvement groups etc.
- The skills and expertise of managers should support the endeavours of the employees.

Unitary approach from an *employer's* view point:
- Staffing policies should try to unify, validate effort, inspire and motivate employees.
- The organisation's wider objectives should be properly communicated and discussed with the staff.
- Reward systems should be designed so as to foster and secure loyalty and commitment.
- Line managers should take responsibility for their team/staffing.
- Staff-management conflicts arise due to lack of information and inadequate presentation of the management's policies.
- The personal objectives of every individual employed in the business should be discussed with them and integrated with the organisation's needs.

2. Pluralistic Perspective: Pluralism, as a theory, believes that the organisation is made-up of powerful and divergent sub-groups, each with its own set of objectives and leaders and their legitimate loyalties. In particular, the two predominant sub-groups in the pluralistic perspective are the management and trade unions. Thus, the role of management leans towards persuasion and coordination and backs away from enforcing and controlling. Trade unions are considered legitimate representatives of employees; conflict is dealt with by collective bargaining. Collective bargaining is viewed as a tool for positive change and evolution, if managed well. This system has a greater propensity towards conflict and realistic managers would expect conflict to occur. Thus, they should be able to anticipate and resolve conflict by securing agreed procedures for settling disputes.

The requirements for following this approach are:
- The firm should have industrial relations and personnel specialists who could give valuable input to managers and provide specialist services in respect of staffing and matters relating to union consultation and negotiation.
- Independent external arbitrators should be used to assist in the resolution of disputes.
- Union recognition should be encouraged and union representatives given the scope to carry out their representative duties.
- Comprehensive collective agreements should be negotiated with the union.

3. Marxist/Radical Perspective: According to the Marxist perspective, in a capitalist society, there is a huge chasm between the interests of the management and labour. This view regards the capitalist economic system as the root of all evil and the basis of inequality of power and economic wealth. Thus, conflict is seen as inevitable and unions as a natural response of workers to their exploitation by the capitalists. This view of industrial relations is a by-product of a theory of capitalist society and social change.

Marx argued that:
- Weakness and contradiction intrinsic to the capitalist system would result in revolution and the rise of socialism over capitalism.
- Capitalism would promote monopolies.
- Wages (costs to the capitalist) would be minimised to a subsistence level.
- Capitalists and workers would compete to win ground and establish their supremacy, constant win-lose struggles would be evident.

4. System Approach/Dunlop's Theory: John Dunlop put forth his theory on Industrial Labour Relations in 1950. According to Dunlop, the modern industrial relations system consists of three players:

(i) management organisations, i.e. employers,

(ii) workers and formal/informal ways they are organised, i.e. labour unions and

(iii) government agencies.

These players and their organisations are located within three environmental constraints: the market, distribution of power in society and technology. Within this environment, the players interact with each other, negotiate and use economic/political power in the process of determining rules that constitute the output of the industrial relations system. Dunlop's model identifies three key factors to be kept in mind while conducting an analysis of the management-labour relationship:

1. Environmental or external factors: economic, technological, political, legal and social forces that impact employment relationships.

2. Characteristics and interactions of the key players in the employment relationship: labour, management and the Government.
3. Rules that are derived from these interactions and which govern the employment relationship.

Effectively, industrial relations is the system which produces the rules of the workplace. Such rules are the result of interactions between the three players, i.e. the workers/unions, employers and associated organisations and the government. It believes that, management, labour and the government possess a shared ideology which helps to define their roles within the relationship and provide stability to the system.

Industrial conflicts are the results of several socio-economic, psychological and political factors. Various lines of thoughts have been expressed and approaches used to explain his complex phenomenon. One observer has stated, "An economist tries to interpret industrial conflict in terms of impersonal markets forces and laws of supply demand. To a politician, industrial conflict is a war of different ideologies – perhaps a class-war. To a psychologist, industrial conflict means the conflicting interests, aspirations, goals, motives and perceptions of different groups of individuals, operating within and reacting to a given socio-economic and political environment".

System Approach (by John Dunlop) focuses on:

(a) Participants in the process

The main participants are:
- Workers and their organisations
- Management and their representatives
- Government agencies

(b) Environmental forces (Context)

Three types of environments
- Technological characteristics of workplace
  (Technological sub-system)
- The market or economic constraints
  (Economic sub-system)
- The 'locus' and 'balance of power' existing in society
  (Political sub-system)

(c) Output

Output is the result of interaction of the parties/actors of the system which is manifested in the network of rules, country's labour policy and labour agreements etc. that facilitate a fair deal to workers.

System Approach studies the above factors and their inter-relationship. Factors are shown in the diagram below:

System approach studies influence of the various factors which have an impact on Industrial Relations. Changes in any may have a positive or negative effect.

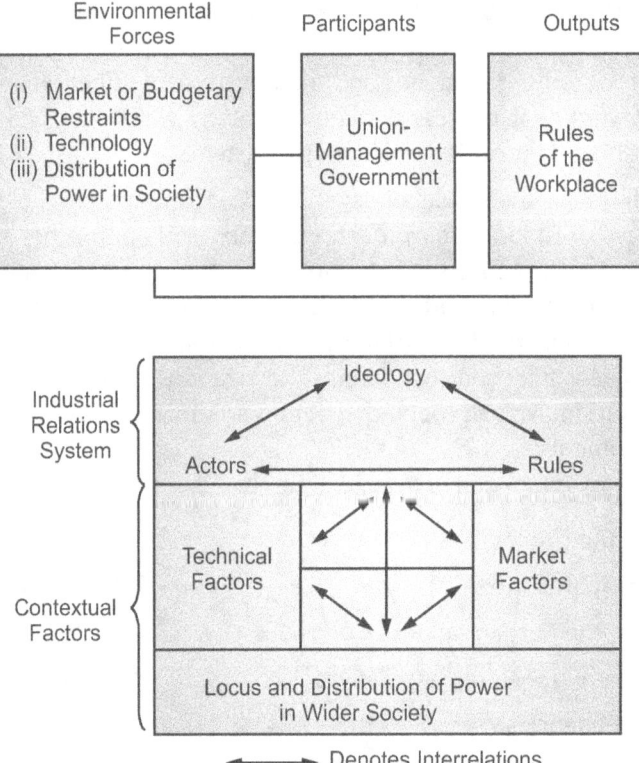

Fig. 5.2: System Approach studies the interaction between the various factors influencing Industrial Relations and their Interrelationship

Psychological Approach

The problems of IR have their origin in the perceptions of the management, unions and the workers. The conflicts between labour and management occur because every group negatively perceives the behaviour of the other i.e. even the honest intention of the other party so looked at with suspicion. The problem is further aggravated by various factors like the income, level of education, communication, values, beliefs, customs, goals of persons and groups, prestige, power, status, recognition, security etc are host factors both economic and non-economic which influence perceptions unions and management towards each other. Industrial peace is a result mainly of proper attitudes and perception of the two parties.

Sociological Approach

Industry is a social world in miniature. The management goals, workers' attitudes, perception of change in industry, are all, in turn, decided by broad social factors like the culture of the institutions, customs, structural changes, status-symbols, rationality, acceptance or resistance to change, tolerance etc. Industry is, thus inseparable from the society in which it functions. Through the main function of an industry is economic, its social consequences are also important such as urbanisation, social mobility, housing and transport problem in industrial areas, disintegration of family structure, stress and strain, etc. As industries develop, a new industrial-cum-social pattern emerges, which provides general new relationships, institutions and behavioural pattern and new techniques of handling human resources. These do influence the development of industrial relations.

Human Relations Approach

Human resources are made up of living human beings. They want freedom of speech, of thought of expression, of movement, etc. When employers treat them as inanimate objects, encroach on their expectations, throat-cuts, conflicts and tensions arise. In fact major problems in industrial relations arise out of a tension which is created because of the employer's pressures and workers' reactions, protests and resistance to these pressures through protective mechanisms in the form of workers' organisation, associations and trade unions.

Through tension is more direct in work place; gradually it extends to the whole industry and sometimes affects the entire economy of the country. Therefore, the management must realise that efforts are made to set right the situation. Services of specialists in Behavioural Sciences (namely, psychologists, industrial engineers, human relations expert and personnel managers) are used to deal with such related problems. Assistance is also taken from economists, anthropologists, psychiatrists, pedagogists, etc. In resolving conflicts, understanding of human behavior – both individual and groups – is a pre-requisite for the employers, the union leaders and the government – more so for the management. Conflicts cannot be resolved unless the management must learn and know what the basic what the basic needs of men are and how they can be motivated to work effectively.

It has now been increasingly recognised that much can be gained by the managers and the worker, if they understand and apply the techniques of human relations approaches to industrial relations. The workers are likely to attain greater job satisfaction, develop greater involvement in their work and achieve a measure of identification of their objectives with the objectives of the organisation; the manager, on their part, would develop greater insight and effectiveness in their work.

Gandhian Approach

Gandhiji can be called one of the greatest labour leaders of modern India. His approach to labour problems was completely new and refreshingly human. He held definite views regarding fixation and regulation of wages, organisation and functions of trade unions, necessity and desirability of collective bargaining, use and abuse of strikes, labour indiscipline, workers participation in management, conditions of work and living, and duties of workers.

Gandhiji had immense faith in the goodness of man and he believed that many of the evils of the modern world have been brought about by wrong systems and not by wrong individuals. He insisted on recognising each individual worker as a human being. He believed in non-violent communism, going so far as to say that "if communism comes without any violence, it would be welcome."

Gandhiji laid down certain conditions for a successful strike. These are: (a) the cause of the strike must be just and there should be no strike without a grievance; (b) there should be no violence; and (c) non-strikers or "blacklegs" should never be molested.

He was not against strikes but pleaded that they should be the last weapon in the armoury of industrial workers and hence should not be resorted to unless all peaceful and constitutional methods of negotiations, conciliation and arbitration are exhausted.

His concept of trusteeship is a significant contribution in the sphere of industrial relations. According to him, employers should not regard themselves as sole owners of mills and factories of which they may be the legal owners. They should regard themselves only as trustees, or co-owners. He also appealed to the workers to behave as trustees, not to regard the mill and machinery as belonging to the exploiting agents but to regard them as their own, protect them and put to the best use they can. In short, the theory of trusteeship is based on the view that all forms of property and human accomplishments are gifts of nature and as such, they belong not to any one individual but to society. Thus, the trusteeship system is totally different from other contemporary labour relations systems. It aimed at achieving economic equality and the material advancement of the "have-nots" in a capitalist society by non-violent means.

Gandhiji realised that relations between labour and management can either be a powerful stimulus to economic and social progress or an important factor in economic and social stagnation. According to him, industrial peace was an essential condition not only for the growth and development of the industry itself, but also in a great measure, for the improvement in the conditions of work and wages. At the same time, he not only endorsed the workers' right to adopt the method of collective bargaining but also actively supported it. He advocated voluntary arbitration and mutual settlement of disputes. He also pleaded for perfect understanding between capital and labour, mutual respect, recognition of equality, and strong labour organisation as the essential factors for happy and constructive industrial relations. For him, means and ends are equally important.

Mahatma Gandhi's views on industrial relations are based on his fundamental principles of:
- Truth, Non-violence, Non-possession, Non co-operation (Satyagarah), trusteeship.
- Workers' right to strike.
- Concept of equality.
- Trusteeship.
- There is no room for conflict of interests between the capitalist and the labourers.
- Workers should have knowledge of the transactions of the organisation.
- Job enrichment.
- Actively supported collective bargaining.
- Advocated Voluntary Arbitration.

Gandhiji expected from workers
- Awakening
- Nurturing faith in their moral strength
- Awareness of its existence
- Unity

Gandhiji advocated
- Demands should be reasonable and through collective action.
- Avoid strikes as far as possible.
- Avoid formation of unions in philanthropic organisations.
- Strikes should be the last resort only.
- In case of organising a strike, workers should remain peaceful and non-violent.

Human Resource Management Approach

The term, human resource management (HRM) in used increasingly in the literature of personnel/industrial relations. The term has been applied to a diverse range of management strategies and, indeed, sometimes used simply as a more modern, and therefore more acceptable, term for personnel or industrial relations management.

Some of the components of HRM are
- Human resource organisation
- Human resource planning
- Human resource system
- Human resource development

- Human resource relationships
- Human resource utilisation
- Human resource accounting
- Human resource audit.

This approach emphasises individualism and the direct relationship between management and its employees. Quite clearly, therefore, it questions the collective regulation basis of traditional industrial relations.

5.1.6 Trade Unions and its Role in IR

Trade unions are formed to protect and promote the interests of their members. Their primary function is to protect the interests of workers against discrimination and unfair labour practices.

A trade union is an organisation of workers, who unite to achieve common goals like, better wages, working conditions and work hours. Trade unions evolved to protect workers' rights against management's atrocities. Workers joined unions as they offered protection. It protected their economic, social and political interests and gave them a sense of belonging. In the earlier times, in the absence of a welfare state, it offered help to its members and later these unions worked to counteract the greater economic strength of employers, to provide legal and other support to members who believe they suffer injustices, and to campaign for reform. Today, a labour or trade union through its leadership, bargains with the employer on behalf of union members and negotiates labour contracts with the employers. This may include the negotiation of wages, work rules, complaint procedures, rules governing hiring, firing and promotion of workers, benefits, workplace safety and policies. The agreements negotiated by the union leaders are binding on the rank and file members and the employer and in some cases even on other non-member workers.

The rapid expansion of industrial society in the 1700s brought women, children, rural workers and immigrants into the workforce. These workers who were unskilled or semi-skilled organised themselves to protect their rights and this is believed to be the true beginning of trade unions.

Objectives of Trade Unions

The main objective of trade unions is to promote the interests of its members and protect them against discrimination and unfair labour practices. Trade unions are formed to achieve the following objectives:

- **Representation:** Trade unions represent individual workers when they have a problem at work. If an employee feels he is being unfairly treated, he can ask the union representative to help sort out the difficulty with the manager or employer. Unions also offer their members legal representation. Normally this is to help people get financial compensation for work-related injuries or to assist people who have to take their employer to court.

- **Negotiation:** When union representatives discuss the issues which affect the workforce of an organisation with its management, it is called negotiation. Many a times there is a difference of opinion between the management and union members. This is when trade unions step in and help find a solution to these differences by negotiating with the employers. Pay, working hours, holidays and changes to working practices are the sorts of issues that are negotiated. When there is a formal agreement between the union and the company, which states that the union has the right to negotiate with the employer, these unions are said to be recognised for collective bargaining purposes.
- **Voice in Decisions Affecting Workers:** The economic security of employees is determined not only by the level of wages and duration of their employment, but also by the management's personal policies which include selection of employees for lay offs, retrenchment, promotion and transfer. These policies directly affect workers. The evaluation criteria for such decisions may, sometimes, not be fair. Intervention of unions in such decisions is a means for workers to have their say in the decision making and thus safeguard their interests.
- **Member Services:** In the last few years, trade unions have increased the range of services they offer their members. These include:
- **Education and training:** Most unions run training courses for their members on employment rights, health, safety and other issues. Some unions also help members who have left school with little education by offering courses on basic skills and courses leading to professional qualifications.
- **Legal assistance:** As well as offering legal advice on employment issues, some unions give help with personal matters, like housing and debt.
- **Financial discounts:** People can get discounts on mortgages, insurance and loans from unions.
- **Welfare benefits:** One of the earliest functions of trade unions was to look after members who go through hard times. Some of the older unions offer financial help to their members when they are sick or unemployed.

Functions of Trade Unions

To achieve its objectives, a trade union has to carry out certain functions. These functions can be classified as:

- **Militant Functions:** Ensuring adequate wages, better working conditions and better treatment from employers are some of the objectives of trade unions. When negotiations and collective bargaining fail to achieve these objectives, trade unions turn militant and put up a fight with the management in the form of go-slows, strikes, boycotts, gheraos etc. These militant methods are used by trade unions to
    (i) achieve higher wages and better working conditions,
    (ii) raise the status of workers as a part of industry and
    (iii) protect labour against victimisation and injustice.

- **Fraternal Functions:** Other objectives of trade unions include rendering help to its members in times of need and improving their efficiency. Trade unions try to encourage a spirit of cooperation and promote friendly industrial relations and undertake many welfare measures for their members. These are its fraternal functions and depend on the availability of funds, which the unions raise by subscription from its members and donations from outsiders, and also on their competent and enlightened leadership. Some of these fraternal functions are:
    (i) to take up welfare measures like school for the education of children, library, reading-rooms, in-door and out-door games, and other recreational facilities, legal aid, publication of journals, further education for workers, loans and financial help, etc. This helps in improving the morale and self confidence of workers.
    (ii) to encourage sincerity and discipline among workers.
    (iii) to provide opportunities for promotion and growth.
    (iv) to protect women workers against discrimination.

Importance of Trade Unions

Industrial peace is a pre-requisite for an industry to flourish. A strong and recognised union is essential for industrial peace. Trade unions help in accelerating the pace of economic development in many ways, some of which are enlisted below:
- by helping in the recruitment and selection of workers.
- by inculcating discipline among the workforce.
- by enabling settlement of industrial disputes in a rational manner.
- by helping social adjustments. Workers have to adjust themselves to the new working conditions, the new rules and policies. Workers coming from different backgrounds may become disorganised, unsatisfied and frustrated. Unions help them in such adjustment.

Trade unions also:
- promote and maintain national integration by reducing the number of industrial disputes.
- incorporate a sense of corporate social responsibility in workers.
- achieve industrial peace.

Reasons Why Workers Join Trade Unions
1. **Greater Bargaining Power:** As compared to an employer an individual employee possesses very little bargaining power. When he joins a union, he joins a collective force of the employees, who can take concerted action against an employer, if the employer is unreasonable. The threat or actuality of a strike by a union is a powerful tool that often causes the employer to accept the demands of the workers for better conditions of employment.

2. **Minimises Discrimination:** The decisions regarding pay, work, transfer, promotion, etc. are highly subjective in nature. The personal relationships existing between the supervisor and each of his subordinates may influence the management. Thus, there is a chance that favouritism and discrimination can occur. A trade union can compel the management to formulate personnel policies that press for equality of treatment to the workers. All the labour decisions of the management are under close scrutiny of the labour union. This has the effect of minimising favouritism and discrimination.

3. **Sense of Security:** Unions give the employees a sense of security as they believe that it is an effective way to secure adequate protection from various types of hazards and income insecurities, such as accident, injury, illness, unemployment, etc. The trade unions secure retirement benefits of the workers and compel the management to invest in welfare services for the benefit of the workers.

4. **Sense of Participation:** By joining trade unions employees can participate in management of matters affecting their interests. They can influence the decisions that are taken as a result of collective bargaining between the union and the management.

5. **Sense of Belonging:** Many employees join a union because their co-workers are members of the union. At times, an employee joins a union under group pressure and to be accepted by the other employees. Also, belonging to a union gives the employees an added stature and respect, in the eyes of their fellow workers. By being a member of the union they have the opportunity to discuss their problems with the trade union leaders.

6. **Platform for Self-expression:** The desire for self-expression is a fundamental human drive for most people. All of us wish to share our feelings, ideas and opinions with others. Similarly the workers also want the management to listen to them. A trade union provides a forum where the feelings, ideas and opinions of the workers can be discussed. It acts as a mediator and conveys the feelings, ideas, opinions and complaints of the workers to the management. The collective voice of the workers is given due consideration by the management, when taking policy decisions.

7. **Betterment of Relationships:** Employees feel that unions can help facilitate and maintain good employer-employee relations. Unions help in betterment of industrial relations among management and workers by solving the problems peacefully.

Role of Trade Unions in IR

The important factors that make the employees join a union are as follows:

1. **Greater Bargaining Power:** The individual employee possesses very little bargaining power as compared to that of his employer. If he is not satisfied with the wage and other conditions of employment, he can leave the job. It is not practicable to continually resign from one job after another when he is dissatisfied. This imposes a

great financial and emotional burden upon the worker. The better course for him is to join a union that can take concerted action against the employer. The threat or actuality of a strike by a union is a powerful tool that often causes the employer to accept the demands of the workers for better conditions of employment.

2. **Minimise Discrimination:** The decisions regarding pay, work, transfer, promotion, etc. are highly subjective in nature. The personal relationships existing between the supervisor and each of his subordinates may influence the management. Thus, there are chances of favouritisms and discriminations. A trade union can compel the management to formulate personnel policies that press for equality of treatment to the workers. All the labour decisions of the management are under close scrutiny of the labour union. This has the effect of minimising favouritism and discrimination.

3. **Sense of Security:** The employees may join the unions because of their belief that it is an effective way to secure adequate protection from various types of hazards and income insecurity such as accident, injury, illness, unemployment, etc. The trade union secure retirement benefits of the workers and compel the management to invest in welfare services for the benefit of the workers.

4. **Sense of Participation:** The employees can participate in management of matters affecting their interests only if they join trade unions. They can influence the decisions that are taken as a result of collective bargaining between the union and the management.

5. **Sense of Belongingness:** Many employees join a union because their co-workers are the members of the union. At times, an employee joins a union under group pressure; if he does not, he often has a very difficult time at work. On the other hand, those who are members of a union feel that they gain respect in the eyes of their fellow workers. They can also discuss their problem with' the trade union leaders.

6. **Platform for Self Expression:** The desire for self-expression is a fundamental human drive for most people. All of us wish to share our feelings, ideas and opinions with others. Similarly the workers also want the management to listen to them. A trade union provides such a forum where the feelings, ideas and opinions of the workers could be discussed. It can also transmit the feelings, ideas, opinions and complaints of the workers to the management. The collective voice of the workers is heard by the management and gives due consideration while taking policy decisions by the management.

7. **Betterment of relationships:** Another reason for employees joining unions is that employees feel that unions can fulfil the important need for adequate machinery for proper maintenance of employer-employee relations. Unions help in betterment of industrial relations among management and workers by solving the problems peacefully.

5.2 Dispute Settlement

State intervention in industrial relations is essentially a modern development with the emergence of the concept of welfare states, new ideas of social philosophy, national economy and social justice sprang up with the result that industrial relations no longer remains the concern of labour and management alone. In India we have realised that for general progress to be assured, economic progress was a must. In no country is a complete laissez faire attitude now adopted in the matter of labour management relations.

An industrial dispute or conflict can be defined as *a withdrawal from work by a group of employees, or a refusal by an employer to allow workers to work.* Conflict refers to disputes, disagreements or dissatisfaction between individuals and/or groups. A dispute is a disagreement.

Industrial disputes are costly and damaging to both, the business and the employees. Grievances held by individual employees or groups of workers can lead to potentially heavy costs if they develop into litigation or industrial action. Ideally, an organisation's culture and procedures should seek to avoid or resolve any potential conflict. Good employee relations, especially communications, are the key to creating an environment that is free of conflict. However, it's not always possible to prevent industrial disputes from arising. Some of the common causes for industrial disputes are wage demands, working conditions, management policy, political goals and social issues. Absenteeism, sabotage, staff turnover, lockouts, pickets, strikes, bans and work-to-rule are some of the forms which industrial conflicts can take.

Conciliation, arbitration, grievance procedures, negotiation, mediation, common law action, business/division closure are some of the dispute resolution processes used by firms for managing disputes.

Causes of Industrial Disputes

The causes of industrial disputes can be broadly classified into two categories:

- **Economic:** Economic issues include issues related to compensation like wages, bonus, allowances, and conditions for work, working hours, leave and holidays without pay, unjust layoffs and retrenchments.

- **Non-economic causes:** The non-economic factors include victimisation of workers, ill treatment by staff members, sympathetic strikes, political factors, indiscipline etc.

1. **Wages and Allowances:** As the cost of living index increases, workers tend to bargain for higher wages to meet the rising cost of living index and to increase their standards of living. It refers to a demand by employees for an increase in their wage rate or changes to the way in which their wages are calculated or determined. Wage demands may relate to pay rates that need to be adjusted to compensate employees in times of inflationary pressures when interest rates become higher.

In India, in 2002, 21.4% of disputes were caused by demands for higher wages and allowances. This percentage was 20.4% during 2003 and during 2004 increased up to 26.2%. In 2005, wages and allowances accounted for 21.8% of disputes.

2. **Management Policies and Retrenchment:** Disputes often result due to inadequate consultation by management with their employees. Disputes over changes that management wishes to implement often cause industrial conflict. Controversial management policies could include terms and conditions of employment, new awards and agreements, award restructuring, outsourcing and technology acquisitions and structural changes. Retrenchment and lay-offs which are also a part of management policy is also a major contributing factor for industrial conflict.

   During the year 2002, disputes caused by management policies other than retrenchment and layoffs were 14.1% while those caused by retrenchment and layoffs were 2.2% and 0.4% respectively. In 2003, a similar trend could be seen, wherein 11.2% of the disputes were caused by management policies other than retrenchment and layoffs, while 2.4% and 0.6% of disputes were caused by retrenchment and layoffs. In year 2005, only 9.6% of the disputes were caused by management policies other than retrenchment and layoffs, and only 0.4% was caused by retrenchment.

3. **Indiscipline and Violence:** Industrial disputes caused by indiscipline have shown an increasing trend over the years. In 2002, 29.9% of disputes were caused because of indiscipline, which rose up to 36.9% in 2003. Similarly, in 2004 and 2005, 40.4% and 41.6% of disputes were caused due to indiscipline respectively.

   During the year 2003, indiscipline accounted for the highest percentage (36.9%) of the total time-loss of all disputes. This was followed by other causes like wages and allowance and management policies with 20.4% and 11.2% respectively. A similar trend was observed in 2004 where indiscipline accounted for 40.4% of disputes.

4. **Bonus:** Bonus has always been an important factor in starting of industrial disputes. 6.7% of the disputes were because of bonus in 2002 and 2003 as compared to 3.5% and 3.6% in 2004 and 2005 respectively.

5. **Working Conditions:** Working conditions include factors like leave entitlements, pensions, compensation, working hours and safety at the workplace. However, leave and working hours have not been important motivating factors to initiate industrial disputes. During 2002, 0.5% of the disputes were because of leave and hours of work while this percentage increased to 1% in 2003. During 2004, only 0.4% of the disputes were because of leaves and working hours.

6. **Political Goals and Social Issues:** This usually refers to non-industrial issues, but involves wider issues directed at persons or situations rather than those relating to the employer-employee relationship. Employee unions, federations and associations will often undertake actions that are unrelated to the basic wages and conditions of their members.

7. **Miscellaneous:** The miscellaneous factors include:
   (a) Inter/Intra Union Rivalry.
   (b) Charter of Demands.
   (c) Work Load.
   (d) Standing orders/rules/service conditions/safety measures.
   (e) Non-implementation of agreements and awards etc.

Nature of Industrial Disputes

The nature of conflict can be cooperative or competitive. The theory of *cooperative conflict* suggests that employers and employees have shared goals; however conflicts arise mainly because both parties have different views on the manner in which they need to work to achieve this goal. The theory of *competitive conflict* indicates that labour and management have opposing goals and interests. There is a high degree of mistrust and a propensity for communication channels to break down, leading to overt conflict. Margerison's behavioural analysis of conflict generation has suggested that there are three levels of conflict. Conflict may occur at the,

(a) **Distributive level:** Conflict at the distributive level suggests that there is discontent regarding the allocation of economic rewards at the workplace. e.g. Who gets what reward for performing a certain role in the organisation? At this level of conflict, the outcome could be a strike or lock out.

(b) **Structural level:** At the structural level, conflict may arise because the organisation is so poorly designed that it is unable to adapt to changes in the business environment. An often observed example is that of a subordinate receiving two conflicting directives from two superiors. As a result, there are demarcation disputes and authority is challenged.

(c) **Human relations level:** Conflict at the human relations level is the most common and recognisable among the three. At this level, conflict may occur due to differing social orientations among individuals, groups or labour and management. The outcome of this is usually individual alienation and group strain.

Industrial disputes can be of two kinds:

(i) **Overt** i.e. the action taken is highly visible and a physical response. It is aimed at gaining maximum awareness and is well organised by unions. It can take the form of lockouts, pickets, strikes, bans, work-to-rule.

(ii) **Covert** i.e. the action taken is a silent and unseen response. It is not openly acknowledged or displayed and is carried out without any organisation. Absenteeism, sabotage and high staff turnover are some of the forms it takes.

Overt Action

- **Lockouts:** This is an action taken by employers wherein employees are not allowed to enter the factory or place of work, i.e. they are locked out of their work place unless they agree to follow management orders and work as directed. It is declared by employers to put pressure on their workers. Thus, a lockout is employers' weapon while a strike is raised on part of employees. According to the Industrial Disputes Act 1947, a lock-out means *the temporary closing of a place of employment or the suspension of work or the refusal by an employer to continue to employ any number of persons employed by him.*

Characteristics of Lockouts

Following are the important characteristics of lock-out:

1. Lock-out is an act of management. It is generally intended to put some pressure on the workers in order to make them agree to the terms of work of their employer.
2. Mere suspension of work (e.g. on account of shortage of raw materials, coal, supply of water etc.) is not lock-out.
3. Lock-out indicates the temporary closure of the place of business and not the closure of the business itself.
4. Lock-out is generally caused by strike, fear of disorder, fear of destruction of the properties of the firm, company etc. Most of these causes are the results of industrial disputes.
5. Lock-out indicates the temporary closing of a place of employment, or the suspension of work or the refusal by an employer to continue to employ any number of persons employed by him.

- **Picketing:** Picketing is when striking workers or a union gather outside the workplace and form a line to prevent entry of other employees, contract labour or suppliers to the workplace, i.e. when workers are dissuaded from work by stationing certain men at the factory gates. Picketing is legal if it does not involve any violence. Pickets are workers who are on strike that stand at the entrance to their workplace. It is basically a method of drawing public attention towards the fact that there is a dispute between the management and employees, to stop or persuade workers not to go to work, to tell the public about the strike and to persuade workers to take their union's side.

- **Strikes:** A strike is a withdrawal of labour from production. Strikes are the most overt form of industrial action and aim to attract publicity and support for the employees' case. Strikes occur when employees collectively cease to work in order to enforce a demand or express a grievance.

According to the Industrial Disputes Act 1947, a strike is *"a cessation of work by a body of persons employed in an industry acting in combination; or a concerted refusal of any number of persons who are or have been so employed to continue to work or to accept employment; or a refusal under a common understanding of any number of such persons to continue to work or to accept employment"*. This definition throws light on a few aspects of a strike. Firstly, a strike is a referred to as stoppage of work by a group of workers employed in a particular industry. Secondly, it also includes the refusal of a number of employees to continue work under their employer.

Types of Strikes

- **Economic Strike:** This type of strike is undertaken by workers to enforce their economic demands such as wages and bonus. In these kinds of strikes, workers ask for increase in wages, allowances like travelling allowance, house rent allowance, dearness allowance, bonus and other facilities such as increase in privilege leave and casual leave.

- **Sympathetic Strike:** When workers of one unit or industry go on strike in sympathy with workers of another unit or industry who are already on strike, it is called a sympathetic strike. The members of other unions involve themselves in a strike to support or express their sympathy with the members of unions who are on strike in other undertakings. E.g. the workers of sugar industry may go on strike in sympathy with their fellow workers of the textile industry who may already be on strike.

- **General Strike:** It means a strike by members of all or most of the unions in a region or an industry. The strike may involve all the workers in a particular region of industry to push for demands which are common to all the workers. These strikes are usually intended to create political pressure on the ruling government, rather than on any one employer. It may also be an extension of the sympathetic strike to express generalised protest by the workers.

- **Sit down Strike:** These strikes are also known as 'pen down' or 'tool down' strike. In this kind of a strike, workers do not absent themselves from their place of work. They keep a control over production facilities, but do not work. Workers show up at their place of employment, but they refuse to work. They however also refuse to leave, which makes it very difficult for an employer to defy the union and take over the workers' places. E.g. In June 1998, all the Municipal Corporation employees in Punjab observed a pen down strike to protest against the non-acceptance of their demands by the state government.

- **Slow Down Strike:** Employees remain on their jobs under this type of strike. They do not stop work, but restrict the rate of output in an organised manner. They adopt go-slow tactics to put pressure on the employers.

- **Sick-out (or sick-in):** In this strike, all or a significant number of union members call in sick on the same day. They don't break any rules; they all just use the sick leave that is allotted to them on a particular day. However, the sudden absence of so many employees, all on one particular day can show the employer just what it would be like if they really went on strike.

- **Wild cat strikes:** These strikes are conducted by workers or employees without the authority and consent of unions. E.g. In 2004, a significant number of advocates went on a wildcat strike at the City Civil Court premises in Bangaluru. They were protesting against some remarks allegedly made against them by an Assistant Commissioner.

- **Gherao: Gherao** in Hindi means to surround. It denotes a collective action initiated by a group of workers under which members of the management are prohibited from leaving the industrial establishment premises by workers who block the exit gates by forming human barricades. The workers can also gherao members of the management such that they are forced to stay within their cabins. Gheraos can often take a violent turn. The main object of gherao is to inflict physical and mental torture to the person being gheraoed and hence this weapon disturbs the industrial peace to a great extent.

- **Bans:** When employees refuse to perform tasks that are not specified in their employment contract, such as overtime.

- **Work-to-Rule:** Working to rule is similar to a work ban and workers perform only those tasks that are contained in their employment contract or award and strictly follow the terms of their employment contract or award.

Covert Action

- **Absenteeism:** Industrial disputes wherein employees views are not taken into consideration can lead to discontent. This discontent can take the form of absenteeism, i.e. the employees may not show up at work, and absent themselves. Employees may undertake mass absenteeism with many being off at the same time, or rotational absenteeism where they roster who will be taking time off. Action of this sort disrupts business but it does not stop the employee's income (as he is entitled sick leave, casual leave, etc), and hence it is favoured by some employees.

- **Sabotage:** Deliberately damaging physical items and causing vandalism in the workplace is called sabotage and is a form of action taken by employees during industrial disputes. Damage is done by employees to either the product or in the production of the product. Employees damage either the product or damage the processes involved in the production of the product. This kind of action by the employees can bring disrepute or even destroy a firm's image.

- **Staff Turnover:** High voluntary labour turnover (resignation) rates are often linked with absenteeism rates as indicators of conflict and dissatisfaction among employees.

5.2.1 Dispute Settlement

Dispute settlement is the process of resolving disputes between parties.

Methods of dispute resolution include:
- Lawsuits (litigation)
- Arbitration
- Collaborative law
- Mediation
- Conciliation
- Many types of negotiation
- Facilitation

Dispute resolution processes fall into two major types:

1. Adjudicative processes, such as litigation or arbitration, in which a judge, jury or arbitrator determines the outcome.
2. Consensual processes, such as collaborative law, mediation, conciliation, or negotiation, in which the parties attempt to reach agreement

5.2.2 Machinery to Dispute Settlement

Prevention of industrial disputes:

The preventive machinery has been set up with a view to creating harmonious relations between labour and management so that disputes do not arise. It comprises the following measures:

(a) Schemes of workers' participation in management such as works committees, joint management councils and shop councils and joint councils.

(b) Collective bargaining.

(c) Tripartite bodies

(d) Code of discipline.

(e) Standing orders.

Settlement of Industrial Disputes (Judicial Machinery)

Preventive measures seek to create an environment where industrial disputes do not arise. Should they, however, arise, every effort is required to be made to settle them as early as possible so that they do not lead to work stoppage. The machinery for the settlement of industrial disputes has been provided under the Industrial Disputes Act, 1947.

This machinery comprises:

(a) Conciliation,

(b) Arbitration, and

(c) Adjudication.

Grievance Procedure

> *Grievance procedure is a formal communication between an employee and the management designed for the settlement of a grievance.*

The grievance procedures differ from organisation to organisation. Grievance procedures fall into two categories:

1. Open door policy
2. Step-ladder policy

Open door policy: Under this policy, the aggrieved employee is free to meet the top executives of the organisation and get his grievances redressed. Such a policy works well only in small organisations.

However, in bigger organisations, top management executives are usually busy with other concerned matters of the company. Moreover, it is believed that open door policy is suitable for executives; operational employees may feel intimidated to go to the top management.

Step ladder policy: Under this policy, the aggrieved employee has to follow a step by step procedure for getting his grievance redressed. In this procedure, whenever an employee is confronted with a grievance, he presents his problem to his immediate supervisor.

If the employee is not satisfied with the superior's decision, then he discusses his grievance with the departmental head. The departmental head then discusses the problem with joint grievance committees to find a solution.

However, if the committee also fails to redress the grievance, then it may be referred to chief executive. If the chief executive also fails to redress the grievance, then such a grievance is referred to voluntary arbitration where the award of arbitrator is binding on both the parties.

Grievance procedure can be defined as, *"a formal communication between an employee and the management designed for the settlement of a grievance"*. We can view the grievance procedure as a tool which:

- Enables solving of problems and settling of disputes.
- Allows the management to detect any flaws in the working conditions or in labour relations and gives them an opportunity to correct the same.
- Provides a channel via which any employee can present his grievance.

- Reassures an employee that his grievance will be addressed promptly and systematically in a dispassionate and detached manner.
- Reassures the employee that he will not be victimised for the complaint.
- Allows a worker to feel cared for and valued as he is allowed to have his say regarding his feelings of dissatisfaction with his job, working conditions or with the management.
- Serves as a check on the arbitrary action of the management, as supervisors are aware that employees are empowered to take their protest to higher management.

Pre-requisites of a Grievance Procedure

For a grievance procedure to be reliable and effective, it should have certain pre-requisites. These are:

(a) **Conformity with statutory provisions:** Due consideration must be given to the prevailing legislation while designing the grievance handling procedure.

(b) **Unambiguity:** Every aspect of the grievance handling procedure should be clear and unambiguous. All employees should know whom to approach first when they have a grievance, whether the complaint should be written or oral, the maximum time in which the redressal is assured, etc. The redressing official should also know the limits within which he can take the required action.

(c) **Simplicity:** The grievance handling procedure should be simple and short. If the procedure is complicated it may discourage employees and they may fail to make use of it in a proper manner.

(d) **Promptness:** The grievance of the employee should be promptly handled and necessary action must be taken immediately. This is good for both the employee and, because if the wrong doer is punished late, it may affect the morale of other employees as well.

(e) **Training:** The supervisors and the union representatives should be properly trained in all aspects of grievance handling beforehand or else it will complicate the problem.

(f) **Follow up:** The Personnel Department should keep track of the effectiveness and the functioning of grievance handling procedure and make necessary changes to improve it from time to time.

Basic Elements of a Grievance Redressal Procedure

The basic elements of a grievance redressal procedure are:

(i) The existence of reliable channels through which a grievance may pass for redressal, especially if the previous stage or channel has been found to be inadequate, unsatisfactory or unacceptable.

(ii) The procedure should be simple, definite and prompt, for any complexity, ambiguousness or delay, may lead to the aggrieved and distressed employee getting increasingly more dissatisfied.

(iii) The steps in handling a grievance should be clearly defined. These should comprise:

   (a) Receiving and defining the nature of the grievance.

   (b) Getting all the relevant information, about the grievance from all parties and then classifying the information as facts, data, opinions, etc.

   (c) Analysing the facts, after taking into consideration the economic, social, psychological and legal issues involved in them.

   (d) Developing alternative solutions to the problem and then selecting the best one.

   (e) Taking an appropriate decision after a careful reconsideration of all the facts.

   (f) Communicating the decisions to the aggrieved employee.

(iv) The decision should be followed-up, such that the reaction to the decision is known. This would help determine whether the issue has been closed or not.

(v) Implementing the solution, if it has been found acceptable by all parties involved.

Grievance procedures differ from organisation to organisation. There are two major policies of which one is usually used. These are:

1. **Open door policy:** Under this policy, the aggrieved employee is free to meet the top executives of the organisation and get his grievances redressed. Such a policy is effective only in small organisations. In bigger organisations, however, top management do not handle grievance procedures as they are extremely busy sorting out the more intricate matters concerning the company. Moreover, it is believed that open door policy is suitable for executives but not for operational employees as they may feel shy to go to top management with their complaints.

2. **Step ladder policy:** Under this policy, an aggrieved employee has to follow a step by step procedure for getting his grievance redressed. In this procedure, whenever an employee has a grievance, he goes to his immediate supervisor, with the problem. If the employee is not satisfied with his superior's decision he can approach the departmental head with the grievance. The departmental head, then, discusses the problem with joint grievance committees to find a solution. However, if the committee also fails to redress the grievance, it can be referred to the chief executive. If the grievance is not satisfactorily redressed by the chief executive, then such a grievance is referred to voluntary arbitration where the award of arbitrator is binding on both the parties.

Chart 1: Three-Step Grievance Procedure

Step	Labour Representative	Management Representative
1.	Shop steward/supervisor and aggrieved employee	Foreman
2.	Shop committee	General Manager
3.	Arbitration by an impartial third party	

Chart 2: Four-Step Grievance Procedure

Step	Labour Representative	Management Representative
1.	Steward/supervisor and aggrieved employee	Foreman
2.	Shop committee	Personnel Manager
3.	Local union officers	President
4.	Arbitration by an impartial third party	

Chart 3: Five-Step Grievance Procedure

Step	Labour Representative	Management Representative
1.	Union steward/supervisor or employee	Employee's immediate supervisor
2.	Chief steward/supervisor or business agent	Superintendent or Industrial Relations Officer
3.	Company grievance committee	Industrial Relations Director/or Plant Manager
4.	Regional or distinct representatives of the Union	Top corporate management
5.	Arbitration by an impartial third party	

Grievance Procedure Steps in Unionised Organisations

In a unionised organisation, the operation of the grievance procedure may contain the following steps:

Step 1: The aggrieved employee verbally explains his grievance to his immediate supervisor in a conference or a discussion specially arranged for the purpose. He may or may not be accompanied by his shop steward. The grievance can be settled if the supervisor has been properly trained for the purpose and if he adheres strictly to a basic problem-solving method.

Step 2: If the supervisor is unable to settle the grievance, the case is sent to a higher level manager. The manager is informed about the situation and the nature of action suggested to which the employee objects. The higher level manager is generally the chief business manager, a superintendent or an Industrial Relations Officer who checks the grievance and gives his decision on the matter.

Step 3: If the matter is not solved by the supervisor and the higher level manager, the matter is submitted to the Grievance Committee. This committee is composed of some fellow employees, the shop steward or a combination of union and management representatives. It evaluates the situation and the records and then suggests a possible solution. It may call upon the grievant to accept the employer's proposed settlement. It may advise him that the trade union will not press for anything more than what has already been suggested. In some cases, it may recommend that the issue be submitted for arbitration.

Step 4: If the decision or suggestion of the Grievance Committee is not accepted by the grievant, he may approach the management or corporate executive.

Step 5: The final step is taken when the grievance is referred to an arbitrator who is acceptable to the employee as well as the management. They may agree beforehand that the arbitrator's award will be final and binding on both the parties. In practice, the grievance procedure differs from company to company. Some contain simple two-step procedures; others may have as many as six or more steps.

Grievance Procedure in Indian Industry

The 15th session of Indian Labour Conference which was held in 1957, emphasised the need of an established grievance procedure for the country which would be acceptable to unions as well as to management. In the 16th session of Indian Labour Conference, a model for grievance procedure was drawn up. This model helps in creation of grievance machinery. According to it, workers' representatives are to be elected for a department or their union is to nominate them. Management has to specify the persons in each department who are to be approached first and the departmental heads who are supposed to be approached in the second step. The Model Grievance Procedure specifies the details of all the steps that are to be followed while redressing grievances. These steps are:

Step 1: In the first step the grievance is to be submitted to departmental representative, who is a representative of management. He has to give his answer within 48 hours.

Step 2: If the departmental representative fails to provide a solution, the aggrieved employee can take his grievance to head of the department, who has to give his decision within 3 days.

Step 3: If the aggrieved employee is not satisfied with the decision of the departmental head, he can take the grievance to the Grievance Committee. The Grievance Committee makes its recommendations to the manager within 7 days in the form of a report. The final decision of the management on the report of Grievance Committee must be communicated to the aggrieved employee within three days of the receipt of report. An appeal for revision of final decision can be made by the worker if he is not satisfied with it. The management must communicate its decision to the worker within 7 days.

Step 4: If the grievance still remains unsettled, the case may be referred to voluntary arbitration.

Successful Grievance Handling Procedures

For grievance procedures to be successful, the attitude, the procedure, the training, etc. need to be evolved and positive. Given below are some points which help in making the procedure successful.

(a) The helpful attitude and support of the management.

(b) Belief on the part of all concerned in the utility of the procedure.

(c) Introduction of the procedure with the agreement of the employees' representative and their trade unions.

(d) A simple, fair, easily understandable and prompt grievance handling procedure which has a time limit for each step.

(e) Codification of the company's policies, rules and practices and the availability of copies at different management levels, involved in the handling of grievance redressal procedures.

(f) Delegation of appropriate authority so that action may be taken at all the levels of the management.

(g) The functioning of the personnel department in an advisory capacity at all the levels of the management.

(h) A fact-oriented, instead of an employee-oriented discussion of grievances.

(i) Respect for the decision taken at each level of the management.

(j) Adequate publicity given to the procedure and its achievements in the company.

(k) A periodic review of the working of the procedure.

Legislative Aspects of the Grievance Redressal Procedure in India

In India, at present, we find that the industries have formulated the grievance procedures formulated by themselves while in some enterprises, the Model Grievance Procedure has been adopted. But there are three important Acts which deal with provisions of the Acts are applicable. These three Acts are –

(a) The Industrial Employment (Standing Orders) Act of 1946.

(b) The Factories Act of 1948.

(c) The Industrial Disputes Act of 1947.

Before Independence, the settlement of the day-to-day grievances of the employees did not receive much legislative attention. However, the Industrial Employment (Standing Orders) Act of 1946 has provided for the framing of standing orders for every establishment employing one hundred or more workers and it is also made clear in the Act that these orders should contain among other things, provisions for redressal of grievances of workers against unfair treatment and wrongful exactions by the employer or his agents. The Act has a limited applicability and it does not provide for bipartite discussions or any powerful measure for a prompt redressal of the grievances.

The Factories Act of 1948 provides for the appointment of a welfare officer in every factory ordinarily employing five hundred or more workers [Section 49 (1)]. These officers, thus appointed, look after the complaints and grievances of the workers employed in the factories to which the Factory Act of 1948 is applied. According to the provisions of the Factories Act, the State Government have framed rules which enjoin upon Labour Welfare Officers to ensure the settlement of grievances.

In the Industrial Disputes Act of 1947, we find certain provisions relating individual industrial disputes relating to discharge, dismissal, retrenchment, etc. Section 9 (c) provides for setting up of "Grievance Settlement Authorities" and reference of certain individual disputes to such authorities.

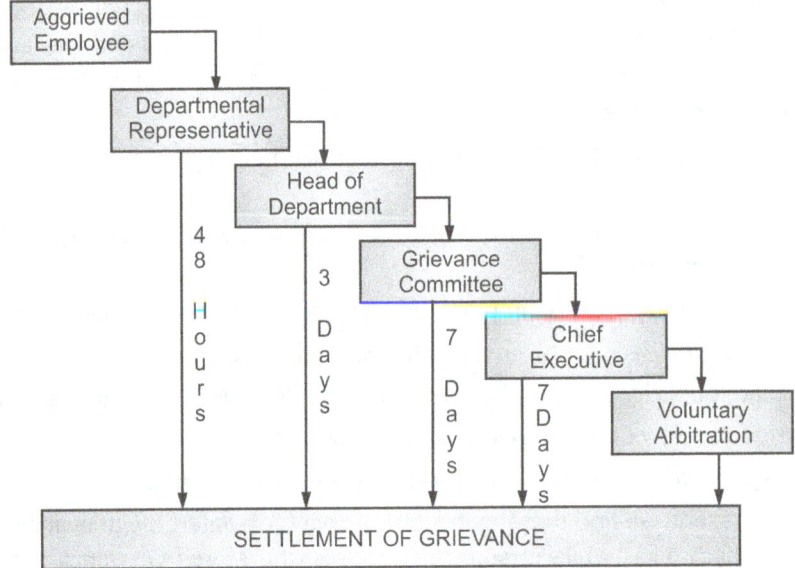

Fig. 5.3

Collective Bargaining

Characteristics of Collective Bargaining

- It is a group process, wherein one group, representing the employers, and the other, representing the employees, sit together to negotiate terms of employment.
- Negotiations form an important aspect of the process of collective bargaining i.e., there is considerable scope for discussion, compromise or mutual give and take in collective bargaining.
- Collective bargaining is a formalised process by which employers and independent trade unions negotiate terms and conditions of employment and the ways in which certain employment-related issues are to be regulated at national, organisational and workplace levels.

- Collective bargaining is a process in the sense that it consists of a number of steps. It begins with the presentation of the charter of demands and ends with reaching an agreement, which would serve as the basic law governing labour management relations over a period of time in an enterprise. Moreover, it is a flexible process and not fixed or static. Mutual trust and understanding serve as the by products of harmonious relations between the two parties.
- It's a bipartite process. This means there are always two parties involved in the process of collective bargaining. The negotiations generally take place between the employees and the management. It is a form of participation.
- Collective bargaining is a complementary process i.e. each party needs something that the other party has; labour can increase productivity and management can pay better for their efforts.
- Collective bargaining tends to improve the relations between workers and the union on one hand and the employer on the other.
- Collective Bargaining is continuous process. It enables industrial democracy to be effective. It uses cooperation and consensus for settling disputes rather than conflict and confrontation.
- Collective bargaining takes into account day to day changes, policies, potentialities, capacities and interests.
- It is a political activity frequently undertaken by professional negotiators.

Importance of Collective Bargaining

Collective bargaining includes not only negotiations between the employers and unions but also includes the process of resolving labour-management conflicts. Thus, collective bargaining is, essentially, a recognised way of creating a system of industrial judicial process. It acts as a method of introducing civil rights in the industry, that is, the management should be conducted by rules rather than arbitrary decision making. It establishes rules which define and restrict the traditional authority exercised by the management.

Importance to employees

- Collective bargaining develops a sense of self respect and responsibility among the employees.
- It increases the strength of the workforce, thereby, increasing their bargaining capacity as a group.
- Collective bargaining increases the morale and productivity of employees.
- It restricts management's freedom for arbitrary action against the employees. Moreover, unilateral actions by the employer are also discouraged.
- Effective collective bargaining machinery strengthens the trade unions movement.

- The workers feel motivated as they can approach the management on various matters and bargain for higher benefits.
- It helps in securing a prompt and fair settlement of grievances. It provides a flexible means for the adjustment of wages and employment conditions to economic and technological changes in the industry, as a result of which the chances for conflicts are reduced.

Importance to employers

- It becomes easier for the management to resolve issues at the bargaining level rather than taking up complaints of individual workers.
- Collective bargaining tends to promote a sense of job security among employees and thereby tends to reduce the cost of labour turnover to management.
- Collective bargaining opens up the channel of communication between the workers and the management, and increases worker participation in decision making.
- Collective bargaining plays a vital role in settling and preventing industrial disputes.

Importance to society

- Collective bargaining leads to industrial peace in the country
- It results in establishment of a harmonious industrial climate which supports which helps the pace of a nation's efforts towards economic and social development since the obstacles to such a development can be reduced considerably.
- The discrimination and exploitation of workers is constantly being checked.
- It provides a method or the regulation of the conditions of employment of those who are directly concerned about them.

Levels of Collective Bargaining

Collective bargaining operates at three levels:

1. National level
2. Sector or industry level
3. Company/enterprise level

Economy-wide (national) bargaining is a bipartite or tripartite form of negotiation between union confederations, central employer associations and government agencies. It aims at providing a floor for lower-level bargaining on the terms of employment, often taking into account macroeconomic goals.

Sectoral bargaining, which aims at the standardisation of the terms of employment in one industry, includes a range of bargaining patterns. Bargaining may be either broadly or narrowly defined in terms of the industrial activities covered and may be either split up according to territorial subunits or conducted nationally.

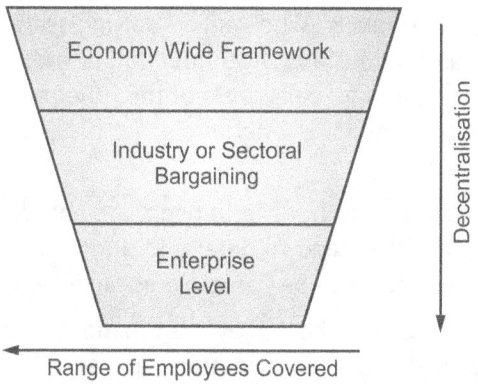

Fig. 5.4: Levels of Collective Bargaining

The third bargaining level involves the company and/or establishment. As a supplementary type of bargaining, it emphasises the point that bargaining levels need not be mutually exclusive.

Negotiation

> *Negotiation is intended to aim at compromise.*

Negotiation is a dialogue between two or more people or parties. It is intended to reach an understanding, resolve point of difference, or gain advantage in outcome of dialogue.

It aims to produce an agreement upon courses of action. It bargains for individual or collective advantage, to craft outcomes. It helps to satisfy various interests of two people/parties involved in negotiation process. Negotiation is a process where each party involved in negotiating tries to gain an advantage for themselves by the end of the process. Negotiation is intended to aim at compromise.

Negotiation can take a wide variety of forms, from trained negotiator acting on behalf of a particular organisation or position in a formal setting, to an informal negotiation between friends.

Negotiation can be contrasted with mediation, where a neutral third party listens to each side's arguments and attempts to help craft an agreement between the parties.

It can also be compared with arbitration, which resembles a legal proceeding. In arbitration, both sides make an argument as to the merits of their case and the arbitrator decides the outcome. This negotiation is sometimes also called positional or hard-bargaining negotiation.

Negotiation styles

R.G. Shell identified five styles/responses to negotiation. Individuals can often have strong dispositions towards numerous styles; the style used during a negotiation depends on the context and the interests of the other party, among other factors. In addition, styles can change over time.

1. **Accommodating**: Individuals who enjoy solving other party's problems and preserving personal relationships. Accommodators are sensitive to the emotional states, body language, and verbal signals of the other party. They can, however, feel taken advantage of, in situations when the other party places little emphasis on the relationship.

2. **Avoiding**: Individuals who do not like to negotiate and don't do it unless warranted. When negotiating, avoiders tend to defer and dodge the confrontational aspects of negotiating; however, they may be perceived as tactful and diplomatic.

3. **Collaborating**: Individuals who enjoy negotiations that involve solving tough problems in creative ways. Collaborators are good at using negotiations to understand the concerns and interests of the other parties. They can, however, create problems by transforming simple situations into more complex ones.

4. **Competing**: Individuals who enjoy negotiations because they present an opportunity to win something. Competitive negotiators have strong instincts for all aspects of negotiating and are often strategic. Because their style can dominate the bargaining process, competitive negotiators often neglect the importance of relationships.

5. **Compromising**: Individuals who are eager to close the deal by doing what is fair and equal for all parties involved in the negotiation. Compromisers can be useful when there is limited time to complete the deal; however, compromisers often unnecessarily rush the negotiation process and make concessions too quickly.

Conciliation

> *Conciliation or mediation signifies third party intervention in promoting the voluntary settlement of disputes.*

The International Labour Organisation has defined conciliation as:

"The practice by which the services of a neutral third party are used in a dispute as a means of helping the disputing parties to reduce the extent of their differences and to arrive at an amicable settlement or agreed solution. It is a process of rational and orderly discussion of differences between the parties to a dispute under the guidance of a conciliator."

The conciliator assists the parties to dispute in their negotiations by removing bottlenecks in communication between them.

Conciliation machinery as provided under the Industrial Disputes Act, 1947 is as under:

(i) **Conciliation Officers:** The Act provides for the appointment of conciliation officers, permanently or for a limited period, for specific area or for a specific industry, to whom, the industrial disputes shall be referred for conciliation. The conciliation officer enjoys the powers of a civil court; he can call and witness parties on oath. The conciliation officer examines all facts relevant to the disputed matter and then gives his judgment.

(ii) **Board of Conciliation:** The Act also empowers the Government to appoint a Board of Conciliation for promoting the settlement of disputes where the Conciliation Officer fails to do so within 14 days. The Conciliation Board is a tripartite adhoc body consisting of a chairman and two to four other members nominated by the parties to the dispute. The mode and procedure of the functioning of the Board are similar to those of the Conciliation Officer.

(iii) **Court of Inquiry:** In case the conciliation proceedings fail to settle an industrial dispute, the Government has yet another option of referring the disputed to the Court of Inquiry. The Court is expected to give its report within six months.

Conciliation is an alternative dispute resolution (ADR) process whereby, the parties to a dispute use a conciliator. The conciliator meets with the parties separately in an attempt to resolve their differences. The conciliators do this by lowering tensions, improving communications, interpreting issues, providing technical assistance, exploring potential solutions and bringing about a negotiated settlement.

> *Conciliation differs from arbitration in that the conciliation process, in and of itself, has no legal standing.*

Conciliation differs from arbitration in that the conciliation process, in and of itself, has no legal standing. The conciliator usually has no authority to seek evidence or call witnesses, usually writes no decision, and makes no award.

Conciliation differs from mediation in that the main goal is to conciliate, most of the time by seeking concessions. In mediation, the mediator tries to guide the discussion in a way that optimises party's needs, takes feelings into account and reframes representations.

In conciliation the parties seldom, if ever, actually face each other across the table in the presence of the conciliator.

Arbitration

Arbitration is a form of alternative dispute resolution (ADR). It is a technique for the resolution of disputes outside the courts, where the parties to a dispute refer it to one or more persons (the "arbitrators", "arbiters" or "arbitral tribunal"), by whose decision (the "award") they agree to be bound.

> *Arbitration is a resolution technique in which a third party reviews the evidence in the case and imposes a decision that is legally binding for both sides and enforceable.*

Arbitration can be either voluntary or mandatory (although mandatory arbitration can only come from a statute or from a contract that is voluntarily entered into, where the parties agree to hold all existing or future disputes to arbitration, without necessarily knowing, specifically, what disputes will ever occur) and can be either binding or non-binding.

Non-binding arbitration is similar to mediation in that a decision cannot be imposed on the parties.

However, the principal distinction is that a mediator will try to help the parties find a middle ground on which to compromise, whereas the (non-binding) arbitrator remains totally removed from the settlement process and will only give a determination of liability, if appropriate, and an indication of the quantum of damages payable. By one definition arbitration is binding and so non-binding arbitration is technically not arbitration.

Arbitration is a proceeding in which a dispute is resolved by an impartial adjudicator whose decision the parties to the dispute have agreed, or legislation has decreed, will be final and binding. There are limited rights of review and appeal of arbitration awards.

Arbitration is not the same as:
- Judicial proceedings, although in some jurisdictions, court proceedings are sometimes referred as arbitrations.
- Alternative dispute resolution (or adr).
- Expert determination.
- Mediation.

Adjudication

Adjudication means "The legal process of resolving a dispute. The formal giving or pronouncing of a judgment or decree in a court proceeding; also the judgment or decision given. The entry of a decree by a court in respect to the parties in a case. It implies a hearing by a court, after notice, of legal evidence on the factual issue(s) involved. The equivalent of a determination. It indicates that the claims of all the parties thereto have been considered and set at rest."

> *Adjudication is the legal process by which an arbiter or judge reviews evidence and argumentation.*

It includes legal reasoning set forth by opposing parties or litigants to come to a decision. It determines rights and obligations between the parties involved.

Three types of disputes are resolved through adjudication:
1. Disputes between private parties, such as individuals or corporations.
2. Disputes between private parties and public officials.
3. Disputes between public officials or public bodies.

The ultimate remedy for the settlement of an unresolved dispute is its reference by the Government to adjudication.

> *Adjudication may be described as a process which involves intervention in the dispute by a third party appointed by the government, with or without the consent of the parties to the dispute, for the purpose of settling the dispute.*

The reference of dispute to adjudication is voluntary when both parties agree to refer the matter of dispute to adjudication at their own accord, and it is compulsory when reference is made to adjudication by the Government without the consent of either or both the parties to the dispute.

The Industrial Disputes Act, 1947 provides a three-tier adjudication machinery comprising:

(i) Labour Courts,
(ii) Industrial Tribunals, and
(iii) National Tribunals.

(i) Labour Courts

The Labour Courts can deal with disputes relating to:

(a) The propriety or legality of an order passed by an employer under the standing Orders.
(b) The application and interpretation of Standing Orders.
(c) Discharge and dismissal of workmen and grant of relief to them.
(d) Withdrawal of any statutory concession or privilege.
(e) Illegality or otherwise of any strike or lock-out.
(f) All matters not specified in the third schedule of Industrial Disputes Act, 1947 (it deals with the jurisdiction of Industrial Tribunals).

(ii) Industrial Tribunals

The Industrial Tribunals can deal with the following matters:

1. Wages including the period and mode of payment.
2. Compensatory and other allowances.
3. Hours of work and rest intervals.
4. Leave with wages and holidays.
5. Bonus, profit sharing, provident fund and gratuity.
6. Shift working in accordance with standing orders.
7. Rules of discipline.
8. Rationalisation.
9. Retrenchment.
10. Any other matter that may be prescribed.

(iii) National Tribunals

These tribunals are meant for those disputes which, as the name suggests, involve the questions of national importance or issues which are likely to affect the industrial establishments of more than one state. The employers and unions use adjudication as a primary measure of resolving disputes.

However, adjudication is not a democratic method and may create bitterness among the parties. It tends to encourage litigation and irresponsible behaviour among employers and labour.

Labour Courts

A **labour court** (or **labour court** or **industrial tribunal**) is a governmental judiciary body which rules on labour or employment-related matters and disputes. In a number of countries, labour cases are often taken to separate national labour high courts.

Detailed Current Functions of the Labour Court are to:

- Investigate trade disputes under the Industrial Relations Acts, 1946 to 2004.
- Investigate, at the request of the Minister for Enterprise, Trade and Employment, trade disputes affecting the public interest, or conduct an enquiry into a trade dispute of special importance and report on its findings, hear appeals of Rights Commissioners' recommendations under the Industrial Relations Acts.
- Establish Joint Labour Committees and decide on questions concerning their operation.
- Register, vary and interpret employment agreements.
- Register Joint Industrial Councils.
- Investigate complaints of breaches of registered employment agreements.
- Investigate complaints of breaches of codes of practice made under the Industrial Relations Act, 1990 (following consideration of the complaint by the Labour Relations Commission).
- Give its opinion as to the interpretation of a code of practice made under the Industrial Relations Act, 1990.
- Investigate disputes (where negotiating arrangements are not in place) under the Industrial Relations (Amendment) Act, 2001 as amended by the Industrial Relations (Miscellaneous Provisions) Act, 2004.

5.3 Define Separation

Generally, an employee separation describes any event that separates the employer and the employee. Some human resources practitioners refer to "separation" as the process of informing the employee of the termination, completing paperwork for continuation of benefits and retrieving company property from the employee. Other HR practitioners distinguish between separation and termination based on why the employee is no longer employed.

> *Employee Separation is one of the very important and crucial function / process of HR Department.*

This process, if not handled in an efficient manner, can lead to various legal complications.

Separated employees include employees who retire. Employee separation, in some instances, is a relatively neutral way to describe the end of the employment relationship. Separation can occur when the employee doesn't necessarily want to leave, but does so anyway for reasons other than leaving the company for a better opportunity or embarking upon a new career path. Employee separation is a phrase also used to describe the end of the employment relationship due to death.

Voluntary Work Separations

A work separation is voluntary if initiated by the employee. An employee initiates the work separation if he or she basically sets the ball rolling toward a work separation. In a true voluntary work separation, the employee has more control than the employer over the fact and the timing of leaving the work.

This can happen in several different ways:

1. **Resignation with advance notice:** The employee gives the employer oral or written notice of leaving in advance.

2. **Retirement:** A special form of resignation with advance notice that involves satisfying some kind of condition for leaving the company with one form or another for continued benefits.

3. **Resignation without advance notice, but with notice given at the time of the work separation:** The employee let the employer know somehow, that he or she will not be returning to work.

4. **Resignation without notice at all:** This can include walking off the job, job abandonment, and failure to return to work after a period of leave.

5. **"Constructive discharge":** For purposes of discrimination, wrongful discharge, anti-retaliation, and other laws, an employee may be considered to have been constructively discharged if working conditions were so intolerable that a reasonable employee would feel forced to resign. However, under the law of unemployment compensation, such a work separation is generally considered to be voluntary.

6. **Failing to return following an unpaid suspension of three days or less see "Unpaid Suspensions" in the article "Unemployment Insurance Law:** Qualification Issues" for details.

As long as the employer did not pressure the employee into resigning, work separations that occur under those circumstances may be considered voluntary.

Involuntary Work Separations

A work separation is involuntary if initiated by the employer.

An employer initiates a work separation by taking some kind of action that makes it clear to the employee that continued employment will not be an option past a certain date.

In such a situation, the employer has more control than the employee over the fact and the timing of leaving the work. There are many ways in which a work separation can be involuntary:

1. Layoff, reduction in force, or downsising - work separation due to economic inability to keep the employee on the payroll.
2. Temporary job comes to an end - work separation due to work no longer being available because the job is simply finished. This includes successful completion of PRN or on-call, as-needed assignments, if no further work is available the next workday.
3. Discharge or termination for misconduct or "cause" - work separation that the employer views as somehow being the claimant's fault.
4. Resignation in lieu of discharge - same as discharge, but the employer gives the employee the option of resigning as a face-saving option.
5. Forced retirement - may be akin to an economic layoff or a discharge for cause, but in this situation, the employee is allowed to qualify under a retirement plan.
6. "Mutual agreement" - in most cases, this form of work separation is viewed as involuntary, since it is usually initiated or encouraged by the employer.
7. Unpaid suspension of four days or longer.

5.3.1 VRS/CRS

In the present globalised scenario, right sizing of the manpower employed in an organisation has become an important management strategy in order to meet the increased competition.

> *The voluntary retirement scheme (VRS) is the most humane technique to provide overall reduction in the existing strength of the employees.*

It is a technique used by companies for trimming the workforce employed in the industrial unit. It is now a commonly used method to dispense off the excess manpower and thus improve the performance of the organisation. It is a generous, tax-free severance payment to persuade the employees to voluntarily retire from the company. It is also known as the **'Golden Handshake'** as it is the golden route to retrenchment.

In India, the Industrial Disputes Act, 1947 puts restrictions on employers in the matter of reducing excess staff by retrenchment, by closures of establishment and the retrenchment process involved lot of legalities and complex procedures. Also, any plans of retrenchment and reduction of staff and workforce are subjected to strong opposition by trade unions.

Hence, VRS was introduced as an alternative legal solution to solve this problem. It allowed employers including those in the government undertakings, to offer voluntary retirement schemes to off-load the surplus manpower and no pressure is put on any employee to exit.

The voluntary retirement schemes were also not subjected to much opposition by the Unions, because the very nature of its being voluntary and not using any compulsion. It was introduced in both the public and private sectors. Public sector undertakings, however, have to obtain prior approval of the government before offering and implementing the VRS.

A business firm may opt for a voluntary retirement scheme under the following circumstances:

1. Due to recession in the business.
2. Due to intense competition, the establishment becomes unviable unless downsizing is resorted to.
3. Due to joint-ventures with foreign collaborations.
4. Due to takeovers and mergers.
5. Due to obsolescence of Product/Technology.

Though the eligibility criteria for VRS varies from company to company, usually, employees who have attained 40 years of age or completed 10 years of service are eligible for voluntary retirement.

The scheme applies to all employees including workers and executives, except the directors of a company. The employee who opts for voluntary retirement is entitled to get forty five days emoluments for each completed year of service or monthly emoluments at the time of retirement multiplied by the remaining months of service before the normal date of service, whichever is less.

Along with these benefits, the employees also get their provident fund and gratuity dues. Compensation received at the time of voluntary retirement is exempt from tax under section 10 (10C) of the Income Tax Act, 1961 up to the prescribed amount upon fulfilling certain stipulated conditions. However, the retiring employee should not be employed in another company or concern belonging to the same management.

The companies can frame different schemes of voluntary retirement for different classes of their employees. However, these schemes have to conform to the guidelines prescribed in rule 2BA of the Income-tax Rules. The guidelines for the purposes of section 10(10C) of the Income-tax Act have been laid down in the rule 2BA of the Income-tax Rules.

The guidelines provide that the scheme of voluntary retirement framed by a company should be in accordance with the following requirements, namely:

1. It applies to an employee of the company who has completed ten years of service or completed 40 years of age.
2. It applies to all employees (by whatever name called), including workers and executives of the company except the Directors of the company.
3. The scheme of voluntary retirement has been drawn to result in overall reduction in the existing strength of the employees of the company.

4. The vacancy caused by voluntary retirement is not to be filled up, nor is the retiring employee to be employed in another company or concern belonging to the same management.

5. The amount receivable on account of voluntary retirement of the employees does not exceed the amount equivalent to one and one-half month's salary for each completed year of service or monthly emoluments at the time of retirement multiplied by the balance months of service left before the date of his retirement on superannuation. In any case, the amount should not exceed rupees five lakhs in case of each employee, and

6. The employee has not availed in the past the benefit of any other voluntary retirement scheme.

> ***Some companies offers very attractive package of benefits to the employees who opt for VRS.***

For example, the VRS scheme may also include providing counselling to employees about their future; managing of funds received under the scheme offering rehabilitation facilities to them, etc.

A company may make the following announcements while implementing a voluntary retirement scheme:

1. The reasons behind downsizing the organisation.
2. The eligibility criteria for voluntary retirement scheme.
3. The age limit and the minimum service period of employees who can apply for the scheme.
4. The benefits that are offered to the employees who offer to retire voluntarily.
5. The rights of the employer to accept or reject any application for voluntary retirement.
6. The date up to which the scheme is open.
7. The income tax benefits and income tax incidence related to the scheme.
8. It should also indicate that the employees who opt for voluntary retirement and accept the benefits under such scheme shall not be eligible in future for employment in the organisation.

Voluntary Retirement Schemes have been legally found to be giving no problem to employers, employees and their unions. But, the retrenchment plans of an organisation must be compatible to its strategic plans.

Its procedure and reasons for introduction must be discussed with all management staff including top management. One needs to identify departments or employees to whom VRS is applicable and thereby formulate its terms and conditions and also state the benefits that would be available to those who took VRS.

Such information should be made available to every employee of the organisation, mentioning the period during which the scheme will be open. Also, existing employees might face insecurity because of fear of losing their job too.

One of the possible drawbacks of the VRS is that the efficient employees would leave the company while the inefficient may stay back. Thus it is the responsibility of the employer to motivate them and remove their apprehensions and fears.

CRS (Compulsory Retirement Scheme)

> *Employees who are undergoing penalty and are retired on compulsory measure as a penalty can be granted compulsory retirement pension.*

This pension has to be authorised by the competent authority that is, empowered to impose the penalty of compulsory retirement.

Resignation

This is the most common way of separation. Employee leaves his job and employment with his employer to pursue better opportunities; a better position at a better compensation package in a branded company (or better known company) in the same city and country or in a different city or different country.

So, an employee resigns for:

1. Better compensation and benefits.
2. Higher position / level.
3. Challenging role.
4. To move from an unknown or lowly branded company to a highly branded and reputed company.
5. For foreign or international assignments.

Superannuation

Definition: *An organisational pension programme created by a company for the benefit of its employees.*

Funds deposited in a superannuation account will grow typically without any tax implications until retirement or withdrawal.

These plans are usually either defined-benefit or defined-contribution plans.

Gratuity

1. It is a lump sum payment granted to an employee or his/her nominee on his/her retirement or medical invalidation.
2. How is it calculated?
3. An employee who has completed 5 years of qualifying service is entitled for retirement gratuity. The gratuity depends upon the qualifying service and the last pay and grade pay drawn by the employee.

4. It is calculated at the rate of half of the emoluments for each completed six monthly period of qualifying service subject to a maximum of sixteen and half times the emoluments and the total amount should not exceed ₹ 10, 00,000/- (Rupees Ten lakhs).
5. The entire gratuity will be withheld in case the employee does not vacate the railway accommodation provided to him.

Formula for Non-Running Staff

Gratuity = (Pay in the Pay Band + Grade Pay + DA) × Qualifying Service/2

Illustration: If an employee is retiring with 33 years qualifying service and his Basic Pay is ₹ 16,050 in pay band ₹ 9,300 – 34,800 with GP ₹ 4,600, current DA @ 58% (as on 01.07.2011) @ ₹ 11,977/-

Retirement Gratuity ₹ (16,050 + 4,600 + 11,977) × 33/2 = ₹ 32,627 × 16.5 = ₹ 5,38,345.50 i.e. rounded off to next rupee = ₹ 5,38,346/-

Formula for Running Staff

In case of Running Staff, 30% of Basic Pay will be treated as Pay rating the Running Allowance. Dearness Allowance as on the date of retirement shall be paid on the basic pay + the pay element of the Running Allowance i.e., 30% of the Basic Pay.

Gratulty = Pay^ + DA^^ × Qualifying Service 2 *Pay = Pay + 55% of Pay** DA = (Pay + 30% of Pay) × DA as on the date of retirement

Illustration

If an employee is retiring with 33 years qualifying service and his Basic Pay is ₹ 18,660 in pay band ₹ 9,300-34,800 + GP ₹ 4,200, current DA @ 58% (as on 01.07.2011) @ ₹ 13,259/- Retirement Gratuity ₹ (18,660 + 4,200 + 12,573) + 17,236 × 33/2 = ₹ 52,669 × 16.5 = ₹ 8,69,038.50 i.e. rounded off to next rupee = ₹ 8,69,039/-

In case of Death Gratuity:

If an employee dies while in service, the amount of death gratuity shall be paid to the family in the manner indicated in the Table below:

Sr. No.	Length of Qualifying Service		Rate of Gratuity
(i)	Less than one year	=	2 times of emoluments.
(ii)	One year or more but less than 5 years	=	6 times of emoluments.
(iii)	5 years or more but less than 20 years	=	12 times of emoluments.
(iv)	20 years or more Half of emoluments for every completed six monthly period of qualifying service subject to maximum of	=	33 times emoluments provided that the amount of death gratuity shall in no case exceed ₹ 10,00,000/-.

Recoveries from Gratuity

Government dues, if any, could be recovered from the retirement gratuity or Death gratuity of an employee even without obtaining his/her consent and in the case of a deceased employee, without obtaining consent of the members of his/her family.

Discharge

> *The term "discharge" is often used to describe an employee who is fired or terminated involuntarily.*

It's common to hear this term used in a union work environment, as in "the employee was discharged for a just cause".

"The terms "discharge" and "just cause" are indicative of employment terms and conditions pursuant to a collective bargaining agreement or an employment contract. Involuntary termination refers to severing the employment relationship due to poor performance, violation of workplace policies, misconduct, absenteeism or other similar reasons.

Dismissal

"Dismissal" simply means termination of employment by the employer. While dismissal can be a disciplinary step, it does not have to be (e.g. dismissal might be for redundancy or for health reasons).

Process

There must be a good reason for a dismissal and the dismissal must be carried out fairly. Otherwise, the employee may have a personal grievance claim against the employer.

What is fair depends on the circumstances. Any relevant provisions in the employment agreement must be followed. If an employment agreement does not have a notice period, then reasonable notice must be given.

Employees have the right to be told what the problem is and that dismissal or other disciplinary action is a possibility. Employees must then be given a genuine opportunity to tell their side of the story before the employer decides what to do.

The employer should investigate any allegations of misconduct thoroughly and without prejudice. Unless there has been misconduct so serious that it warrants instant dismissal, the employee should be given clear standards to aim for and a genuine opportunity to improve.

If an employee is dismissed, he or she has the right to ask the employer for a written statement of the reasons for dismissal. This request can be made up to 60 days after they find out about the dismissal. The employer must provide the written statement within 14 days of such a request. If the employer fails to provide this written statement, the employee may consequently be able to raise a grievance after the required 90 day limitation period.

Dismissal during a trial period

Employers are able to employ new workers on a trial period of up to 90 calendar days and may dismiss them during that time. The employer does not have to provide a written statement of the reasons for dismissal if an employee is dismissed while on a trial period and the employee cannot pursue a personal grievance for unjustified dismissal during the trial period.

Forced resignation or "constructive dismissal"

If an employer puts pressure (directly or indirectly) on an employee to resign, or makes the situation at work intolerable for the employee, it may be a forced resignation often known as a "constructive dismissal".

A constructive dismissal may be where, for example, one or more of the following occurs:

- The employer has followed a course of conduct deliberately aimed at coercing the employee to resign.
- The employee is told to choose between resigning or being dismissed.
- There has been a breach of duty by the employer (i.e. a breach of the agreement or of fair and reasonable treatment) such that the employee feels he or she cannot remain in the job.

If an employee has been forced to resign, they may have a personal grievance case.

Suspension

Suspension is a form of punishment that people receive for violating rules and regulations.

Suspension is a common practice in the workplace for being in violation of an organisation's policy, or major breaches of policy.

Work suspensions occur, when a business manager or supervisor deems an action of an employee to be a violation of policy. Whether the action is intentional or unintentional, it should result in a course of punishment, and when the employee's absence during the suspension period does not affect the company. This form of action hurts the employee because she/he will have no hours of work during the suspended period and therefore will not get paid, unless the suspension is with pay, or is challenged and subsequently overturned.

Some jobs, which pay on salary, may have paid suspensions, in which the affected worker will be prevented from coming to work but will still receive pay. Generally, suspensions are deemed most effective if the affected worker remains unpaid.

Suspensions are deemed most effective if the affected worker remains unpaid.

Suspensions are usually given after other means of counselling statements have been exhausted, but some violations may result in immediate suspension.

Suspensions are tracked, and any number of them, even one may prevent one from receiving raises, bonuses or promotions, or could cause dismissal from the company.

Suspension clauses are common components of collective bargaining agreements.

Suspensions may be challenged by employees in unionised organisations through the filing of a grievance.

Suspension on full pay can also be used when an employee needs to be removed from the workplace to avoid prejudicing an investigation. This is used not as a punishment, but in the employer's best interest. For example, a police officer who shoots a person while on duty will be given a suspension with pay during the investigation, not to punish, but to enable the department to carry out its investigation. Most officers involved in such shootings end up receiving no punishment.

Layoff

> ***Separation due to layoff happens when the employer does not have enough work for his current employers.***

Employee termination and employee separation are both appropriate ways to describe when an employee layoff occurs. Although the word termination sounds like the employee was at fault, termination in the case of a layoff means the employment relationship ended due to business closure or a lack of available work.

Where there is an indefinite layoff, such as business closure, the termination process is more likely to be called a separation because there exists a slim possibility employees may be called back.

Retrenchment

Retrenchment is something similar to downsizing. When a company or government goes through retrenchment, it reduces outgoing money or expenditures or redirects focus in an attempt to become more financially solvent. Many companies that are being pressured by stockholders or have had flagging profit reports may resort to retrenchment to shore up their operations and make them more profitable. Although retrenchment is most often used in countries throughout the world to refer to layoffs, it can also label the more general tactic of cutting back and downsizing.

Companies can employ this tactic in two different ways. One way is to slash expenditures by laying off employees, closing superfluous offices or branches, reducing benefits such as medical coverage or retirement plans, freezing hiring or salaries, or even cutting salaries.

There are numerous other ways in which a company can employ retrenchment. These can be non-employee related, such as reducing the quality of the materials used in a product, streamlining the process in which a product is manufactured or produced, or moving headquarters to a location where operating costs are lower.

The second way in which a company may practice retrenchment is to downsize in one market that is proving unprofitable and build up the company in a more profitable market. If one market has become obsolete due to modernisation or technology, then a company may decide to change with the times to remain profitable.

5.4 Safety and Security

Safety management is generally understood as the application of a set of principles, framework, processes and measures to prevent accidents, injuries and other adverse consequences that may be caused by using a service or a product.

Safety management implies a systematic approach to managing safety, including the necessary organisational structure, accountabilities, policies and procedures. Safety management is an organisational function, which ensures that all safety risks have been identified, assessed and satisfactorily mitigated.

Safety and health of the employees has a significant bearing on the productivity of an organisation. Organisations are always known for product, production and employees. The employees of an organisation develop the organisational culture and climate. For an organisation the employees are equally or more important than production is. An organisation can only move as fast as its slowest members and if those members are injured, production will grind down or stop. Once safety is compromised, the company's insurances (Health, Life, Workers' Compensation etc.) will take a major bite off any profits. Also, the morale of all employees will go down.

If safety is not a priority, the lack of it will become a major liability. There is a balance between safety and production based on the degree of risk. One should always advocate the attitude of 'Safety First' or "Be Careful". Neither of the terms really means more than be safe to the average worker nor is its connection to production tenuous. If you ask a few people what the meaning of these terms is, you may get the same kind of non-specific statement like, 'don't get hurt' or 'watch out for hazards'.

For the smooth functioning of an organisation, the employer has to ensure safety and security of his employees. Health and safety form an integral part of work environment. A work environment should enhance the well being of employees and thus should be accident free.

The terms health, safety and security are closely related to each other.

- **Health** is the general state of well being. It not only includes physical well being, but also emotional and mental well being.
- **Safety** refers to the act of protecting the physical well being of an employee. It will include the risk of accidents caused due to machinery, fire or diseases.

Definitions of Safety
1. **Safety:** The condition of being safe; freedom from danger, risk or injury.
2. **Safety:** The state of being certain that adverse effects will not be caused by some agent under the defined conditions.
3. **Safety:** The quality or condition of being safe; free from danger, injury or damage; of being secured.

Significance of Safety
1. If an organisation has no safety culture it might result in 1 or more of the following:
2. Damage to plant and machinery.
3. Loss to the organisation due to decrease in production.
4. Increased expenses on medical aid to the injured employees.
5. Pain and suffering to the injured employees which might result in loss of morale.
6. Loss of reputation of the organisation.
7. Deterioration in the employer and employee relationship.
8. High attrition rates or premature death of employee.
9. Added expenditure on recruitment and training of new employees.
- **Security** refers to protecting facilities and equipments from unauthorised access and protecting employees while they are on work.

5.4.1 Employee Safety

Since 1950, the International Labour Organisation (ILO) and the World Health Organisation (WHO) have shared a common definition of occupational health. It was adopted by the Joint ILO/WHO Committee on Occupational Health at its first session in 1950 and revised at its twelfth session in 1995. The definition reads:

"Occupational health should aim at: the promotion and maintenance of the highest degree of physical, mental and social well-being of workers in all occupations; the prevention amongst workers of departures from health caused by their working conditions; the protection of workers in their employment from risks resulting from factors adverse to health; the placing and maintenance of the worker in an occupational environment adapted to his physiological and psychological capabilities; and, to summarise, the adaptation of work to man and of each man to his job".

The main focus in occupational health is on three different objectives:
(i) The maintenance and promotion of workers' health and working capacity;
(ii) The improvement of working environment and work to become conducive to safety and health and
(iii) Development of work organisations and working cultures in a direction which supports health and safety at work and in doing so also promotes a positive social climate and smooth operation and may enhance productivity of the undertakings.

The concept of working culture is intended in this context to mean a reflection of the essential value systems adopted by the undertaking concerned. Such a culture is reflected in practice in the managerial systems, personnel policy, principles for participation, training policies and quality management of the undertaking."

– Joint ILO/WHO Committee on Occupational Health

> *Occupational safety and health is an area concerned with protecting the safety, health and welfare of people engaged in work or employment.*

The goals of occupational safety and health programmes include fostering a safe and healthy work environment.

5.4.2 Types of Safety

Safety is the state of being "safe". Safety comes from the French word SAUF. Safety is the condition of being protected against harm. Harm from or against physical. We commonly know that being safe is being kept from harm from physical harm. However there are other factors or issues that may hurt us- such as social, financial, political, emotional, occupational, psychological, educational, incidents, accidents, errors or other types or consequences of failure. Whether intentional or unintentional. Safety is being safe from harm or any other event which could be considered non-desirable.

Safety can also be defined to be the control of recognised hazards. Recognition of hazards leads to being able to mitigate these hazards or provide control measures to these hazards such that they (or the events that are undesirable) are not released and work/play is within an acceptable level of risk.

Safety should be seen as a component in Quality, Reliability, Availability and Maintainability. Safety is critical to quality, productivity and profitability.

Normative Safety

Normative safety is a term used to describe products or designs that meet applicable design standards. It is the compliance of products, services and designs to a set specification or standards of safety

Substantive Safety

Substantive safety means that the real-world safety history is favourable, whether or not standards are met. Substantive safety is how safe a person actually is. It is the objectionable degree of safety, based on historical circumstance or facts.

Perceived Safety

Perceived safety refers to the level of the comfort of users. Perceived safety describes the comfort level of people. People may have a perceived value of safety. Essentially, perceived safety refers to how safe a person feels, generally due to an external tool or measure such as a seatbelt, airbag or a "five-star" crash safety rating.

For example, traffic signals are perceived as safe, yet under some circumstances, they can increase traffic crashes at an intersection. Traffic roundabouts have a generally favourable safety record, yet often make drivers nervous.

Security

Also called social safety or public safety, security is the risk of harm due to intentional criminal acts such as assault, burglary or vandalism.

Because of the moral issues involved, security is of higher importance to many people than substantive safety. For example, a death due to murder is considered worse than a death in a car crash, even though in many countries, traffic deaths are more common than homicides.

Workplace Hazards and Safety Measures

1. Physical and Mechanical Hazards

Physical hazards are a common source of injuries in many industries. They are perhaps unavoidable in many industries such as construction and mining, but over time people have developed safety methods and procedures to manage the risks of physical danger in the workplace. Employment of children may pose special problems.

Falls are a common cause of occupational injuries and fatalities, especially in construction, extraction, transportation, healthcare, and building cleaning and maintenance.

Example: In an engineering workshop specialising in the fabrication and welding of components it is an employer's duty to provide 'all equipment (including clothing affording protection against the weather) which is intended to be worn or held by a person at work which protects him against one or more risks to his health and safety'. In a fabrication and welding workshop an employer would be required to provide face and eye protection, safety footwear, overalls and other necessary proper protection equipments.

Machines are common in many industries, including manufacturing, mining, construction and agriculture, and can be dangerous to workers. Many machines involve moving parts, sharp edges, hot surfaces and other hazards with the potential to crush, burn, cut, shear, stab or otherwise strike or wound workers if used unsafely. Various safety measures exist to minimise these hazards, including lockout procedures for machine maintenance and roll over protection systems for vehicles.

Machines are also often involved indirectly in worker deaths and injuries, such as in cases in which a worker slips and falls, possibly upon a sharp or pointed object. The transportation sector bears many risks for the health of commercial drivers, too, for example from vibration, long periods of sitting, work stress and exhaustion. More drivers die in accidents due to security defects in vehicles.

Confined spaces also present a work hazard. The National Institute of Occupational Safety and Health defines "confined space" as having limited openings for entry and exit and unfavourable natural ventilation, and which is not intended for continuous employee occupancy. These kinds of spaces can include storage tanks, ship compartments, sewers, and pipelines. Confined spaces can pose a hazard not just to workers, but also to people who try to rescue them.

Noise also presents a fairly common workplace hazard: Noise is not the only source of occupational hearing loss; exposure to chemicals such as aromatic solvents and metals including lead, arsenic, and mercury can also cause hearing loss.

Temperature extremes can also pose a danger to workers. Heat stress can cause heat stroke, exhaustion, cramps, and rashes. Heat can also fog up safety glasses or cause sweaty palms or dizziness, all of which increase the risk of other injuries. Workers near hot surfaces or steam also are at risk for burns. Dehydration may also result from overexposure to heat. Cold stress also poses a danger to many workers. Overexposure to cold conditions or extreme cold can lead to hypothermia, frostbite, trench foot, or chilblains.

Electricity poses a danger to many workers. Electrical injuries can be divided into four types: fatal electrocution, electric shock, burns, and falls caused by contact with electric energy.

Vibrating machinery, lighting, and air pressure can also cause work-related illness and injury. Asphyxiation is another potential work hazard in certain situations.

Musculoskeletal disorders are avoided by the employment of good ergonomic design and the reduction of repeated strenuous movements or lifts.

2. **Other Safety Hazards include**
   - **Biological and chemical hazards**
   - **Biological hazards**
   - **Exposure to** Bacteria, Virus, Fungi, Blood-borne pathogens, Tuberculosis

Chemical hazards: Acids, Bases, Heavy metals, Lead, Solvents, Petroleum, Particulates, Asbestos and other fine dust/fibrous materials, Silica, Fumes (noxious gases/ vapours), Highly-reactive chemicals, Fire, conflagration and explosion hazards: Explosion, Deflagration, Detonation, Conflagration

Psychological and social issues: Work-related stress, whose causal factors include: excessive working time and overwork, Violence from outside the organisation, Sexual harassment, Mobbing, Burnout, Exposure to unhealthy elements during meetings with business associates, e.g. tobacco, uncontrolled alcohol.

In organisations the responsibility of employee health and safety falls on the supervisors or HR manager. An HR manager can help in coordinating safety programmes, making employees aware about the health and safety policy of the company, conduct formal safety training, etc. The supervisors and departmental heads are responsible for maintaining safe working conditions.

Responsibilities of Managers

- Monitor health and safety of employees.
- Coach employees to be safety conscious.
- Investigate accidents.
- Communicate about safety policy to employees.

Responsibilities of Supervisors/Departmental heads

- Provide technical training regarding prevention of accidents.
- Coordinate health and safety programmes.
- Train employees on handling facilities an equipments.
- Develop safety reporting systems.
- Maintaining safe working conditions.

5.4.3 Safety and Health Programmes

An effective safety and health programme depends on the credibility of management's involvement in the programme; inclusion of employees in safety and health decisions; rigorous worksite analysis to identify hazards and potential hazards, including those which could result from a change in worksite conditions or practices; stringent prevention and control measures; and thorough training. It addresses hazards whether or not they are regulated by government standards.

An effective occupational safety and health program will include the following four elements:

- Management commitment and employee involvement.
- Worksite analysis
- Hazard prevention and control
- Safety and health training

Reasons for Health and Safety Programs or Policies in the Workplace

There are several reasons why workplaces need a health and safety policy or programme, including:

- to clearly demonstrate management's full commitment to their employee's health and safety;
- to show employees that safety performance and business performance are compatible;
- to clearly state the company's safety beliefs, principles, objectives, strategies and processes to build buy-in through all levels of the company;

- to clearly outline employer and employee accountability and responsibility for workplace health and safety;
- to comply with all legislation regarding Health and Safety; and
- to set out safe work practices and procedures to be followed to prevent workplace injuries and illnesses.

Safety Programmes

A safety programme is constituted to:

(a) Establish when, where and why accidents are occurring.
(b) Identify measures to be implemented to reduce accidents and losses associated with them.
(c) Implement measures and evaluate achievements.

5 Es of a Safety / Programme are:

(i) Engineering i.e. to build safety into plant, processes and operations.
(ii) Education i.e. to educate employees in safe practices.
(iii) Enforcement i.e. to enforce adherence to safety rules and safe practices.
(iv) Enlistment i.e. to create safety consciousness among the employees and arouse their interest in accident prevention.
(v) Examples i.e. to lead employees by following rules.

Key element of the safety programme are as under:

- Safety manual/procedures
- Safety organisation
- Safety engineering
- Safety audit
- Accident reporting and investigation
- Hazards and danger anticipation
- On-site and off-site emergency plan
- Safety rewards and motivation
- Safety awareness programme
- Training and education
- Safety discipline (enforcing safety rules)

A safety programme involves systematic investigation and accidents which includes:

- Accident reporting.
- Analysis of accidents (i.e. operationwise, machinewise, injured body partwise, age and sexwise of the injured etc.).
- Accident prevention measures.
- Cost of accidents.

Key elements of safety controls are:
- Employment of safety / medical officer.
- Formation of safety committee / safety groups.
- Safety monitoring / safety rounds.
- Safety meetings.
- Safety rewards and motivation.
- Involving union in company's safety efforts.

Legislation on occupational health and safety has existed in India for over 50 years.

Legal framework

Safety and health occupy a significant place in India's Constitution, which prohibits employment of children under the age of 14 in factories, mines and hazardous occupations. This policy aims to protect the health and strength of all workers by discouraging employment in occupations unsuitable to the worker's age and strength. It is the policy of the State to make provisions to secure just and humane conditions at work. The Constitution provides a broad framework under which policies and programmes for occupational health and safety can be established.

The principal health and safety laws are based on the British Factories Act. The Factories Act, 1948 has been amended from time to time, especially after the Bhopal gas disaster, which could have been prevented. The amendment demanded a shift away from dealing with disaster (or disease) to prevention of its occurrence. The Factories (Amendment) Act came into force on December 1, 1987.

A special chapter on occupational health and safety to safeguard workers employed in hazardous industries was added. In this chapter, pre-employment and periodic medical examinations and monitoring of the work environment are mandatory for industries defined as hazardous under the Act. A maximum permissible limit has been laid down for a number of chemicals.

The Act is implemented by state factory inspectorates, supported by industrial hygiene laboratories. There are similar provisions under the Mines Act. The Factories Act is applicable only to factories that employ 10 or more workers; it covers only a small proportion of workers.

The Directorate General of Factory Advice Service and Labour Institutes (DGFASLI) assists the labour ministry in formulating national policies on occupational safety and health in factories and docks, and enforcing them through inspectorates of factories and inspectorates of dock safety. Similarly, the Director General of Mines Safety (DGMS), Ministry of Labour, is responsible for the health and safety of mine workers and implementation of the Mines Act, 1952.

There are also two key laws covering worker compensation and welfare. They are:
- Workmen's Compensation Law, by which a worker can claim compensation under establishments covered by the Factories Act.
- Employees Sate Insurance Act (ESI Act), which is a contributory social insurance scheme that protects the interests of workers in contingencies such as sickness, maternity, employment injury causing temporary or permanent physical disability or death, loss of wages or loss of earning capacity. As of March 2006, there were 35.4 million beneficiaries under this scheme.

5.4.4 Statutory Provisions of Safety in India

Occupational Health and Safety (OH & S)

> *Health and safety of the employees is an important aspect of a company's smooth and successful functioning.*

It is a decisive factor in organisational effectiveness. It ensures an accident-free industrial environment. Companies must attach the same importance towards achieving high OH&S (Occupational Health & Safety) performance as they do to the other key objectives of their business activities. This is because, proper attention to the safety and welfare of the employees can yield valuable returns to a company by improving employee morale, reducing absenteeism and enhancing productivity, minimising potential of work-related injuries and illnesses and increasing the quality of manufactured products and/ or rendered services.

The Constitution of India has also specified provisions for ensuring occupational health and safety for workers in the form of three Articles i.e. 24, 39(e and f) and 42. The regulation of labour and safety in mines and oil fields is under the Union list. While the welfare of labour including conditions of work, provident funds, employers' invalidity and old age pension and maternity benefit are in the Concurrent list.

> *The Ministry of Labour, Government of India and Labour Departments of the States and Union Territories are responsible for safety and health of workers.*

Directorate General of Mines Safety (DGMS) and Directorate General Factory Advice Services & Labour Institutes (DGFASLI) assist the Ministry in technical aspects of occupational safety and health in mines and factories & ports sectors, respectively.

DGMS exercises preventive as well as educational influence over the mining industry. Its mission is the reduction in risks of occupational diseases and casualty to persons employed in mines, by drafting appropriate legislation and setting standards and through a variety of promotional initiatives and awareness programmes. It undertakes inspection of mines, investigation of all fatal accidents, grant of statutory permission, exemptions and relaxations in respect of various mining operation, approval of mines safety equipment, appliances and material, conduct examinations for grant of statutory competency certificate, safety promotional incentives including organisation of national awards and national safety conference, etc.

DGFASLI is an attached office to the Ministry of Labour and relates to factories and ports/docks. It renders technical advice to the States/Union Territories in regard to administration and enforcement of the Factories Act. It also undertakes support research facilities and carries out promotional activities through education and training in matters concerning occupational safety and health.

Major Initiatives undertaken by DGFASLI during the Xth Five Year Plan are:

- Improvement and strengthening of enforcement system for safety and health of dock workers in major ports.
- Development of safety and health information system and data bank.
- Establishment of Regional Labour Institute at Faridabad.
- Setting up of a National Board on occupational safety and health.
- Legislations.

The statutes relating to OH&S are broadly divided into three:

1. Statutes for safety at workplaces.
2. Statutes for safety of substances.
3. Statutes for safety of activities.

At present, safety and health statutes for regulating OH&S of persons at work exist only in four sectors:

1. Mining,
2. Factories,
3. Ports,
4. Construction.

The major legislations are:

The Factories Act, 1948

It regulates health, safety, welfare and other working conditions of workers in factories.

It is enforced by the State Governments through their factory inspectorates. The Directorate General Factory Advice Service & Labour Institutes (DGFASLI) co-ordinates matters concerning safety, health and welfare of workers in the factories with the State Governments.

DGFASLI conducts training, studies and surveys on various aspects relating to safety and health of workers through the Central Labour Institute in Mumbai and three other Regional Labour Institutes located at Kolkata, Chennai and Kanpur.

Mines Act, 1952

It contains provisions for measures relating to the health, safety and welfare of workers in the coal, metalliferous and oil mines.

The Mines Act, 1952, prescribed duties of the owner (defined as the proprietor, lessee or an agent) to manage mines and mining operation and the health and safety in mines. It also prescribes the number of working hours in mines, the minimum wage rates, and other related matters.

Directorate General of Mines Safety conducts inspections and inquiries, issues competency tests for the purpose of appointment to various posts in the mines, organises seminars/conferences on various aspects of safety of workers.

Courts of Inquiry are set up by the Central Government to investigate into the accidents, which result in the death of 10 or above miners. Both penal and pecuniary punishments are prescribed for contravention of obligation and duties under the Act.

Dock Workers (Safety, Health & Welfare) Act, 1986

It contains provisions for the health, safety and welfare of workers working in ports/docks.

It is administered by Director General Factory Advice Service and Labour Institutes, Directorate General FASLI as the Chief Inspector there are inspectorates of dock safety at 10 major ports in India viz. Kolkata, Mumbai, Chennai, Visakhapatnam, Paradip, Kandla, Mormugao, Tuticorin, Cochin and New Mangalore

The overall emphasis in the activities of the inspectorates is to contain the accident rates and the number of accidents at the ports.

Other legislations and the rules framed there under:

- Plantation Labour Act, 1951.
- Explosives Act, 1884.
- Petroleum Act, 1934.
- Insecticide Act, 1968.
- Indian Electricity Act, 1910.
- Indian Boilers Act, 1923.
- Indian Atomic Energy Act, 1962.
- Building and Other Construction Workers (Regulation of Employment and Conditions of Service) Act, 1996.
- Beedi and Cigar Workers' (Conditions of Employment) Act, 1966.

National Safety Council of India (NSCI)

The National Safety Council of India (NSCI) was set up to promote safety consciousness among workers to prevent accidents, minimise dangers and mitigate human suffering, arrange programmes, lectures and conferences on safety, conduct educational campaigns to arouse consciousness among employers and workers and collect educational and information data, etc. It has launched new initiatives in three sectors:

- Road Transportation Safety
- Safety of Health in Construction Sector
- Safety, Health and Environment in Small and Medium Scale Enterprises(SMEs)

At the international level, NSCI has developed close collaboration with International Labour Organisation (ILO); United Nations Environment Programmes (UNEP); World Bank ; Asian Disaster Preparedness Centre (ADPC), Bangkok; World Environment Centre (WEC), New York; and the member organisations of Asia Pacific Occupational Safety and Health Organisation (APOSHO) of which NSCI is a founder-member.

The National APELL (Awareness and Preparedness for Emergencies at Local Level) Centre (NAC) has been established since April 2002 in the NSCI Headquarters under the MoU with the Division of Technology, Industry & Economics (DTIE) of UNEP, Paris. It is the first APELL Centre in the world. It has the technical support and information from UNEP and other international sources and the Ministry of Environment & Forests, Government of India and the stakeholders. It is dedicated primarily to strengthen chemical emergency preparedness and response in India through the use of the internationally accepted APELL process.

Policy

Announcement of the National Policy On Safety, Health And Environment At Work Place was also a step towards improvement in safety, health and environment at workplace performance.

Objectives of the policy were:

- Continuous reduction in incidence of work related injuries, fatalities, diseases, disaster and loss of national assets.
- Continuous reduction in the cost of work place injuries and diseases.
- Extend coverage of work related injuries, fatalities, and diseases for a more comprehensive data base as a means of better performance and monitoring.
- Continuous enhancement of community awareness regarding safety, health and environment at workplace related areas.

Awards

In order to encourage occupational health and safety, certain awards have also been instituted by the Government:

- The National Safety Awards for factories and docks were instituted in 1965, to give recognition to good safety performance on the part of the industrial undertakings and to stimulate and maintain the interest of both management and workers in accident prevention programmes.

- The National Safety Awards for mines were instituted in 1983, to give recognition to outstanding safety performances of mines of national-level which comes within the purview of the Mines Act, 1952.
- The Shram Vir Awards, now known as Vishwakarma Rashtriya Puraskar were instituted in 1965. These are meant for workers of factories, mines, plantations and docks and are given to them in recognition of their meritorious performance, which leads to high productivity or economy or higher efficiency.

Indian Standard on OH&S management systems

Occupational Health and Safety demands adoption of a structured approach for the identification of hazards, their evaluation and control of risks in the organisation. Hence, Bureau of Indian Standards has formulated an Indian Standard on OH&S management systems. It is called as the IS 18001:2000 Occupational Health and Safety Management Systems. This standard prescribes the requirements for an OH&S Management Systems, to enable an organisation to formulate a policy, taking into account the legislative requirements. It also provides information about significant hazards and risks, which the organisation can control in order to protect its employees and others, whose health and safety may be affected by the activities of the organisation.

> *Organisations interested in obtaining licence for OH&S Management System as per IS 18001 should ensure that they are operating the system according to this standard.*

The organisation should apply on the prescribed proforma (Form IV) at the nearest Regional Office of BIS along with Questionnaire (Form X) and the prescribed application fee. The application shall be signed by the proprietor or the Chief Executive Officer (CEO) of the organisation or any other person authorised to sign on behalf of the organisation. The name and designation of the person signing the application must be recorded legibly in a space set apart for the purpose in the application form. Each application must be accompanied by a documented Occupational Health and Safety Management System Documentation (such as OHS manual etc.).

ILO conventions

The International Labour Organisation frames key conventions for protecting the rights of workers; many of them are specifically on occupational health and safety. These conventions, once ratified by member states, form guiding principles for the formulation of national policies and laws. The ILO has 18 conventions that are targeted at addressing the issue of occupational safety and health (OSH). Though India has ratified 41 ILO conventions and treaties on labour welfare and labour rights to date, it has ratified only three conventions on OSH. India is still to ratify important conventions like Convention 155 on occupational safety and health and the working environment, Convention 161 on occupational health services, Convention 167 on safety and health in construction, Convention 176 on safety and health in mines, Convention 184 on safety and health in agriculture, Convention 187, the promotional framework for occupational safety and health.

Lax implementation

> *In spite of having a good legal framework for the protection of workers, India suffers from the chronic problem of lax implementation.*

Regulatory bodies, including the inspectorates, are ill-equipped and severely understaffed. According to a DGFASLI report (1998), the country has 1,400 safety officers, 1,154 factory inspectors, and 27 medical inspectors. These numbers are grossly inadequate even for the inspection of formal units that only employ about 10% of India's total workforce.

Occupational diseases and their diagnosis

> *In most places, occupational safety and health invariably means prevention of accidents; very little attention is paid to occupational diseases.*

Accidents, despite being visible, are still grossly underreported in the Indian context. The reporting of insidious occupational diseases therefore stands little chance. If we analyse the details of workers who die because of their work environment, we find that, surprisingly, most of them succumb to occupational cancers and other work-related illnesses. This is contrary to the common belief that most work-related deaths are caused by accidents. In most places, occupational safety and health invariably means prevention of accidents; very little attention is paid to occupational diseases. An accident-free workplace by no means implies a safe workplace.

Occupational diseases - including cancers caused by various materials in the workplace, including asbestos, carcinogenic (cancer-causing) chemicals, silica, cotton, dust, and radiation, job stress and work shifts - usually take a long time to develop (from a few months to more than 10 years). And given changing work practices, most industries tend to hire workers on short-term contract. By the time they develop a disease, therefore, it is almost impossible to link it to their work.

Non-communicable diseases result in more deaths than communicable diseases, except in Africa. Overall, people are more likely to die of work-related diseases than childhood or infectious diseases.

Not many doctors are able to correctly diagnose an occupational disease. In fact, certain occupational diseases like byssinosis (a lung disease caused by cotton dust) and silicosis (a lung disease caused by silica dust) are often wrongly diagnosed as tuberculosis. In a community where having a doctor is a privilege, an OSH specialist is simply out of the question.

Informal sector problems

Most workers in India (90%) work in the vast informal sector. The variable and insecure nature of the work means that more and more workers are pushed into taking up hazardous and precarious employment both in the informal economy as well as informal work in the formal sector. For these workers, employment not only fails to bring about a successful escape from poverty, it may contribute to existing vulnerabilities.

There are other contributory factors that lead to poor working conditions in the informal sector:

There is very little awareness about workplace hazards due to lack of access to information, or even any kind of formal education. Then too, OSH is given very low priority among informal workers, as having work is more important than the quality of the job. As many workers say: "We might die of work, but if we don't work our families will die of hunger."

No proper work hours; piece-rate work often leads to exploitation and extended exposure to hazardous chemicals and processes.

> *Diagnosis of occupational diseases is difficult even in the formal sector.*

Diagnosis of occupational diseases is difficult even in the formal sector; in the informal sector it is almost impossible. In the absence of proper diagnosis, treatment of occupational illness is next to impossible for workers in this sector.

No clear distinction between living and working area complicates the problem and exposes relatives and others living in the vicinity to work-related risks.

Effects on women and children

> *Working pregnant women expose their unborn children to great risks.*

If information on OSH hazards among informal workers is poor, their impact on women's health is even less understood. In addition to paid work, women also do other demanding jobs like cooking, cleaning and taking care of the children. The extended work hours puts tremendous pressure on women's bodies and minds. Women also face an increased risk of musculo-skeletal disorders because of the repetitive nature of the jobs they perform, and having to work in uncomfortable positions for long hours (sometimes they work with babies in their laps or on their backs). Women who work with chemicals like solvents in adhesives, in home-based work, or pesticides out in the fields are also in danger of chemical poisoning. Working pregnant women expose their unborn children to great risks.

> *Child labour is a big problem in the informal sector in India.*

Children in the informal sector sometimes have to help their parents, for economic reasons. The growing bodies of children are more susceptible to hazards at the workplace, but since children (legally) are not supposed to work, very few initiatives are targeted at improving their working conditions.

India and International Labour Organisation (ILO)

India is a founder member of International Labour Organisation. The principal means of action in ILO is the setting up the 'International Labour Standards' in the form of Conventions and Recommendations. Conventions are international treaties and are the instruments which create legally binding obligations on the countries ratifying them.

Recommendations are non-binding guidelines which orient national policies and actions. ILO has so far adopted 182 conventions and 190 recommendations, encompassing subjects such as worker's fundamental rights, worker's protection, social security, labour welfare, occupational safety and health, women and child labour, migrant labour, indigenous and tribal population, etc

> *The approach of India with regard to International Labour Standards has always been positive.*

India has accordingly evolved legislative and administrative measures for protection and advancement of the interests of labour in India. The practice followed by India so far has been that a Convention is ratified only when the national laws and practices are in conformity the provisions of the Convention in question. India has so far ratified 41 ILO Conventions. The unratified Conventions of the ILO are also reviewed at appropriate intervals in relation to our National laws and practices.

Points to Remember

- **Grievance procedure** is a formal communication between an employee and the management designed for the settlement of a grievance.
- **Negotiation is** intended to aim at compromise.
- **Conciliation** or mediation signifies third party intervention in promoting the voluntary settlement of disputes.
- Conciliation differs from arbitration in that the conciliation process, in and of itself, has no legal standing.
- **Arbitration** is a resolution technique in which a third party reviews the evidence in the case and imposes a decision that is legally binding for both sides and enforceable.
- Adjudication is the legal process by which an arbiter or judge reviews evidence and argumentation.
- Adjudication may be described as process which involves intervention in the dispute by a third party appointed by the government.
- **Employee separation** is one of the very important and crucial function / process of HR Department.
- A work separation is involuntary if initiated by the employer.
- **The Voluntary Retirement Scheme (VRS)** is the most humane technique to provide overall reduction in the existing strength of the employees.
- Some companies offers very attractive package of benefits to the employees who opt for VRS.

- Employees who are undergoing penalty and are retired on compulsory measure as a penalty can be granted compulsory retirement pension.
- The term **"discharge"** is often used to describe an employee who is fired or terminated involuntarily.
- Suspensions are deemed most effective if the affected worker remains unpaid.
- Separation due to layoff happens when the employer does not have enough work for his current employers.
- Occupational safety and health is an area concerned with protecting the safety, health and welfare of people engaged in work or employment.
- Health and safety of the employees is an important aspect of a company's smooth and successful functioning.
- The Ministry of Labour, Government of India and Labour Departments of the States and Union Territories are responsible for safety and health of workers.
- In spite of having a good legal framework for the protection of workers, India suffers from the chronic problem of lax implementation.
- Organisations interested in obtaining licence for OH&S Management System as per IS 18001 should ensure that they are operating the system according to this standard.
- In most places, occupational safety and health invariably means prevention of accidents; very little attention is paid to occupational diseases.
- Diagnosis of occupational diseases is difficult even in the formal sector.
- Working pregnant women expose their unborn children to great risks.
- Child labour is a big problem in the informal sector in India.
- The approach of India with regard to International Labour Standards has always been positive.

Questions for Discussion

1. Define IR
2. Enumerate Concepts and Objectives of IR
3. List Parties to IR
4. Describe Approaches to IR
5. Illustrate Trade Unions and its Role in IR.
6. Define the Machinery to Dispute Settlement.
7. Explain Grievance Procedure.

8. List the features of Collective Bargaining.
9. Describe any two: Negotiation, Conciliation, Arbitration, Adjudication.
10. Illustrate Labour Courts.
11. Define Separations.
12. Enumerate VRS/CRS.
13. List features of Resignation.
14. Describe Superannuation, Gratuity.
15. Illustrate procedures of Discharge and Retrenchment.
16. Define Employee Safety.
17. Enumerate Types of Safety.
18. Describe Safety and Health Programs.
19. Explain the Statutory provisions of safety in India.

Case Study

Mahesh was just promoted as a shift officer. The promotion became effective when his immediate superior Mr. Verma was out of town for a few days. Due to illness of Mahesh's subordinate the work schedule was not being met. He decided to pitch in and help spending about four hours daily in production. When Mr. Verma returned to his work, Mahesh was not available, as he was not working on the shop floor. He is upset and tells him that it is the function of the supervisor to accomplish work with and through other people and not do it himself.

Question:

Do you agree with Mr. Verma? Justify your answer.

Activity

Prepare a questionnaire on Industrial Relations problems and interview an IR/HR manager in an establishment in your vicinity.

Objective Questions

(Questions: 1-10) Fill in the Blanks:

1. Grievance procedure is a _____ communication between an employee and the management designed for the settlement of a grievance.
2. Negotiation is intended to aim at _____
3. Conciliation or mediation signifies _____ party intervention in promoting the voluntary settlement of disputes.

4. Conciliation _____ from arbitration in that the conciliation process, in and of itself, has no legal standing.
5. Arbitration is a _____ technique in which a third party reviews the evidence in the case and imposes a decision that is legally binding for both sides and enforceable.
6. Adjudication is the _____ process by which an arbiter or judge reviews evidence and argumentation.
7. Adjudication may be described as a process which involves intervention in the _____ by a third party appointed by the government.
8. Employee Separation is one of the very important and crucial function / process of _____ Department.
9. A work separation is _____ if initiated by the employer.
10. The voluntary retirement scheme (VRS) is the most _____ technique to provide overall reduction in the existing strength of the employees.

(Question: 11-15) True or False:
11. Companies do not offer very attractive package of benefits to the employees who opt for VRS.
12. Employees who are undergoing penalty and are retired on compulsory measure as a penalty can be granted compulsory retirement pension.
13. The term "discharge" is not used to describe an employee who is fired or terminated involuntarily.
14. Suspensions are ineffective if the affected worker remains unpaid.
15. Separation due to layoff happens when the employer does not have enough work for his current employers.

Answers:
1. Formal
2. Compromise
3. Third
4. Differs
5. Resolution
6. Legal
7. Dispute
8. HR
9. Involuntary
10. Humane
11. False
12. True
13. False
14. False
15. True

References

- Personnel Management by C.B Mamoria
- Human Resource Management by Garry Dessler
- Human Resource Management by Aswathappa
- https://en.wikipedia.org/wiki/Industrial_relations
- http://industrialrelations.naukrihub.com
- http://business.gov.in/manage_business
- http://rulemaster.wordpress.com/2012/03/31/retirement-benefits-for-railway-employees-in-general

www.ingramcontent.com/pod-product-compliance
Lightning Source LLC
Chambersburg PA
CBHW080924180426
43192CB00040B/2705